More Praise for Fiduciary Management

"Fiduciary management is an answer to the increasing complexity of the investment environment in which trustees of pension funds and endowments have to fulfil their role. The step from outsourcing individual mandates to appointing a fiduciary manager is a logical one in a process which leads to ever greater demands on the professionalism of trustees. This book helps to understand the complexities and pitfalls of institutional asset management and gives a clear answer to basic questions as what are the key responsibilities of a board of trustees and how to take care of them. Organizing beauty parades is not one of them. Hiring a fiduciary manager might help.

Institutional investment management is a profession and should be organized as such. This book shows what professional management is all about and why you should not enter this field without the help of a fiduciary manager. Reading this book is a must. I can highly recommend it."

Jean Frijns, professor of investments, University of Amsterdam, The Netherlands, chairman of the Dutch governmental commission on governance

"Fiduciary Management is a monument to good pension fund governance and transparency. The author demonstrates enormous knowledge of the unique pillar of services to pension fund boards or trustees which Fiduciary Management can be. A must for all those involved in servicing pension funds."

Koen De Ryck, managing director of Pragma Consulting N.V., Belgium

"Not having been able to read the book as carefully as I should, my conclusion is that this is a nice book on a rather new phenomenon, which will become a reference book for a lot of people taking complex decisions which are needed constantly nowadays in order to create an optimal pension fund design."

Piet Duffhues, professor emeritus of finance, Tilburg University

"Fiduciary Management gives the interested reader a concise perspective on fiduciary investment management, and adds to this a well structured perspective on institutional portfolio management. Anton van Nunen has been a successful pioneer from the early days of fiduciary management, and his insight and experience will prove a helpful guide for many who are venturing into this area."

Roderick Munsters, chief investment officer, ABP Pension Fund, The Netherlands

"This book explains in a lucid fashion how fiduciary management allows those who are responsible for advancing the interests of the beneficiaries of a pension fund to harness the specialized expertise of investment managers. This timely book is about the continuous quest for institutional innovations that ensure that the ultimate stakeholders of pension funds benefit from the increasing potential of financial markets. In this way, it helps to raise the value created by one of the most ingenious inventions in the history of mankind: pension funds offering credible promises about old-age income."

Arij Lans Bovenberg, economics professor, Tilburg University, and scientific director, Network for Studies on Pensions, Aging, and Retirement, Tilburg University

Fiduciary Management

Founded in 1807, John Wiley & Sons is the oldest independent publishing company in the United States. With offices in North America, Europe, Australia and Asia, Wiley is globally committed to developing and marketing print and electronic products and services for our customers' professional and personal knowledge and understanding.

The Wiley Finance series contains books written specifically for finance and investment professionals as well as sophisticated individual investors and their financial advisors. Book topics range from portfolio management to e-commerce, risk management, financial engineering, valuation and financial instrument analysis, as well as much more.

For a list of available titles, visit our Web site at www.WileyFinance.com.

Fiduciary Management

Blueprint for Pension Fund Excellence

ANTON VAN NUNEN

Foreword by Don Ezra

John Wiley & Sons, Inc.

Published by John Wiley & Sons, Inc., Hoboken, New Jersey.
Published simultaneously in Canada.

Wiley Bicentennial logo: Richard J. Pacifico.

For general information on our other products and services or for technical support, please contact our Customer Care Department within the United States at (800) 762-2974, outside the United States at (317) 572-3993 or fax (317) 572-4002.

Wiley also publishes its books in a variety of electronic formats. Some content that appears in print may not be available in electronic books. For more information about Wiley products, visit our Web site at www.wiley.com.

Library of Congress Cataloging-in-Publication Data:

Nunen, Anton van, 1950-
  Fiduciary management : blueprint for pension fund excellence / Anton van Nunen.
        p. cm. — (Wiley finance series)
  Includes bibliography references and index.
  ISBN 978-0-470-17103-5 (cloth)
 1.   Pension trusts – Management. I. Title
  HD7105.4.N86 2008
  331.25'2068 – dc22

                                                              2007023238

Printed in the United States of America.

10 9 8 7 6 5 4 3 2 1

Contents

Foreword   xi

Preface   xiii

CHAPTER 1
The Pendulum Swings Back in Asset Management   1

The Forces of History   1
The Rise of Modern Portfolio Theory   3
Support for Shares   4
The New Paradigm   6
The Rise of Indexing   9
Discontent with the Paradigm   10
The Need for Fiduciary Managers   12

CHAPTER 2
Pension Plans: The Principal Setting for Fiduciary Management   15

The Historical Idea of Pensions   15
A Patchwork of Pension Provisions   18
Organization and Regulation of the Pension System in
     several OECD Countries   23
     Denmark   23
     France   25
     Germany   26
     The Netherlands   27
         Marking to Market   28
         Sufficiency Test   29
     Sweden   30
     Switzerland   31
     United Kingdom   31
     The United States   32
     Australia   33

Similarities and Differences   34
Commonalities on the Asset Side   36

CHAPTER 3
The Role of the Fiduciary Manager as Chief Advisor   **39**

The Asset-Liability Study   39
Thinking through Risk and Return   41
Portfolio Construction   42
Selecting and Overseeing Investment Managers   43
Measuring and Benchmarking   43
Education   44
The Trusted Counselor, the Fellow Fiduciary   46

CHAPTER 4
Shaping the Fundamental Investment Policies   **47**

Liability-Driven Investments   51
Choosing an Active Investment Policy   52
Integrating Active Policy in the Overall Portfolio   55
Completion Account as a Necessary Adjunct to Active Policy   58
The Fiduciary Platform to Integrate Active Policy in the
    Overall Investment Portfolio   59
A Special Case: Bridging the Duration Gap   67
What a Fiduciary Manager's Report Looks Like   68

CHAPTER 5
Asset-Liability Modeling and the Fiduciary Manager   **73**

The Role of the Fiduciary Manager   74
The Asset-Liability Model (ALM)   75
Policy Instruments Used in Asset-Liability Modeling   78
Calculations to Cope with Uncertainty   80
The Crucial Role of ALM   81
Asset-Liability Modeling in Practice   82
    Prognosis of Future Reserves without Policy Changes   84
    Future Financial Situation with Flexible Premium
        Levels under the Regime of a Fixed Compound Rate   85
    Future Financial Situation with Flexible Premium
        Levels under the Regime of Compound Rates Equal
        to Market Interest Rates   88
    Future Financial Situation with Changes
        in Investment Policy   100

Policy Changes   102
Where Does Fiduciary Management Fit In?   102

CHAPTER 6
Fiduciary Management In Practice—Portfolio Construction   **105**

Defining Appropriate Asset Classes   106
Hedge Funds: Weighing the "New" Alternative   106
Burrowing In: Defining Sub-Allocations   109
Thinking about Style   111
Apportioning the Fixed Income Portfolio   112
Measure for Measure   112
Formulating Mandates for Managers   114

CHAPTER 7
**Horses For Courses—Selecting And Overseeing Investment
Managers**   **115**

Creating the Beauty Parade   116
Investment Performance   117
Investment Process and Philosophy   117
Investment People   118
Operational Risk   119
Managing the Beauty Parade   121
Managing the Transition   122
Overseeing the Managers   123

CHAPTER 8
Performance Measurement and Benchmarking   **127**

Why Has Benchmarking Grown More Important?   128
The Use of Different Types of Benchmarks   131
Liability-Driven Benchmarks   133
Strategic Benchmarks   134
    Fixed Income   136
    Equities   137
    Real Estate   139
Detailed Benchmarks in the Context of Active
    Investment Policy   140
Active Overlay Management   143
Rebalancing   144
Measurement of Active Policy   145

CHAPTER 9
The Fiduciary Manager Experience in the Netherlands and Beyond   **151**

Changes in Investment Policy   152
Changes in the Role of a Fund's Investment Committee   153
Changes in the Breadth and Depth of Discussions with Asset
   Managers   153
Changes in the Communication Process   154
Changes in the Level and Structure of Costs   155
Changes in the Importance of the Custodian   156
Overseeing the Fiduciary   157
Future Developments of the Market for Fiduciary Services   159
Beyond the Netherlands   165
Fiduciary Management Plus   165

CHAPTER 10
Summing Up Fiduciary Management: What It Is and Is Not   **167**

Goals, Policy, and Responsibilities   167
Fiduciary Management Can Enhance Productivity   173
What Fiduciary Management Is Not: A Simplification   174
Comparisons with Other Investment Management Models   175
The Concept's Claims   176

Appendix: Suppliers of Fiduciary Services   **181**

Notes   **259**

Bibliography   **265**

Index   **269**

Foreword

I first met Dr Anton van Nunen at a conference organized by my company, Russell Investment Group, in the Netherlands in May 2006. Having ascertained that our views were broadly similar on pension fund governance (my topic at the conference), Dr van Nunen introduced himself to me. And now that I've read his book, I've ascertained that our views are broadly similar on a wide variety of topics. Hence this foreword.

I can start in two ways, either of which leads quickly to my main point.

One is to assert that good governance is worth money. I've never seen definitive proof of that statement, either for pension funds or for corporate boards, but it hardly needs proof. Think of any hypothetical organization. Superimpose on it either good governance (characterized by clear delegation and decision rights) or poor governance (characterized by overlapping responsibilities and confusion as to who is responsible for what). Which do you think is more likely to be successful? It's as obvious as that.

The other is to recall the statement that good people can make any organizational structure work. That may well be true, but why create a structure that's an obstacle they have to jump over? Why not give them a structure that is helpful in itself? Wouldn't that increase the chances of success in their venture?

My point is that governance, by which I mean the way in which decision rights are assigned, is a worthwhile issue to treat seriously, and an essential ingredient if success is to be achieved by plan rather than by chance. And "fiduciary management" is an essential feature in the governance of defined benefit pensions.

Since terminology differs from country to country, and this book is clearly designed to have international appeal, let's clarify what "fiduciary management" means. Think first of a corporation. Consider three broad layers. It has a board that sets or approves direction. It has workers who create the product or service. And it has management that hires workers and organizes them to facilitate production. So too with a pension plan. It has (or ought conceptually to have) three layers. There's a board of trustees (or its equivalent with a name that varies from country to country) with ultimate fiduciary responsibility. There are investment managers who produce investment judgments (the pension fund's investment product). And there is the "fiduciary manager," playing the equivalent of the corporate role of "management."

Most pension funds are too small to have a full-time fiduciary manager in-house. Their best bet is to hire a company that specializes in this role. It's likely to work better than having a part-time board over-reach itself and play the role of full-time fiduciary manager, or have someone in-house, with other corporate responsibilities, play the role part-time. Outsourced fiduciary management is the model that is used in this book.

Dr van Nunen goes much further than to discuss governance. He discusses all aspects of what should be done in making a defined benefit plan successful, and expresses his opinions forthrightly. We may not agree on every point (do any two advisers ever?), but he backs his opinions solidly and clearly, and following them should increase a fund's chances of success.

His analysis is up-to-date: for example, he deals with hedge funds, liability-driven investing, and transitions of portfolios from one manager to another. And he not only traces the history of pension arrangements, but supplements it with a fascinating chapter comparing arrangements around what I think of as the funded world. His primary focus is on the Netherlands, where in my view defined benefits are more prominent, and administered more sensibly, than anywhere else in the world. But his ideas are relevant to fiduciaries around the funded world. I'm very glad that he asked me to write this foreword and I hope you find his book as interesting, engaging and useful as I did.

Don Ezra
Director, Investment Strategy, Russell Investment Group
Coauthor, *Pension Fund Excellence*
New York, June 2007

Preface

A good advisor not only provides a sounding board for one's own ideas, he or she contributes their own valuable ideas as well. This is always the case with Dr. Kees Cools, Professor of Finance at Groningen University and a partner at Boston Consulting Group, who is what we call in Holland a *commissaris*, or advisor, to my company. I have the pleasure of sitting down with him periodically to hold rather high-level discussions about what our company is doing. Some years ago, after I had completed several Fiduciary Management mandates on behalf of various pension funds, he suggested that I write a book about these experiences. The result of that advice is now in front of you.

One of the main reasons for writing this book was the success that has been achieved as a result of the first fiduciary contract between an institutional investor and a major financial services firm. This contract received a certain amount of publicity in the financial press, and after a gestation period, it led several parties to copy various parts of it. As various arrangements have been negotiated, however, this has gradually blurred the picture of Fiduciary Management. This book tries to restore some clarity to the concept. It indicates where and how—and why—Fiduciary Management can be employed, and it spells out the attributes and merits of this approach to organizing the management of an institutional investment portfolio.

I am indebted to Boudewijn Dessing and Hans Kestens of the board of VGZ-IZA, a major Dutch health insurance company, and to its financial officer, Guus Sommerdijk, for giving me the opportunity to work through the idea of structuring an investment process in which an institutional investor that does not have in-house investment expertise can nonetheless be in control of its pension fund, which is an increasingly vital part of the activities at many companies. I am grateful to them for enabling me to put these ideas in practice.

As I gradually worked out the necessary tasks and controls inside, and especially outside, at VGZ-IZA and other organizations, the concept of what would become Fiduciary Management began to take shape. I am grateful to the officers mentioned previously for enabling me to put these ideas in practice and for having the courage to give this assignment to a one-man shop. Their company became the first institutional investor to hire a Fiduciary Manager.

The content of this book has been enlarged and greatly improved by in-depth discussions with peers such as Dr. Con Keating of the Finance Development Centre Limited in the UK ("You should write a book, not a pamphlet"), Koen De Ryck of Pragma Consulting in Belgium, Professor Amin Rajan of Create Research, and by the writings of Don Ezra of the Russell Investment Group. I appreciate their comments and stimulating discussions. After reading one of my articles on the subject, valuable comments were offered by my dear friend, Professor Jean Frijns, Professor of Investment Theory at the University of Amsterdam. Jean, formerly chief investment officer of ABP, one of the largest pension funds in the world, helped me validate the ideas of Fiduciary Management.

Another long time friend and colleague, Haitse Hoos, read most of the manuscript, and his additions and critical questions have substantially improved the content. Martijn Vos and Ridzert van der Zee, distinguished researchers at Ortec, a leading Dutch operations research company specializing in financial planning and asset-liability management improved the chapter on asset-liability modeling. Numerous colleagues in the field—indeed too many to mention here—took great interest in the book and convinced me it was worth carrying on in times when the work did not move ahead as smoothly as I expected.

Last but not least, my wife Francine and daughter Lot were not only kind enough to set me free of all duties on the weekends, they consistently supported me when I was less content with the pace of the writing and with the quality of the content.

I hope that the support of all those people has resulted in a book that can shed some light on issues that I think are highly relevant to pension funds and insurance companies now and will remain critical in the future: What organizational structures and actions should be undertaken by pension funds if they are to successfully carry out their important mission of providing retirement incomes? What is the most effective way to organize and carry out their duties?

Despite all the help received, I am afraid there will inevitably be errors and omissions. They are mine, and that brings to mind a comment from John Thain, the chairman of the New York Stock Exchange and the NYSE Euronext Group but formerly the head of Goldman Sachs. During the celebration of the first fiduciary mandate won by his company, he told me, "Anton, if something is wrong, you call me."

Anton van Nunen
The Netherlands
Summer 2007

CHAPTER 1

The Pendulum Swings Back in Asset Management

Fiduciary Management is a way of organizing the management of sizable investment portfolios. The growing interest in this phenomenon reflects the beginnings of an historic shift in the approach many institutions are taking to investment management. After several decades of expanding the range of actors involved in managing an institutional portfolio, there is increasing recognition of the problems created by the involvement of this large cast of characters. When many are involved, it turns out, no one is fully responsible.

Fiduciary Management can be viewed in Hegelian terms: thesis, antithesis, synthesis. In the context of investment management, the thesis was the balanced manager: As institutional investment was growing more than a century ago, the initial response was to turn money over to a single manager who would select all investments, manage the portfolio, and take full responsibility for all investment issues and decisions. Antithesis came about half a century later in the form of Modern Portfolio Theory. It encouraged the view that specialized managers could achieve better results than generalists, and this led institutions to put together armadas of managers under the guidance of investment consultants. But this has created problems in achieving comprehensive risk management, strategic decision making, and effective organizational governance.

The Fiduciary Manager is the synthesis: This Fiduciary Manager oversees a decentralized, outsourced array of investment managers, but the Fiduciary Manager also centralizes responsibility in one person or organization.

THE FORCES OF HISTORY

In order to understand the need for the Fiduciary Manager approach that is being advocated here, it is important to understand the evolution of

1

investment management in the advanced industrial countries. Much of the appeal for the concepts underpinning the idea of a Fiduciary Manager is a response to the shortcomings that many investors see in the current approach to managing institutional portfolios, especially pension funds. Thus, it is valuable to understand the course of events that has led to the current model.

As pension funds began to be created in the developed nations more than a century ago, employers had to decide what to do about funding these plans. Should they simply pay pension benefits out of current revenues, or should they put aside money on an ongoing basis to reflect the growing future pension obligations that they were incurring?

In the United States, tax policy accorded with accounting principles and led to the development of funded plans. Accountants said that since liabilities were accruing each day an employee worked, then assets should be set aside to match those liabilities. Because tax law permitted deducting the funds that were set aside as a business expense, thereby lowering a company's tax burden, employers were prepared to embrace the advice of the accounting profession and put aside funds for their pension plans. The Netherlands took a similar approach, as did Japan, the UK, and several Commonwealth countries, including Canada, Australia, and South Africa. In certain European countries, meanwhile, some plan sponsors chose to fund their plans but others operated them on a pay-as-you-go basis or on a book reserves basis.

Among those plan sponsors who decided to fund their pension plans, a few decided they could and would manage their pension assets in house. However, most companies concluded that they were not specialists in managing investments, so they sought outside expertise for their pension monies. Some companies turned the money over to an insurance company. This permitted them to make actuarially determined contributions that would be invested by the insurance companies. The insurance company would take the risk of underfunding; if investment results did not yield enough to pay the promised benefits, the insurance company would make up the difference, and, conversely, if investment results created a surplus in the pension account, the insurance company would get to keep this money.

Others turned the monies over to a bank, typically the trust department or investment management department of the company's lead bank in the case of a large national company, or the main local bank or house bank of a smaller company. Public employee pension funds did precisely the same thing: some hired insurance companies, and others hired one of the banks in their locality to manage the growing pool of pension assets.

In almost all of these cases, when banks received money from corporate or public employee pension funds, they invested the money using a *balanced fund* approach. This meant that all of the pension assets were invested in a single account, and these monies were invested in securities. Originally, most of the money was invested in bonds, but a number of pension funds began to add shares of stock to portfolios, particularly since the early 1950s.

In this balanced approach, the investment managers would occasionally shift the allocations between stocks and bonds based on their outlook for the respective markets. The principal investment objective was preservation of capital with some modest incremental returns. The portfolio was viewed as having two parts: the original principal and the returns on that principal, which were measured in terms of the interest received on the large proportion of bonds in the portfolio and the dividends earned by the equities that were owned.

General Mills, the cereal and foods company based in Minneapolis, Minnesota, provides an example of this early approach. In 1940, General Mills established its first Employee Retirement System Pension Fund. The fund, which was managed by Bankers Trust Co. of New York, was originally invested almost entirely in fixed income securities. In the mid-1950s, however, with the encouragement of the plan sponsor, Bankers Trust began moving into equities. And by the beginning of the 1960s, the fund would be 70 percent invested in stocks.[1]

While there were certainly many exceptions to this pattern, the General Mills story was typical of pension plans in several countries: They were invested in a balanced fund that emphasized fixed income securities until the 1960s, when important developments in investment theory began to work their way through the investment community.

THE RISE OF MODERN PORTFOLIO THEORY

In the early 1950s, Professor Harry Markowitz and other academics, principally in the United States., had begun to systematically analyze investment patterns and returns. The growing availability of computers would soon mean that for the first time, it was possible to analyze massive amounts of data about the movement of prices of investment instruments as well as the returns that were, or could be, generated by large numbers of alternative portfolios.

This academic work generated a series of important ideas, which would take hold in the investment community in two ways. First of all, investors read and noted the work of academics. Perhaps more importantly, the Master of Business Administration (MBA) degree was becoming an increasingly important credential among those entering the professional investment world, and those who studied for that degree took finance courses in which the new ideas, called Modern Portfolio Theory, were taught to them. There were several elements of Modern Portfolio Theory, or MPT, that significantly altered the investment landscape.

One was the idea that asset allocation was the principal source of a portfolio's returns. Being in the right markets, it was said, was far more important than being in the right securities. In a landmark article published in the *Financial Analysts Journal* in 1986, Gary P. Brinson, Randolph Hood, and Gilbert Beebower argued that asset allocation was responsible for 90 percent of the variability of returns achieved by a portfolio, while securities selection and the timing of transactions accounted for less than 10 percent of the returns that were earned.[2]

A second important finding had to do with the management of risk. Until the middle of the twentieth century, investors were advised to avoid risky assets. The "prudent man rule" in the United States, and similar concepts in other countries, took the view that each investment had to be "prudent." But Modern Portfolio Theory argued that the risk and return associated with a single investment was essentially immaterial. As long as risky investments had a low correlation coefficient with each other, it was possible for investors to modulate the risks by creating a diversified portfolio. This meant it was safe for investors to hold riskier individual investments in the hopes of generating incremental returns.

This mode of analysis sharply altered perceptions of what was appropriate for an institutional portfolio.[3] As these ideas took hold, "the prudent man rule" would be refocused to examine an entire portfolio rather than individual investments. The prudent man rule in the United States, and similar standards developed by the courts in other countries, essentially said that an investment manager could not be held responsible for an investment that performed badly if the investment was something that a prudent investor could have purchased in good faith. In this realm, too, MPT shifted the focus to the entire portfolio; within reason, risky investments were acceptable as long as the portfolio in the aggregate reflected a prudent approach to risk.

In 1974, the U.S. Congress enacted The Employees' Retirement Income Security Act (ERISA) which established standards for the fiduciaries of retirement plans. The Act stipulated that fiduciaries act with the "care and skill of a prudent person familiar with such matters...."

SUPPORT FOR SHARES

A third important theme of MPT was that stocks consistently outperformed bonds. The emergence of new levels of computing power in the 1960s made it possible to demonstrate what many observers had always believed: that over the long run, and on average, stocks significantly outperform bonds, and bonds outperform cash. Nowadays this is simply seen as proof of the iron law of the financial markets. On average in the longer run, an asset delivers a higher return because the risks associated with that asset are greater in terms of periodic volatility.

The Center for Research in Securities Prices at the University of Chicago amassed monthly securities prices going back to 1926, and a variety of academics used this data to provide rigorous analyses of the returns that could have been generated by various combinations of securities and various investment strategies. These showed that over the long run, despite the 1929 Stock Market Crash and the Great Depression, for almost every extended period of time, stocks outperformed bonds. This research spelled out the extent of the differences and made a convincing case that prudent long-term investors could safely increase their holdings of equities.

There would be a series of further refinements of this idea. A University of Chicago graduate student named Ralf Banz would use the CRSP data as the basis for a doctoral dissertation in which he would demonstrate that the shares of smaller listed companies outperformed the shares of larger companies. Banz, who would return to his native Switzerland and become an investment manager at a private bank in Geneva, essentially created the concept of small cap stocks as well as the view that these were highly attractive investments.

Going forward, other scholars would demonstrate that using different time frames, small cap stocks did not always outperform large cap stocks. But the importance of Banz's work was not so much that he discovered the characteristics of small stocks, but that he essentially framed a debate in which different segments of the equities market were identified and compared with others.

Concepts like small, medium, and large cap stocks, or growth stocks versus value stocks would become standard tools in examining the market. Academia provided fodder for the old Wall Street adage that there was not a stock market, there was a market of stocks. Moreover, this marketplace was a highly variegated and differentiated forum for trading investments that fell into a wide range of categories.

Another important step in the evolution of investment management was the promulgation of the total return approach. History and legal principles had led many institutions to think in terms of principal and interest. The principal was to be left untouched while the interests could be spent. But several landmark reports published by the Ford Foundation in 1969 altered that view. The first was a report by a blue ribbon panel of investment experts, which concluded that educational endowments ought to take a "total return" approach to their investments.[4]

At any point in time, these institutions had a single pool of capital, the reports said, and there was no need to make a dichotomy between principal and interest. Similarly, there was no reason to treat returns that came in the form of dividends or interest differently from returns that came in the form of capital appreciation. The report argued that institutions should take a total return approach: A portfolio was essentially marked to market at various points in time; its value was then compared against previous points in time; and its total return was the most accurate and meaningful measure of how well it was faring.

In essence, this approach said that a dollar's worth of income was equal to a dollar's worth of growth. These two sources of value were completely fungible, and the only thing that mattered was that the portfolio be worth more at the end of a period than it was at the beginning. The Ford Foundation helped institutions understand and implement the total return approach by publishing another report, called *The Law and the Lore of Endowment Funds.*[5]

In 1972, in the United States, the National Conference of Commissioners on Uniform State Laws recommended the adoption of the Uniform Management of Institutional Funds Act, which sought to codify the findings of the two Ford Foundation reports. If an institution needed cash to meet certain liabilities, that did not mean that it had to invest in fixed income securities that would generate interest to meet those obligations. It was appropriate to invest in equities and then to sell some of those equities to generate the required cash.

Yet another theme that began percolating up at this point was that investment managers who specialized in specific, narrowly defined segments of the market did better in those segments than generalist managers who placed some portion of their portfolio in those segments. Specialization was a major theme in many endeavors throughout the twentieth century, and research was indicating that it was important for investing as well. Large cap growth stock managers typically did better in large cap growth stocks than balanced fund managers; small cap specialists did better at small cap investing than generalists; and so on.

THE NEW PARADIGM

The results of this theoretical revolution created a new paradigm for investors. Once investing seemed to be defined by a bottom-up approach: Astute investors watched the market, and one by one they perceived opportunities. Did Daimler-Benz shares appear to be undervalued? Then buy a little of that. Did Kellogg have a popular new cereal? Then buy some shares of that company. Suddenly, theory said that was wrong; investors needed to take a top-down approach. They needed to specify their expectations for various markets going forward, then determine an asset allocation, and then invest money within the various asset classes. Moreover, the investments within those asset classes should be made by managers who specialized in those asset classes. Their job was not to decide how much to put in those areas or, indeed, whether to be in the market at any point in time. That was for some central decision-making authority. Instead, these managers were given money that was to be invested in their specialty.

These changes worked their way through both the supply and demand side of the market for investment services. In terms of the demand side, institutional investors became increasingly likely to conclude that the balanced fund approach was not good enough. How could a single manager decide how much to put into equities versus fixed income? And how could that manager then choose among the thousands of stocks and bonds that were available in the U.S. market, never mind foreign markets that were just coming into the consciousness of U.S. institutional investors? The new approaches that were emerging said that a balanced manager would inevitably produce less than optimal results because that manager did not have skills equal to those of the various specialists.

As discontent was rising among institutions, on the supply side, as the 1960s unfolded, substantial numbers of American investment professionals would leave the trust departments and the investment departments of insurance companies in the United States, and they would set up investment management firms. These firms would not propose to be all things to all men, like their previous employers. Rather, they would specialize. Fisher Francis Trees & Watts managed only bonds, for example, and, at a later stage, specialist bond houses would specialize further in government bonds, higher yield corporate bonds, and other specific types of fixed income investments. Many other new firms invested only in growth stocks, or value stocks, or they focused on small versus large caps, and so on.

As these firms were created during the heady days of the 1960s, they developed track records based on a total return approach, and their results were frequently vastly superior to the returns being generated by highly cautious banks running balanced accounts.

Pension funds took note of the differences in returns, and they began hiring groups of managers, giving each a portion of the pension fund portfolio to invest in a specific asset class. The new paradigm said the pension fund's management should determine the asset allocation, along with a range of sub-allocations, and then the plan sponsor should hire specialized managers to invest in each of these asset classes.

But how was a plan sponsor to make these important decisions? Remember, the reason plan sponsors had hired outsiders to manage pension investments in the first place was because the sponsors felt that they did not have the investment expertise to do the job themselves. How then were they to make decisions on asset allocation and on the selection of managers?

The answer was that they would use investment consultants. A vast army of consultants would arise to provide the expertise plan sponsors needed to oversee their portfolios in the new paradigm. Originally, these consultants gathered and analyzed data about the returns achieved by investment managers. But the consulting services that were being created in the 1960s would soon go on to offer plan sponsors advice on asset allocation. They would then help the plan sponsor select investment managers. And they would also help monitor and oversee the managers that had been selected, assisting in the termination of those who were not meeting expectations and the selecting and hiring of managers to replace them. The consultants would also help the plan sponsor determine whether there were new asset classes that could and should be added to the asset allocation.

Again, the General Mills pension fund demonstrates the changes that were taking place. After several decades of having Bankers Trust manage its entire pension fund, in the mid-1960s, it replaced this bank with four independent investment management firms.[6]

As the new paradigm played out, institutions would be moving to large numbers of managers. By the 1980s, it was not at all unusual for a pension plan to have two dozen managers. The finest expression of this view was the AT&T pension plan. By 1974, it had 75 fund managers. AT&T (which then consisted of the parent company, which provided long distance telephone service, and a group of local operating telephone companies that would later be separated from AT&T in an antitrust case) had initially used only large U.S. banks as managers. But in 1971, it hired T. Rowe Price, an independent investment management firm, and in the ensuing two years it added 16 more investment advisory firms and two insurance companies to its ranks of managers.[7]

A few years later, however, AT&T and others began to call into question some aspects of the specialized manager approach. A pension plan that had a large number of managers would inevitably find that some managers were buying what others were selling, and surely the above-average performance being achieved in some segments of the market had to be offset by the below-average performance being achieved elsewhere.

THE RISE OF INDEXING

There was also growing concern about *closet indexing*. One of the most controversial academic ideas that grew out of the 1960s was the efficient market hypothesis. This said that the stock market was an efficient market. Efficiency in this context did not mean that a market operated effectively in terms of completing transactions and handling the record keeping associated with these transactions. Rather in the academic context, *efficiency* meant that the stock market quickly incorporated information, so that at any point in time the prices of securities rather accurately reflected all that was known and knowable about the issuer's prospects. In the nineteenth century, perhaps, a company might discover oil in Texas or in Indonesia, and the news would not arrive in New York or London for days. Or a company's main factory might have a serious fire in Cleveland or Düsseldorf, and the market would not hear about it. But by the mid-twentieth century, advances in telecommunications and disclosure regulations meant that news quickly arrived at the stock market and was immediately factored into the share prices. If British Petroleum found a major oil field Tuesday morning, the market would quickly know that, and the price of BP shares would quickly change that same morning to reflect the company's enhanced prospects.

As information flows were accelerating, in the same period regulations with respect to the use of nonpublic information were imposed in many markets, so that those who were privy to inside information were not allowed to use it in buying and selling investments.

To be sure, not all segments of all markets were efficient all the time. The market for small cap stocks, for example, was less efficient because there were fewer analysts and others watching smaller companies. And sometimes major markets would act irrationally as investors were caught up in emotional responses to events. But the theorists argued that most major securities markets in the United States and Western Europe, for example, were generally very efficient.

The efficient market hypothesis said two things to investors. On the one hand, there was substantial evidence that the stock market did better than the bond market over the long run, which was a consequence of the existence of a risk premium as a reward for taking on higher risks. On the other hand, efforts to pick the best-performing individual stocks were essentially doomed; the average investment manager could not outperform an efficient market, and once a manager's fees and transaction costs were deducted, their performance was often below that of the market as a whole. Managers who had extraordinary skills could beat the market, but the average investor could expect to do about average.

How could investors gain exposure to the broad market without incurring the costs of management? Again, the rise of computing power made it possible to achieve this objective. It was possible to develop and maintain a portfolio that would contain all of the stocks comprising a major index. A little later, computer programs would indicate that it was possible to shadow the index using fewer stocks than the universe, making these portfolios even more cost-effective. In the U.S. market, the Dow-Jones Industrial Average had only 30 stocks and was not regarded as reflective of the broader market, but the Standard & Poor's 500 Stock Index was considered representative of the U.S. equity market. And beginning in 1971,[8] several investment management firms, with Wells Fargo taking the lead, began to offer index funds.

Indexing was a very controversial approach. Indeed it was decried in some U.S. investment circles as "un-American," perhaps even unpatriotic. Choosing to index essentially said that the plan sponsor agreed that it couldn't beat the market, so it would settle for matching the market, giving up the opportunity to outperform in return for the guarantee that it would not underperform. This form of "passive" management was attacked by "active" managers who insisted that there were plenty of examples of managers who had, in fact, beaten the market, not only in any given year, but often year after year. The theoreticians of indexing agreed that outperformance was possible, just as gamblers sometimes beat the house, but beating the market was a zero sum game; those who outperformed had to be matched by others who underperformed. And they argued that mathematically, those who outperformed, even for an extended period of time, did not necessarily have any more skill than a gambler who kept winning at the roulette wheel. Institutional investors were being told that there might be exceptional managers who might be able to find managers who could outperform the markets in which they were investing, but it would be exceedingly difficult to find those managers and achieve exceptional results consistently over the long term.

DISCONTENT WITH THE PARADIGM

While some turned to indexing, by the 1990s, others were seeking ways to revise the MPT-driven investment paradigm in a fashion that corrected what they saw as weaknesses in it.

One major concern was that the fleet of managers used by pension funds had often grown too large and unwieldy. The response at some institutions was a decrease in the number of managers. In some cases mandates were defined more broadly. In others, plan sponsors simply hired fewer managers in each of the categories that they had established.

A more basic concern was that the MPT paradigm meant that nobody really had broad responsibility. The division of labor among plan sponsors, consultants, and investment managers meant that everybody had a narrow range of interests. In a legal sense, the plan sponsor was a fiduciary, responsible for advancing the interests of the plan participants. However, the various investment managers and service providers were not necessarily fiduciaries in the legal sense, and in a practical sense they were simply hired hands who had a specific job to do with little reason to concern themselves with the overall status of the plan. Those who had expertise had little overall responsibility for the plan, and those who had responsibility sometimes had little expertise.

The plan sponsor was an amateur. At many corporations, the pension plan was overseen by an assistant treasurer, one of two or three people holding that title within the company's treasury department. Individuals would be rotated through the job of overseeing the pension fund and then moved on to other treasury functions in order to groom them for broader financial responsibilities at the company.

In the case of public employee pension funds, there would be a small staff that worked for a pension board that was typically composed of representatives of the government agency. In the case of U.S. teachers' retirement funds, for example, the board would consist of a number of teachers. In the case of police and firefighters' funds, the board would contain representatives of the various categories, including police patrolmen and uniformed firefighters as well as senior officers from these two corps. The board members were typically chosen because they had been active in their labor union or other employee associations, and there was no test of their financial knowledge or acumen.

These people depended heavily on their consultants and their investment managers, but the managers had limited purviews, as did the consultants.

There was one brief attempt to rectify this in the United States during the late 1980s. Several corporate pension plans, including that of GTE, which was then a major telecommunications company, sought to develop a "strategic partnership" with their investment managers. In the case of GTE, the company singled out four major investment management firms and placed the bulk of the pension assets with these firms. They were to have rights and responsibilities that were far broader than what was contained in typical investment management mandates. These managers could, for example, allocate funds under their control among various asset classes and categories of investments. This approach was an attempt to enhance the plan sponsor's relationship with its investment managers. From the point of view of the manager, meanwhile, this was a welcome way to strengthen the commercial ties with a large customer.

It was seen by some as a return to balanced management. But this time around it was being done with managers who had teams of specialists within their own organization. Thus, it seemed to offer the benefits of specialization along with the benefits of a single manager who would exercise broad responsibility for the pension plan.

This approach did not catch on in the United States or elsewhere, however. One concern was that it was unlikely that a single asset-management firm could, in fact, effectively shift assets from one asset class or strategy to another. While it might have the requisite expertise under one roof, there would be institutional constraints that could prevent the manager from taking money from one department and giving it to another.

Despite a brief flurry of interest during which GTE officials and others discussed their approach at assorted conferences, little would be heard about this approach after the initial flurries of discussion. There were simply too many flaws in this approach. How could plan sponsors decide who would be the best strategic partners? And could these partners be equally good at managing equities, bonds, and other assets, or would some partner have more expertise in a certain area? Would partners shift between assets for the benefit of the fund, even if that would mean their overall level of fees would decline? Would assets be shifted for the benefit of the plan sponsor or to meet the needs of the manager?

THE NEED FOR FIDUCIARY MANAGERS

Thus, as the twenty-first century began to unfold, there was substantial discontent among plan sponsors and other institutions regarding the prevailing investment management structure. Too many people had a role while no one had overall responsibility. The fund managers were not allowed to share their expertise; their job was simply to manage funds according to the style that had led to their selection; to do otherwise was evidence of *style drift* and grounds for termination. The consultants were paid a per diem and gave their advice accordingly. Cynics postulated that some consultants might seek to increase their own returns and recoup the costs of their research by doling out the same data, and, perhaps the same advice as well, to their roster of clients.

Meanwhile, having outsourced much of the work of running a pension plan, the plan sponsor was likely to be a small organization with limited expertise. It was deeply dependent on both its consultants and managers, just as it was dependent on its actuaries and other experts for specialized counsel.

Fiduciary Management came into being in response to these problems. Fiduciary Management seeks to reunite expertise and responsibility. It seeks to ensure that those who oversee managers and consultants have both the expertise to do this job and also to have close enough ties to the plan sponsor to do this job effectively.

The Fiduciary Manager cannot be an individual: it has to be a firm, and a rather large one. It can be a firm that does nothing other than serve as a Fiduciary Manager, or it can be a department of a firm with other activities and businesses, such as investment management. The only requirement is that the Fiduciary Manager be responsible to the plan sponsor—and only the plan sponsor—and that it have the expertise to oversee the funds' advisors and investment managers.

Turning to a Fiduciary Manager does not mean reducing reliance on specialized investment managers. In fact, the Fiduciary Manager is supposed to provide the expertise that a plan sponsor requires to manage a large fleet of specialized managers effectively. Similarly, having a Fiduciary Manager does not mean reducing reliance on the classic pension fund investment consultants. Again, interposing a Fiduciary Manager means that the expertise of these consulting firms could be tapped more effectively because the plan sponsor would have a better understanding of what a pensions consultant could and could not do. Indeed, the traditional pension fund consultant can stay on board, although his or her responsibilities will be more focused and redirected (for instance, in the direction of reporting on the fiduciary).

As the first decade of this century continued to unfold, a number of pension plans around the world began to examine and adopt the principle of Fiduciary Management. And their experiences suggest that there is much that other institutions could learn from their experiences.

CHAPTER 2

Pension Plans

The Principal Setting for Fiduciary Management

Fiduciary Management is best understood as an organizational structure and set of relationships that are most frequently utilized in connection with pension funds, although these ideas are certainly applicable to the management of investment assets belonging to insurance companies and other institutions. Pension funds, however, represent one of the largest pools of capital in the world, and the principles of Fiduciary Management are particularly applicable in that setting.

Consequently, it is important for the reader to understand the issues and ideas that provide the underpinnings for pension funds and shape the requirements of their investment management process.

THE HISTORICAL IDEA OF PENSIONS

The idea of paying an income to sizable numbers of people who are no longer working is an idea largely associated with modern times. It grows out of several developments whose role is not always examined. The first is the idea of old age: For most of human history, most people died young. In the mid to late nineteenth century, however, improvements in personal and social hygiene, in coordination with new developments in medical science, unleashed an extension in longevity that continues to this day. Decade after decade, people have been living longer. Today, people in the advanced developed countries can generally expect to live well into their eighties. This is double the life expectancy during much of the nineteenth century.

Increasing life expectancy gave rise to the idea of retirement. People who lived to an advanced age could not be expected to continue working their entire life, particularly since most jobs involved physically demanding

15

tasks. There was a gradual acceptance of the view that at some advanced age, people could and should retire and live out their days without working.

But that raised the question about how they would be supported financially. For much of human history, the old, like the infirm, were taken care of by their extended family. Indeed, one reason people had large numbers of children was to ensure that there would, in fact, be someone who would take care of them in their old age.

However, the growth of urbanization and industrialization meant that more and more individuals did not live among their extended families but rather in a nuclear family setting. Meanwhile, as industrialization took hold in the nineteenth century, more and more individuals were also working in large organizations in which personal relationships with their employer were being replaced by rules and regulations.

It was largely in this context that the idea of large-scale pension plans was born. To be sure, there are examples of pensions in settings dating back to antiquity. In many of these cases, however, these pensions were no more than individual arrangements granted as a favor or honor; at most they were applicable to a few high-ranking people. In ancient Rome, there were the beginnings of what could be labeled a pension system, which was open to soldiers who made regular contributions and in exchange obtained the right to receive a pension for themselves and their relatives after active duty.

There were also several early attempts to create pensions in the sixteenth and seventeenth centuries. There were, for example, provisions for sailors (France from 1673), miners (Germany from the sixteenth century), and naval officers (England around the 1670s). But many trace the beginning of a coherent system of pension fund benefits to nineteenth-century France. Starting in 1817, some government workers were offered pension benefits, and in 1831 military personnel were also offered retirement pensions. In 1850, the National Retirement Fund was founded in France. It lasted until 1910, when legislation was enacted to cover a broader group of workers. In 1930, all workers were covered.

As these changes were unfolding in France, in Germany, Otto von Bismarck enacted a social security system in 1881 that provided financial protection against the income consequences of old age and ill health. It is generally agreed by historians that labor unions were a major force in spurring the development of social protection for the weak, and it has been argued that Bismarck introduced his pension system in order to curb the popularity of the left which demanded it. The law originally only covered blue-collar workers, and it took years before all workers were protected. England followed in 1908 with modest, means-tested state pensions for people over 70 years of age who had "good character."

In 1935 the United States introduced its Social Security system, as a form of social insurance providing pensions to older people. This system covered some 60 percent of the total workforce. Before that date, however, federal civil servants and military personnel were already covered by a federal government pensions law. It took until the 1950s before Social Security reached something approaching total coverage.[1] Even today, ironically perhaps, many government workers at the federal, state, and local levels are not covered by Social Security.

Many of the systematic first steps to creating pensions were in the public sector, where the idea of the welfare state would eventually become the successor to the "poor laws." That meant the state slowly replaced charity in providing basic relief for people in poverty, and for the aged as well.

Meanwhile, from the late nineteenth century onward, private-sector employers were also urged to create pension plans for their workers. Slowly they did so. A number of the earliest plans were set up in mass-production industries, such as steel, autos, and others in which there were large cadres of workers and trade unions to bargain on behalf of employees.

European immigrants brought the desire for pensions to the United States in the early 1900s, and a few pension plans were created early in the century. Generally, however, private-sector pensions in the United States were put off, first by the Great Depression, and then by World War Two. Following the war, however, in the late 1940s and early 1950s, collective bargaining agreements in such industries as steel, automobile manufacturing, coal mining, and other heavy industries began to include pension plans. This would be followed by substantial portions of the textile and garment industry.

Until the beginning of the 1980s, the concept of a pension was largely synonymous with the idea of a *defined benefit* (DB) plan; that is, the promise of a pension meant that upon retirement, an individual would receive a predetermined amount for the rest of his or her life. That amount could be fixed well in advance. Or it could be based on some formula related to the individual's salary during some period of time, such as the last year of working prior to retirement.

Beginning in the 1980s, there was substantial growth in *defined contribution* (DC) plans. In these plans, the employer does not specify what benefits the retiree will receive. Instead, an investment account is opened for an employee, the employer and/or the employee make contributions to it, and upon retirement the individual can draw upon the money in the account. Depending on how much is contributed and how well it is invested, the retiree could have more than enough for a comfortable retirement, or less than enough. But the employer did not have a role in doling out benefit payments, nor in guaranteeing that there was enough money available to provide some specific level of retirement income.

There are both important similarities and important differences in the social insurance and retirement income systems among the industrial countries. Flora and Heidenheimer (New Brunswick, 1982) summarize the historical development of these plans in Table 2.1.

The conclusion from the table is that, despite a long history of pensions, the pension system as a coherent entity with its place in legislation and social policy is fairly recent and lags behind other social legislation in the majority of countries.

A PATCHWORK OF PENSION PROVISIONS

Once the idea of paying a pension was accepted, the next question was: Where would the money come from? Governments essentially paid the pensions they offered to the populace out of current tax revenues. Because they have the power to levy taxes, governments can pay pensions through an intergenerational transfer of wealth: Those who are working are taxed to pay the benefits to those who have retired. (This worked well until birth rates declined sharply, and now governments are straining to generate the revenues needed to pay promised benefits.) Companies in certain countries, including Germany, also chose to treat pension obligations as a current expense.

But in other countries, as noted in the previous chapter, a different view took hold. Pensions were obligations that a company was incurring bit by bit, and therefore the funds to pay those pensions should also be accumulated bit by bit. The same principle was used in matching the development of other assets and liabilities, and it seemed to accord with sound accounting principles to accrue both liabilities and assets in the pension field. Since tax laws typically provided for tax deductions for money that was contributed to a pension plan, this provided further encouragement for the establishment of pension plans.

These pension plans would accumulate funds that would be used to pay pensions in the future. A body of law grew up regarding the nature of these plans, and a body of experience began to develop regarding the investment of the funds being accumulated.

The role of funding has differed markedly among countries. The United Kingdom, the United States, and the Netherlands differ from many other countries in that the majority of future pension benefits have been funded. Many other countries depend to a much higher degree on a pay-as-you-go system.

TABLE 2.1 Core Social Insurance Laws in Western Europe and America

Country	Industrial Accident Insurance		Sickness Insurance		Pension Insurance		Unemployment Insurance	
	Employer's Liability	Compulsory Insurance	Subsidized Voluntary	Compulsory	Subsidized Voluntary	Compulsory	Subsidized Voluntary	Compulsory
Austria		1887		1888		1906		1920
Belgium	1903		1894	1944	1900	1924	1907	1944
Denmark	1898	1916	1892	1933 (semicomp)		1891	1907	
Finland		1895		1963		1937	1917	
France	1898	1946		1930		1910		1914
Germany		1884		1883		1889		1927
Italy		1898	1886	1928	1898	1919		1919
Netherlands		1901		1913		1913	1934	
Norway		1894		1909		1936	1906	1938
Sweden	1901	1916	1891	1910		1913	1934	1934
Switzerland		1911	1911			1946	1924	
United Kingdom	1906	1946		1911		1908		1911
United States	1930				1935	1935	1935	1935
Canada	1930			1971		1927		1940

Source: Flora, P. and Heidenheimer, A.J., New Brunswick, 1982, page 59. Copyright © 1982 by Transaction Publishers. Reprinted by permission of the publisher.

In the case of funded pension plans, by custom and then by law, in several nations, the pension fund came to be seen as separate from the employer who was accumulating funds in it. In the American legal system, there was a *pension plan*, and it was created and operated by a *plan sponsor* (i.e., the employer). A body of law in the United States and some other countries was developed that stipulated that once the plan sponsor contributed money to a pension plan, that money no longer belonged to the sponsor but rather to the plan itself.[2,3] Other countries, however, did not take that view. For instance, Germany, Canada, and Sweden, hold part of the assets, earmarked for future pensions, in so-called book reserves, which are defined as "sums, entered in the balance sheet of the plan sponsor as reserves or provisions for pension benefits. Some assets may be held in separate accounts for the purpose of financing benefits, but are not legally or contractually pension plan assets."[4]

In most countries with funded pension plans, the plan sponsor had a fiduciary duty to manage the plan on behalf of the plan participants. Self-dealing would be prohibited, and the plan, whether governed by a board of trustees or a set of managers, had to be operated in the interests of the plan participants, even though those overseeing the plan were employees of the plan sponsor.

An indication as to the degree countries differ in funding their pension liabilities can be derived from Table 2.2.

As pension fund assets grew, they came to represent important pools of assets in terms of the investment management industry and also the capital formation process. In a substantial number of countries with funded pension plans (9 out of the 29 countries with data published), pension assets represent weights of 5 percent of GDP or less, but in five countries pension assets have weights of 50 percent or more, and in Iceland, Switzerland, and the Netherlands these investments actually exceed the nation's GDP.

It is noteworthy that several non-OECD countries have created funded pension plans in recent years, and these plans have grown rapidly. Chile, Malaysia, and Singapore, for example, each have accumulated pension fund assets equal to some 60 percent of GDP.

For many years, pension assets have grown rapidly in many countries. In the OECD countries, total investment of pension funds increased by almost 20 percent, raising the ratio of investments to GDP from 57.3 in 2002 to 87.6 percent in 2005 (redefining pension fund assets in Finland and Sweden in this period increased the share in their GDP's substantially with 35 and 4.7 percentage points respectively, but this explains just 0.25 percent of the rise in OECD GDP). The fastest growth is recorded in the countries that started from a relatively small base (between 24 and 58 percent in countries such as Spain, Norway, Hungary, and the Czech Republic). But in more

TABLE 2.2 Size of Pension Funds' Investments, Absolute and Relative to GDP, 2005

OECD Countries	Total Investment (Millions of US Dollars)	Total Investment (Share of Gross Domestic Product, %)
Australia	409,372	58.0
Austria	14,291	4.7
Belgium	15,430	4.2
Canada	569,216	50.4
Denmark	87,032	33.6
Finland	127,691	66.1
France	123,660	5.8
Germany	107,856	3.9
Iceland	19,517	123.2
Italy	49,520	2.8
Japan	864,707	18.8
Netherlands	779,843	124.9
Sweden	51,716	14.5
Switzerland	428,634	117.4
United Kingdom	1,541,100	70.1
United States	12,348,250	98.9
Total OECD	17,914,971	87.6
Euro area	1,451,074	21.8

Source: Pension Markets in Focus—October 2006—Issue 3, © 2006 OECD.

mature countries, growth rates have been between 4 and 15 percent over the period 2001–2003. The years 2003–2005 saw strong growth in Poland and, remarkably for a more mature country, France, while Italy, recording strong growth until 2003, fell back.

The true picture of saving for retirement cannot be grasped only by looking at pension plans themselves. In many countries funded arrangements include huge amounts in pension insurance contracts and pension plans managed by other financial institutions, such as banks and investment companies. Broad data is not available for most countries, especially for retail products (i.e., personal pension plans). Yet these figures can alter the financial picture in a country very significantly. Table 2.3 provides an indication for 2004. Compared to 2003, Italy, for example, shows a strong deterioration of the pension fund share for the benefit of book reserves, while Sweden has increased the pension fund share to the detriment of pension insurance contracts.

Book reserves, in which employers indicate how much money they are obliged to pay out in pensions but do not actually set aside that money in

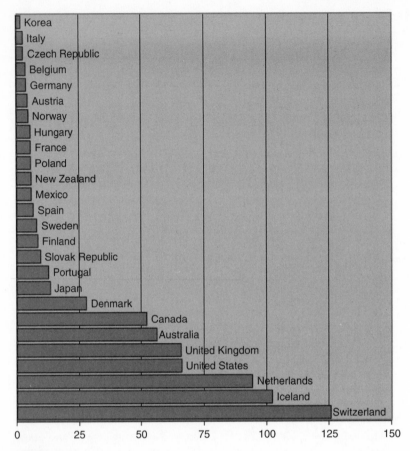

FIGURE 2.1   Importance of Pension Funds in OECD Countries, 2005 (% GDP)
Source: Pension Markets in Focus—October 2006—Issue 3, © 2006 OECD.

a separate account, are obviously different from funded plan assets, but an estimate of a nation's overall pensions assets can be obtained by combining pension fund assets and life-insurance assets. These aggregations are shown for the most important countries in Table 2.4 (The data is for 2003 as later issues of *Pension Markets in Focus* do not specify the combined figures).

While countries such as France, Italy, and Denmark showed a relatively small base of pension fund assets, life insurance contracts compensate to a large extent. France's pension funds assets are only one-eighth of Canada's (in terms of GDP) and one-third of Japan's. Thus, though France does not have substantial amounts in funded pension plans, when insurance contracts are included, France's asset position is comparable with these countries.

TABLE 2.3 Private Pension Plans Assets by Type of Financing Vehicles, 2004

Country	Pension Funds		Book Reserves		Pension Insurance Contracts	
	Millions of USD	Share of Total (Percent)	Millions of USD	Share of Total (Percent)	Millions of USD	Share of Total (Percent)
Canada	477,439	73	126,821	19	50,189	8
Denmark	73,095	29	—	—	179,684	71
Finland	84,271	87	—	—	12,748	13
Italy	44,351	87	4,197	8	2,671	5
Korea	11,516	25	—	—	35,309	75
Spain	95,185	85	16,648	15	—	—
Sweden	43,402	32	6,463	5	86,403	63
United States	11,638,070	85	—	—	1,986,963	15

Source: Pension Markets in Focus—October 2006—Issue 3, © 2006 OECD.

By contrast, the countries with the largest pension fund presence do not lose their top position by adding insurance arrangements.

It is obvious that pension savings are an extremely important portion of the financial and economic system in many countries and in the global economy as well. Because of the differences in pension structures from country to country, it is useful to review in more detail the structure of pension plans in several advanced industrial countries (The figures used here refer to the years 2004 and 2005).

ORGANIZATION AND REGULATION OF THE PENSION SYSTEM IN SEVERAL OECD COUNTRIES[5]

Denmark

The fundamental concept underpinning the first of the three pillars of the Danish retirement income system is a national pension provided by the government. The second pillar is the ATP (Arbejdmarkedets Tillaegs Pension) occupational pension system, which was established in 1963 and is compulsory for the majority of wage earners. It is a fully funded scheme in which employers and employees both contribute, roughly at a ratio of two to one. It covers approximately 90 percent of the workforce and offers defined benefits. Its funds are managed externally. The third pillar consists of mandatory occupational retirement and disability schemes, which take the

TABLE 2.4   Pension Funds and Life-Insurance Assets in OECD Countries (2003)

Countries	Millions of USD	Share of GDP (Percent)
Australia	337,385	82
Austria	45,793	23
Belgium	89,978	37
Canada	501,153	69
Denmark	163,950	95
Finland	33,119	25
France	813,085	57
Italy	258,071	22
Japan	1,949,909	49
Netherlands	539,343	129
Switzerland	497,241	186
United Kingdom	2,004,478	128
Unites States	8,450,761	81
Total	15,932,747	88

Source: *Pension Markets in Focus*—June 2005—Issue 1, © 2005 OECD.

form of industry-wide pension funds, as well as a number of labor-market funds and individual corporate plans or insured schemes with private insurance companies.

On top of this whole system, banks and insurance companies offer personal retirement products. Some 80 percent of employees contribute to voluntary occupational plans, mainly defined contribution plans.

Both the compulsory and the voluntary schemes can be funded in three ways: group insurance schemes, pension funds, or bank schemes. Insurance schemes are the most popular, offering a guarantee of minimum returns. The level of investments in certain areas is regulated (for instance, plans may be required to have a minimum of 30 percent of assets in government bonds and no more than 50 percent in equities). A minimum guarantee is imposed as well, which goes hand in hand with investment restrictions. There are two types of bank schemes: group schemes and individual schemes, which are organized as pools and separate accounts, respectively.

The regulator uses two stress tests to ensure that pension funds (and life-insurance companies) meet risk-based capital measures. This traffic light system differentiates between scenarios regarding equity losses and movements in interest rates. The yellow scenario, for instance, calls for a certain amount of capital to be set aside when equity prices decline by more than 30 percent and interest rates move up or down at least 100 basis points. Failing this test implies that funds have to report on capital adequacy regularly and publicly because the assets are viewed as "potentially in danger." In the red test, the shocks in equity prices and interest rates are smaller. Failing this test has more severe consequences, such as increased regulatory oversight, mandatory sale of risky assets, or even the assumption of management duties by the regulator. Future liabilities of the pension funds are marked-to-market.

There are two and a half times as many industry-wide pension funds as corporate plans in the survey (33 versus 13), but the assets of corporate plans are twice those of the industry-wide plans. (One major corporation represents 60 percent of all the assets of corporate pension funds.) Two public pension funds are about one-third larger than all the corporate pension funds together. The assets under management, according to the survey, are as follows: industry-wide plans: € 61 billion; corporate plans: € 31 billion; public authorities: € 40 billion.

France

The first pillar, comprised of the social security system, and the second, the complementary Caisses de Retraite, which is compulsory for private sector employees, both operate on a pay-as-you-go basis and offer defined benefits. Both schemes are in deficit and threaten to sink further into the red with the rapid aging of French society. The reserve fund, introduced to cope with these deficits in 1999, is already experiencing a shortfall. Compulsory schemes are generally organized on an industry-wide basis, and they predominate. Funding is provided by contributions from both employers (60 percent) and employees (40 percent).

Occupational pension funds hardly exist, as almost all employees are members of the mandatory schemes. Book reserves are not common, either. Funding of occupational schemes is not set by regulation but rather is determined through collective bargaining between employers and employees.

Employees can supplement their retirement income by making additional contributions to the mandatory schemes and by savings through voluntary plans, including company savings plans, group insurance, and individual insurance. Both employees and employers can contribute to the savings plans, which have a minimum investment period.

There are no consistent standards in such areas as accounting and actuarial treatments, funding ratios, or investment guidelines. Voluntary occupational schemes must grow at least 2.5 percent per year, and they are usually insured under life insurance contracts. There is a strong link between the pension schemes and the life insurance business, in that investment regulations are guided by prudential requirements concerning the insurers' overall life insurance portfolio.

Germany

Germany's social security system, which is one of the most comprehensive in the world, is organized on a pay-as-you-go basis. In 2002, social security costs represented some 42 percent of average salary, of which 19 percent represented retirement, survivor, and disability benefits.

The first pillar is a compulsory defined benefit plan, financed equally by employers and employees. In the second pillar, retirement schemes, mostly industry-wide, are offered by many companies, and they can be defined benefit, defined contribution, or defined contribution with a minimum benefit. Employees can also opt for deferred compensation schemes, in which present payments are reduced to finance higher pensions.

With a wary eye on the very fast growth of future liabilities, the pension system was reformed in 2001. One of the goals was to stimulate supplementary private pension plans by subsidizing contributions (the so-called Riester-subsidy). The occupational retirement benefit system is supported by a complex web of five funding vehicles: book reserves, support funds, pension funds, *Pensionskassen*, and direct insurance. Each vehicle has its own investment guidelines and mode of assessing its liability structure. Book reserves and unsubsidized support funds generally offer defined benefits, whereas Pensionskassen, pension funds, and direct insurance mostly offer defined contribution.

Pension funds can be set up by a single company, a financial services provider, or on an industry-wide basis under the sponsorship of an employers association and the trade unions in that industry. Asset classes and the principles of diversification are regulated by the Ministry of Finance. Investments are guided by the prudent person principle. Investments are restricted by a capital maintenance guarantee granted by the pension fund and the employer. *Pensionskassen* have separate regulations, but they are comparable to that of the pension funds. To guarantee that future retirement obligations will be met, the regulator requires companies to take out insurance to protect pension assets.

Starting around 2006, the increasing burden of pension costs in the graying German society led to a discussion about the way the *Investivlohn* should be invested. This part of the yearly wage increase, is not to be doled out as normal wages but should be invested in the company itself or in other companies. Many experts argue that pension funds are the place where those monies should be allocated. This procedure would alleviate the problem of reinvesting this part of the wage sum in the smaller companies that pay these wages and would strengthen the benefits of efficient large-scale investors. However, the biggest advantage of this approach is that future returns would be more stable and/or higher. This would be a welcome counterbalance to the fact that the larger part of the "Riester money" has gone to insurance companies, which typically invest around 80 percent of their funds in fixed income and only some 10 percent in shares.[6] While 6.5 million of the overall 8 million "Riester-agreements" have been contracted with insurance companies, the return prospect of this pension money would be enhanced by allocating it to pension funds.

The Netherlands

The Dutch social security system offers flat rate pensions as a basic retirement provision, financed on a pay-as-you-go basis with contributions made entirely by employees.

Occupational schemes are not mandatory, except in the industry-wide schemes, but they cover more than 90 percent of employees. Virtually all of them are defined benefit plans, but defined contribution is growing strongly. In fact, almost all new pension contracts, whether they are industry-wide or with a specific company, are defined contribution plans.

The funding for occupational schemes can take two forms: pension funds (industry-wide and single employer) or insurance schemes. Most schemes are industry-wide, but investment restrictions are the same for single-employer plans. Both employers and employees make compulsory contributions. Insurance contracts are executed either as individual insurance contracts or as group insurance contracts.

Investment regulation is guided by the prudent person principle: assets must be invested in a prudent manner, which means that sources of risk and return should be well diversified. The investment management of the pension funds can be internal or external. Before 2007, liabilities and fixed income investments were not marked-to-market; instead, both were increased at an annual rate of 4 percent, although pension funds were allowed to value their fixed income investments at market prices. Starting in 2007, however, liabilities and fixed income portfolios are required to be marked-to-market.

Pension funds are subject to a minimum funding level of 105 percent of liabilities at all times. In addition, pension funds require different buffers for the specified asset classes (35 percent for equities, 8 percent for bonds, etc.).

There are a number of unique features of the Dutch pension fund world. First of all, although the Netherlands can be called a medium-sized country at most, it is home to some of the largest pension funds in the world. This is because several occupational schemes draw their participants from across the nation. As a result, the pension funds for civil servants (ABP) or health care workers (PGGM) are huge. In addition, Dutch pension funds are permitted to raise subordinated debt. Another distinctive feature is the reversion clause, which says that if pension funds are solvent (meaning that the funding ratio is greater than 160 percent), the corporate plan sponsor has the right to take cash out of the plan.

While historically most pension schemes were defined benefit plans, defined contribution plans are becoming more common, largely as a consequence of new, more strict, regulation. Many regard this as a deterioration in one of the best national systems of employment-related pension funds. The issue is not only about the level of benefits provided by most DC plans but also the concern that going from DB to DC implies the transfer of risk from the employer to the employee.[7] Under an individual DC plan, the individual employee has to balance risks and returns in deciding his or her portfolio mix. But most employees lack the level of know-how and/or do not spend enough attention to this underestimated matter. Nowadays, collective defined contribution schemes are created and gain popularity in order to make use of the economies of scale of pension funds and, more importantly, to have a framework in which individual decisions are replaced by the policy decisions of the pension fund board. This way, two disadvantages of individual DC schemes are avoided. Moreover, risk management is more effective: the larger entity can assume more risk and the decisions on the risk budget are taken by people who can make better-informed decisions. However positive this latest development may be, the fact remains that going from DB to DC still implies the transfer of risk from the employer to the employee. In an excellent, very outspoken, study, Keating uses the two types of schemes to define insurance contracts (defined benefits) and saving plans (defined contribution).[8] Regulation is tailored to this distinction.

During the last few years major changes have altered the Dutch pension landscape. The Dutch central bank, which oversees financial institutions, devised a new regulatory scheme that served as a prelude for new legislation in this field. The most important changes relate to the valuation of both assets and liabilities and the application of a *sufficiency test*, which measures the ability of a pension fund to meet its present and future liabilities. The solvency test has had a particularly large impact on the investment and contribution strategy of pension funds.

Marking to Market   In recent years, long-term interest rates have been lower than the fixed compounding rate of 4 percent, which means that the change from fixed compounding rates to market interest rates increases the value of the fixed income portfolio. However, the liability side is affected to a much larger extent. This is because the fixed income portfolio typically represents only part of the assets covering the liabilities and also because a duration gap exists most of the time, causing interest rates to have a greater effect on liabilities than on fixed income assets. Dutch pension funds generally have a fixed income portfolio whose duration is far shorter than the duration of the liabilities. For these two reasons, the value of the fixed income portfolio changes less with interest rate levels than the compounded value of the

TABLE 2.5 Balance Sheet

Fixed income portfolio (duration 6 years)	250	Liabilities (duration 12 years)	400
Equities and real estate	300	Reserves	150
	550		550

liabilities. Thus, the interest rate risk is only partially hedged. This situation is illustrated in Table 2.5:

In case interest rate levels decline by 1 percentage point:

- Liabilities rise by 12 * 1% * 400 = 48;
- Fixed income portfolio rises by 6 * 1% * 250 = 15;
- Hedge = 15/48 = 31.25%
- The hedge being lower than 100 percent is caused by the fact that the fixed income portfolio is smaller than the value of the liabilities and by the longer duration of those liabilities compared to the fixed income portfolio.

When interest rates decline, both effects lead to a sharp deterioration in the asset-liability surplus (or deficit, for that matter), and for most pension funds, this gap represents the biggest risk in their balance sheet. It can be bridged in several ways. Buying longer fixed income securities is one, but this is not very attractive because it will drive down long-term rates even further. There may also be concerns about the availability of such securities.[9] The gap also requires more fixed income to be bought, so the asset allocation for equity and other higher-returning assets declines, leaving fewer opportunities to earn sufficient returns for indexing future liabilities to reflect cost-of-living increases. One way to close the duration gap without excessive effects on the asset mix is to use derivatives (especially swaps and swaptions), but the other disadvantages remain.

Sufficiency Test   This test measures the ability of a fund to meet its future liabilities over various time horizons. As noted, Dutch pension funds are required to have a minimum solvency ratio of at least 105 percent at all times. The solvency test is an indication of the degree to which a fund is affected by adverse developments in financial markets and by certain developments in the real economy, such as inflation. The surplus should be sufficient to absorb adverse shocks on a one-year basis. Moreover, a pension fund should be able to absorb the impact of significant changes in interest rates, major declines in equities prices, and perhaps a rise in inflation as well, and still have a probability of 97.5 percent that it will remain in surplus.

If the minimum test is not passed, the plan must rectify the situation within three years. If the institution fails the solvency test, a plan has to be submitted for restoring buffers. The restoration period in this case can be up to 15 years. The continuity test assesses the adequacy of an institution's risk management policies over the longer term. The solvency test can be applied using either a standardized methodology or an internally developed risk model. The internally developed risk model must be approved by the regulator, and the results must be reconciled with the outcome of the regulator's standardized method, which serves as a benchmark. A simpler model can be used as well, but it is permitted only when the risk profile of the fund and its operational management meet certain standards.[10]

Sweden

Sweden's social security system, which is supplemented by the national pension scheme, is essentially a pay-as-you-go model. There have been recent changes, however, which provide for partial funding, and there has also been a move toward a defined contribution model paid for by both employers and employees.

The overwhelming majority (some 95 percent) of private and public sector employees participate in occupational pension schemes in the second pillar. The two main private schemes are the ITP schemes for white collar workers and the STP schemes for blue collar employees. ITP schemes can either be defined benefit or defined contribution plans, while STP schemes are compulsory defined contribution plans. Above a certain income threshold, employees have the choice to opt out of the defined benefit scheme and put money into an investment scheme of their own. These are typically defined contribution schemes.

Pension funds, group insurance, and book reserves are the most important ways of funding occupational plans. Pension funds, which are dominantly defined benefit plans, tend to be organized by company, and they can be separate legal entities. Minimum funding rules are not mandatory, and there are no specific investment restrictions besides the prudent person rule and a solvency requirement. However, pension funds are under obligation to participate in a credit insurance system, which protects the pension assets and guarantees that future pensions will be paid. Most of the defined contribution plans are funded by group insurance contracts, and these plans also have to participate in the credit insurance system. The employees choose their investment vehicle (bank or insurance company).

As in Denmark, a traffic light system is in operation for both pension funds and insurance companies. Companies have discretion in selecting a market-consistent discount rate.

Switzerland

The Swiss federal social security system is a compulsory scheme that covers retirement, survivor, disability, accidents, and unemployment. Employers and employees contribute equally. In addition to the state plan, private occupational (second pillar) and personal schemes (third pillar) also provide pensions.

The occupational pension system has a compulsory component, a voluntary part, and an autonomous or semiautonomous part. Company schemes have been mandatory since 1985, and they offer a minimum level of benefit, which means that, implicitly, they have to generate a guaranteed minimum return. Supplementary defined benefits or defined contributions can be offered by companies. Companies are allowed to offer supplementary defined benefit or defined contribution schemes.

In general, investment restrictions are fairly comprehensive. Not only is external financing obligatory for occupational schemes, the entity must also be an employee welfare foundation. Book reserves and other unfunded assets are not permitted. There is a clear definition of permitted assets, and their proportion is limited.

United Kingdom

In the UK, the first pillar consists of a basic state pension (BSP) and the State Second Pension (S2P). The state pension, financed by pay-as-you-go contributions, does not provide adequate retirement income. (It generates less than 20 percent of average earnings.) S2P replaced the former State Earnings-Related Pension Schemes or SERPS arrangement dating back to 1978, but the basic principles have essentially been intact. BSP and S2P both offer no more than a basic level of retirement income.

The second pillar consists of supplementary benefit plans, offered on a noncompulsory basis by most medium and large-sized employers. These are trust funds with a board of trustees making the investment decisions. The majority of private plans are defined benefit arrangements, covering as many as 85 percent of all participants, but increasingly there are signs of a shift towards defined contribution plans. This reflects several forces, including rising longevity, increased accountability of trustees, and the new accounting standards for defined benefit plans (FRS 17), which make pension liabilities more visible on corporate balance sheets.

Instead of contributing to the S2P plan, employees and their employers can contract out the management of their retirement contributions to alternative schemes as long as the benefits promised by these plans are proportional to the future (rather low) rights that the S2P would have offered. Contracting out is conditional on other, more specific tests. Employees may also select hybrid pension plans, which offer a mixture of defined benefit and defined contribution characteristics and which can also be contracted out.

Employees are allowed to increase their retirement savings through additional voluntary contributions (AVCs) or other contribution private accounts. The companies offering pension plans are also obliged to offer savings opportunities through AVCs. In the case of standard AVCs, employees contribute to individual accounts, which are administered by their employer. When free-standing AVCs exist, the retirement savings plans have to be managed outside of the company.

Either personal pension plans or stakeholders plans (mainly for the larger companies) can be used by employees and employers to make further contributions for retirement. They are personal or group plans, offering defined contributions and managed by an external provider. Employers can contribute to the scheme as well, and contracting out of state pension schemes is allowed. Stakeholder plans tend to be defined contribution schemes, and although the employer selects the plan provider, neither the employer nor employee is required to make contributions into the plan.

Pension funds and insurance companies are the main operators of occupational pension schemes. These schemes are generally company-affiliated although industry-wide pension plans are permitted. Insurance companies provide insured schemes directly, while pension benefits are secured by one or more insurance policies or annuity contracts. They are set up under trust and are legally treated the same way as pension funds.

There are no explicit investment restrictions for pension funds, but the presence of employer's and employee's trustees does constrain the use of certain investment vehicles.

The Pension Protection Fund, operational since 2005, pays compensation to members of eligible defined benefit schemes in case of insolvency of the employer and when there are insufficient assets to cover certain levels of compensation. All eligible schemes pay levies to the fund.

The United States

For a number of years, the occupational pension system in the United States consisted of defined benefit plans and supplemental savings schemes. In a relatively short period of time, however, defined contribution plans have gained ground at the cost of defined benefit plans. The former covered 87 percent of pension plan participants in 1975, but only 20 percent in 1999.

The supplementary employer-linked defined contribution scheme includes 401(k) plans for employees of for-profit companies and 403(b) plans for those working at not-for-profit organizations. There is also an assortment of plans open to the self-employed, such as Keogh plans.

Companies are not required by law to provide pension benefits, but many pension plans are required under collective bargaining agreements. The majority of occupational pension schemes are funded pension funds. Most are linked to a single employer, but there are also multi-employer pension funds. These so-called Taft-Hartley plans, named for the authors of the enabling legislation, pool contributions from a range of employers in an industry into a single industry-wide plan. There are various insurance schemes available for companies that want to terminate their defined benefit schemes.

Investment regulations for pension funds are not strict in terms of the range of asset classes in which a plan can invest. The focus of investment rules has more to do with prohibitions against self-dealing and intermingling the assets of the plan and those of the plan sponsor. As in most countries, there are limits on the extent to which a plan can invest in the shares of the plan sponsor. The U.S. government guarantees future retirement benefits through the Pension Benefit Guaranty Corporation.

In recent years, there have been signs of an accelerating movement away from defined benefit plans toward defined contribution plans, with employers closing down existing DB plans and new companies favoring DC schemes. Pension legislation enacted in August 2006 seemed destined to accelerate that shift. This law, the Pensions Protection Act, required plan sponsors to take various steps to ensure that their plans were adequately funded. But many believed that although these efforts might shore up existing defined benefit plans, they would ultimately result in a decline in the number of defined benefit plans as employers found the burden of funding such plans too onerous. While clearly in decline, the U.S. system of defined benefit plans is destined to remain one of the largest pools of capital in the world for many years to come.

Australia

As in many other countries a three-pillar system is in operation in Australia. The state old age pension is a modest, means-tested, pay-as-you-go-based flat-rate entitlement system. The second pillar is a superannuation scheme, which is generally funded with contributions from employers and is managed privately. Some 90 percent of full-time workers are covered by these schemes, and this percentage continues to grow since the system became compulsory in 1992. Employees without employer's support, together with the self-employed, enjoy tax breaks when arranging their own superannuation through life insurance products. Trustees are responsible for management and control of these funds. They can be classified as corporate or enterprise funds, industry funds, and public sector funds. A number of public sector schemes have huge unfunded employer liabilities. The vast majority offer defined contribution. The whole system is topped by retail funds and super-annuation products offered directly to households by insurance companies; almost all of them are defined contribution schemes.

SIMILARITIES AND DIFFERENCES

Over the course of their rather brief history, funded and insured pension plans have assumed an important function in several spheres: In the social sphere, they have come to play a critical role in providing retirement income for older people who are forming a larger and larger propor-tion of the population in so many of the industrialized countries. In the economic sphere, these pools of capital are an important element in the capital formation process. And in the asset management industry, pension assets are far and away the largest source of institutional capital to be managed.

Pension systems in countries around the world have each had their own course of development, and as a result, there are significant differences between regulations and structures in the different countries. Even within the European Union, although there are efforts aimed at harmonization, the systems differ markedly from country to country. Differences in the economic environment as well as in the history and traditions of each country have shaped a range of patterns.

The global system of pension arrangements can best be classified as a patchwork, with some ingredients used in many countries and others unique to a single country.

At first glance these differences may seem surprising. Since the basic principle is the same—taking care of the elderly after their working life is over. Moreover, these plans all share a desire to minimize the burden on the plan sponsors, whether they are taxpayers or employers. And increasingly employment-related plans are investing in financial markets that are all affected by the same global economic trends and developments. So why then, did the systems grow so differently?

A number of factors have been put forward to explain these huge differences. Political ideology has clearly been a major issue. Europe's socialist parties placed a major emphasis on providing substantial social welfare benefits, including pensions for the elderly. Party politics also played a role: offering and expanding pension benefits has been a major bargaining chip in seeking the support of aging voters. The power of labor relative to employers is another factor having a bearing on the way pension funds and other arrangements were structured over the last few decades.

Pension regulations on a national level have been deeply affected by the level of industrialization in a country, the state of development of the financial markets and financial sector, and ideological views regarding the role of the state versus the role of the market.

However, a number of ideas about pensions that once held sway in certain countries have been reversed by economic and social developments. In the Netherlands, for example, some years ago the government sought legislation to tax away so-called surpluses of pension funds. Later that same government sought legislation that ordered pension funds to build surpluses and enlarge their buffers, leading to a complete overhaul of the way the sector is being run.

Moreover, in recent years, the division between the Anglo-Saxon and the Rhineland approach seems to be narrowing as more and more policy makers in German-speaking countries become more inclined to favor market forces and individual decisions as opposed to government involvement in this field.

Finally special events have had an influence on the thinking of how arrangements should be adapted. In the UK, for example, the raid on the pension fund of the Mirror Group by Robert Maxwell and the mistakes made by Equitable Life (an insurance company that nearly collapsed in 2000 and had to cut the pensions and retirement savings of its policyholders in order to stay afloat) probably shaped changes, as regulators sought to shore up the finances of pension plans and to restore confidence in the system as well.

Some of the differences in the European situation with respect to corporate pensions provisions are summarized in Table 2.6.

It is surprising that one of the most striking differences is situated in the highly technical issue of life expectancy. Cass Business School found very large differences in the suppositions made in the various countries with respect to liabilities. Where life expectancy for men of 65 years old does not differ greatly between countries, the assumptions used by corporate pension funds do. While government statistics show the expected retirement period in European countries varies between 15.5 years (low, The Netherlands) and 17.2 years (high, Switzerland), pension funds calculate with figures ranging from 16.4 years (low, The Netherlands) and 24.2 years (high, France).[11] These differences result in sizable differences in calculating the discount factor to be used. This discount factor varies between 2.5 percent in France to 3.0 percent in the UK and to 4.2 percent in The Netherlands. As a result, if Dutch longevity figures are used, liabilities are lower in the UK and therefore, the Dutch discount rate should have been 4.2 percent, as compared to 3.0 percent in the UK, while for France, where liabilities are higher, the discount factor should be 0.5 percentage point lower than in the UK.

TABLE 2.6   General Picture of European Corporate Pension Provision Structure

Importance of corporate pension funds	Strong	The Netherlands, Switzerland, and UK
	Middle (insurance companies and industry-wide funds important as well)	Belgium, Denmark, Finland, Germany, Norway, Sweden
	Low (state pensions most important)	France, Italy
DB versus DC	DB paramount	The Netherlands, Sweden (white collar workers)
	DB and DC with guarantees	Belgium (mostly DB), Denmark (CDC), Germany (mostly DB), Switzerland
	DB and DC mainly DC	Finland, France, Norway, UK Sweden (blue collar workers), Spain
Trust versus nonfinanced liabilities on the balance sheet	Nonfunded arrangements not permitted	Belgium, Denmark, Finland, The Netherlands, Norway, Switzerland, UK
	Nonfunded arrangements permitted	Germany, Sweden, Luxemburg, Spain, Austria
	No requirement to recognize a liability as such on the balance sheet	France

Source: Courtesy of J.P. Morgan Asset Management. Franceries, Unravelling the Liability Challenge: An Investment Management Perspective Date, Is there a United Europe for Pension Risk? Berlin, December 1, 2005.

COMMONALITIES ON THE ASSET SIDE

It is clear that pension funds and the pension arrangements with insurance companies around the world do not share one grand design; rather they are a reflection of the political and economic situation of each country. Nonetheless, insofar as there are funded plans, there have been signs of some convergence regarding the management of their assets. There continue to be substantial differences in the amounts allocated to various asset classes: Pension funds in the United States and UK typically have much more invested in equities than pension plans in Continental Europe, for example. But the range of asset classes pension funds invest in, and the approaches and modes of analysis of these assets classes are closer together than they were in the past.

This reflects several factors. One is that they share many similar investment objectives: they either seek to maximize returns within certain risk parameters or to achieve investment profiles in which their assets roughly match their liabilities. Moreover, in many countries pension fund investment processes are increasingly guided by the management theories and portfolio theories developed by academicians, often grouped under the name Modern Portfolio Theory. And the investment instruments and markets they invest in are increasingly global in nature. By the same token, the asset management firms who are mandated to manage pension fund assets are increasingly global firms that not only invest in many markets but that also gather funds to invest from many countries as well.

When plan sponsors first began to put aside money in the pension plans to meet future obligations, the question quickly arose—who would manage this money? While many plans kept the asset management duties in house, most looked outside their organization to a bank or insurance company. And whether a bank or an insurance company was chosen to invest a plan's pension assets, they typically put the money into fixed income securities. Property was soon added to this mix. It was not until after World War Two that pension assets began to be invested more heavily in equities.

In the last three or four decades, many pension plans became more interested in maximizing investment returns rather than simply matching liabilities. It was in pursuit of that goal that many pension funds began to divide the plan assets among a number of investment managers, including substantial numbers of the new, independent, specialized investment management firms that were being created. And in recent years, a growing number of Anglo-Saxon pension funds have once again been showing more interest in matching assets and liabilities.

Despite the underlying differences in pension structures from country to country, there are substantial similarities in the investment setting and investment processes at many pension funds. Pension funds in different countries may have different asset allocations, but they have the same kind of managerial issues and concerns, and that suggests that Fiduciary Management has the potential to improve the way institutional investors execute their tasks. The next chapters deal with some of the possibilities in this respect.

CHAPTER 3

The Role of the Fiduciary Manager as Chief Advisor

W hile they may have billions of dollars or euros or yen in assets, most pension funds have very small staffs. Thus, the range and depth of their expertise is limited, and they rely heavily on outside experts. To be sure, a small number of large pension funds around the world have chosen to manage their pension plans in house. They have assembled large staffs with expertise that is both broad and deep. The ABP and PGGM in Holland, the General Motors Investment Corporation in New York, and a few others know as much about investments as any organization in the world. But these are exceptions to the rule.

For most pension fund organizations, the Fiduciary Manager can play an important role in bringing valuable advice and counsel to the plan. The Fiduciary Manager offers a pension fund a unique combination of the expertise that is gained from existing consulting arrangements plus an ongoing commitment to the overall management of the plan. There are a range of areas within the plan management process in which the Fiduciary Manager can inject his or her expertise. These areas include asset-liability studies, balancing risk and return considerations, guiding portfolio construction, selecting and monitoring investment managers, measuring and assessing investment results, and generally educating plan sponsor staffs and trustees about the range of issues confronting them. Each of these areas is briefly outlined below.

THE ASSET-LIABILITY STUDY

The starting point of the institutional investment process is an asset-liability study. It needs to be undertaken when any institutional fund is created, and it needs to be repeated periodically. There are different views as to just how often such a study needs to be undertaken, but it is clear that it needs to be done on a regular basis, and it definitely needs to be done on an ad hoc basis whenever there are significant changes in the financial circumstances of the plan or in the financial markets in which it invests. Such a study also needs to be undertaken when new regulatory directives are issued or when the plan sponsor restructures its business activities and its employment policies.

The liability side of a pension fund's balance sheet—meaning the benefits it is committed to paying—needs to be examined closely. This, after all, is why the fund exists. In the case of pension funds, too often the prospect of changes on the liability side is not scrutinized sufficiently. Two things can happen. One is that the level of benefits being promised may change. At most employers in most countries, wages tend to rise over time, and those examining liabilities must be prepared to recognize in some fashion, formally or informally, that the benefits that will ultimately be paid are probably going to be higher than those currently being promised by the plan.

The other major liability issue is longevity. Liabilities are based on the longevity of employees and are calculated on the basis of actuarial assumptions, which vary from country to country. As in the case of life insurance, in pension plans, it is not clear when any one individual will die, but for large numbers of people there is a statistical basis for estimating average life expectancy. For more than a century, however, life expectancy has been increasing. Mortality tables are typically revised only every five or ten years. With each revision in the past few decades, average life expectancy has been extended. That means that a pension plan may base its planning on the assumption that the average retired worker will live to, say, age 82, and therefore collect his or her benefits, for 17 years, from age 65 to age 82. But updated actuarial data may reveal that the average employee will, in fact, live to be 84 or 94.

Most of us presumably welcome this increasing longevity as we contemplate our own mortality and that of our family and friends. In economic terms, however, we need to be aware that asset-liability modeling is a decidedly tricky undertaking that rests on constantly shifting sands. It requires forecasting both the rates of return on investments and the longevity of pensioners. The only thing we know for sure about rates of return is that they won't necessarily match the past. And it turns out that longevity is also uncertain.

So is the game worth the candle? Absolutely. However tentative and uncertain asset-liability calculations may be, a fund is far better off having some sense of where it stands than no sense at all. It is better to have explicit assumptions and alter them in response to new information than to operate without acknowledging that there are assumptions guiding a plan.

The asset-liability study needs to be undertaken by a specialist who is able to bring together actuarial principles with an understanding of the vagaries of financial markets. A Fiduciary Manager can play a crucial role in this in several ways. One is to convince the fund that an asset-liability study is a necessary tool for good management. Another is help provide critical information needed for the study. Yet another is to evaluate the outcome of such a study.

The Fiduciary Manager can also generate ideas about the investment side of the study, by, for example, offering new ideas about asset classes, additional data about correlations between investments, and so on. The Fiduciary Manager also provides a dispassionate view—a firm but fair-minded approach that does not simply tell the plan sponsor what it wants to hear but speaks the hard truths about rates of return and longevity. If a pension fund assumes 15 percent annual returns and average participant longevity of 70 years, it is easy to say the plan will be well-funded, but it will soon become clear that those assumptions bear little relation to reality.

The Fiduciary Manager's role in asset-liability modeling grounds the plan in reality, and this helps to upgrade the quality of the plan. Even more important is the Fiduciary's ability to help the fund decide what exactly to do with the outcome of the study. A pension fund's board, which generally has limited knowledge of, and experience in, investing, should choose a risk budget that is stated in neutral terms, such as a maximum probability of having a certain amount of underfunding. But in many cases, the board selects a strategic asset mix and a permissible level of risk for asset managers that is too aggressive or not aggressive enough. This situation can be avoided by having the Fiduciary Manager translate the neutrally defined risk budget into investment terms. The board confines itself to decisions it can oversee, and the Fiduciary is responsible for the appropriate translation of this neutral risk budget into budgetary limits that asset managers can work with. In this fashion the outcomes of the asset-liability study lead to investment alternatives that provide a firm basis for developing and implementing a sound investment strategy. The issues involved in mounting asset-liability studies will be examined more fully in Chapter 5.

THINKING THROUGH RISK AND RETURN

Once a plan sponsor has examined its assets and liabilities at any point in time, it then needs to consider the risks and returns associated with various investment approaches. The principal risk facing a pension fund is that it will not have enough money in the fund to pay its pension obligations. The extreme case is that of a pension fund with substantial obligations and a financially troubled plan sponsor.

There are a several investment approaches that a pension fund can pursue. The fundamental dichotomy is between approaches that essentially seek to match assets and liabilities and those that seek to achieve higher investment returns in order to reduce the costs and contributions faced by the plan sponsor or to be able to offer more generous pensions in the future.

As a result of the introduction of more stringent funding regulations, there are a growing number of pension funds that seek to match assets and liabilities as closely as possible. This strategy involves such approaches as adding more and longer-duration fixed income investments at the expense of equities in order to narrow the so-called duration gap. The advantages of diversification among asset classes and the prospect of generating higher returns are increasingly sacrificed for lower risk. Indeed, it is no exaggeration to say that security and peace of mind for the board of an institutional investor are gained at the expense of future retirees.[1]

Once a plan has come to grips with the broad issues associated with its approach to investing, it then can formulate the specifics of its investment approach.

These issues are so important that they will be dealt with in the following chapter. For the moment, however, it is sufficient to say that the Fiduciary Manager can and should be an integral part of decisions about a fund's fundamental approach to investing.

PORTFOLIO CONSTRUCTION

Whatever approach to investing is employed, the Fiduciary Manager can play a significant role in putting together an investment portfolio. In earlier times, a portfolio was simply an aggregation of discrete investment ideas that seemed to hold promise. These days, a portfolio is supposed to be *constructed* on a top-down basis. The starting point is an allocation of assets among a set of asset classes, followed by sub-allocations within some of those asset classes. Careful attention is paid to achieving diversification and managing risks.

All of these tasks can benefit from the involvement of a Fiduciary Manager, as portfolio construction is a highly complicated matter.

In earlier times, only two or three traditional asset classes (bonds, equity, and real estate) existed; nowadays there is a vast array of investment categories considered appropriate for prudent institutional investors. These include hedge funds, private equity, infrastructure investments, currency strategies, derivatives, overlay products, high yield bonds, emerging market debt, structured credits with different sorts of collateral, and a host of tailor-made structured products. The difficulty in fitting all the right categories into a portfolio is hugely complicated by the fact that correlations are different and may vary over time. This makes appropriate diversification a difficult goal to reach.

The Fiduciary brings expertise to these tasks as well as a holistic approach that ensures the broad needs of the plan sponsor are not lost in the details associated with the various aspects of portfolio construction. It should be stressed here that the Fiduciary can advise, but cannot decide. The choice of the investment approach, the number of asset classes and their weights in the portfolio are to be decided by the fund. These decisions cannot be delegated. These matters will be discussed further in Chapter 6.

SELECTING AND OVERSEEING INVESTMENT MANAGERS

This is another important role for the Fiduciary Manager. The allocation of assets among a specific set of asset classes needs to be followed by mandating specialized investment managers to actually invest the funds that have been allocated to each asset class or category of investments. Specialized managers have demonstrated an ability to achieve better results within their specialties than investment managers claiming to manage all kinds of investments with equal facility.

The task of defining the specialties to pursue and identifying the best managers for each of those specialties is one that the Fiduciary Manager can undertake on behalf of an institutional investor's board. The Fiduciary Manager brings to bear extensive experience and a thorough understanding of the investment management industry, so that he or she can spell out the categories of managers to be sought. Then, the Fiduciary Manager can locate the best managers within these categories and give the fund a list from which to make their final decisions. The choices are based on characteristics of the asset managers and their organizations. (This will be dealt with in the chapter on active management.) However, it is not only necessary to scrutinize individual managers but also to examine the combinations of managers to assess the overall risk return pattern they are likely to generate. We will return to this topic in Chapter 7.

MEASURING AND BENCHMARKING

The last of the essential tasks for the Fiduciary Manager is measuring and benchmarking risk and return in all their facets. It is a tenet of modern management that every aspect of any managerial task should be measured and monitored to evaluate how well it is being performed. This requires the development of yardsticks for measuring and benchmarks for evaluating the meaning of those measurements.

The world of investment management is replete with well-developed conventions for measuring investment results in various dimensions. There is also an assortment of benchmarks against which results can be compared and evaluated.

The task facing the Fiduciary Manager is to help the plan sponsor choose the right measuring rods so that the fund can understand the results it is getting and then help the fund choose the right benchmarks so that it can also understand the meaning of those results. What returns have been obtained from various investments, and what is to be thought of those returns? Are we doing better than average? Are we doing better than other similarly situated funds? What are the sources of the results we are getting? Are the risks we are taking being rewarded appropriately? And what can we do to improve our results?

All of these are standard questions in managing an activity. But all of them require the use of specific instruments and approaches when applied to investment management. The Fiduciary Manager brings the knowledge and experience required to assist an institutional investor create the appropriate measurement function and build the feedback loop that makes it possible for past results to be interpreted and used to improve future results. This topic will be examined more fully in Chapter 8.

EDUCATION

At the end of the day, a plan sponsor must decide on its own vision of what its pension fund can and should do. To develop this vision and put it into practice, however, the plan sponsor not only needs informed advice from an insider—the Fiduciary Manager—it also needs education for the fund's board members and senior staff so that they can make informed decisions. In this era of outsourcing, a plan sponsor can hire firms to perform virtually every function associated with running a pension fund. But it cannot outsource its fiduciary responsibility. That's why it needs good advice in order to make good decisions. By the same token, once a fund has engaged a Fiduciary, it should also be able to assess the contributions of this important adviser (this important issue will be dealt with more thoroughly in Chapter 9).

Because of the complexities associated with operating a pension fund, the plan sponsor needs to educate itself about all of the issues and choices that it faces. This is another critical function in which the Fiduciary Manager can play an important role. There is no shortage of people and organizations prepared to tell plan sponsors what to do. Employees want the assets to be as secure as possible, but they also want additional money available for higher benefits. Senior management at the plan sponsor wants to limit and often fix contributions, and they also want the fund's balance sheet to look as good as possible. Investment managers claim their services would bring a unique blend of higher returns and lower risks. A variety of other advisors have products and services that they insist would make life easier and simpler for the plan sponsor.

And how is the plan sponsor to make these critical decisions? How is the corporate plan sponsor to decide when the pension plan is overseen by an assistant treasurer who is single-handedly overseeing a multi-billion dollar pension fund while the company's most senior financial executives only review the plan quarterly? How is the public employee pension plan to make these decisions when it is governed by a board composed of civil servants who may well be fine school teachers or fire fighters or social welfare program administrators but who have no background in financial matters?

The Fiduciary Manager can play a crucial role not only in providing informed but dispassionate advice but also in educating the relevant executives at the plan sponsor so that they can make informed decisions. This education process can take several forms.

At a minimum, it means presenting issues in a context and setting that enable the decision makers to look beyond the details and understand the broad parameters of the decision. It means, for example, not simply saying, "Here are the historic risks and returns associated with having 70 percent of assets in equities versus 60 percent." It means describing the broad parameters of investing so that trustees or board members or executives can, perhaps for the first time, have a sense of what pension funds can and should do and have done with regard to investing in the equity markets. There are, of course, a vast array of other investment possibilities and asset classes, and their addition to a portfolio only underscores the importance of education.

Beyond presenting issues in a context, the Fiduciary Manager can also help plan sponsor decision-makers step back from the day-to-day issues and examine the panoply of issues facing their plan. What are the trends and developments in investment markets? What are other plans doing? What is this news about pension funds beginning to invest in hedge funds, and what relevance does it have for us? How should I position my fund with regard to socially responsible investments? Should ecologically responsible production methods be a factor in deciding where to invest? What are regulators saying? What do accountants or securities analysts or others want from pension plans?

THE TRUSTED COUNSELOR, THE FELLOW FIDUCIARY

In the commercial world, it is not always easy to get disinterested advice. Those who know the most are often those who have things to sell. This is precisely why it is so important for plan sponsors to have advisors who are not only knowledgeable about the market but also knowledgeable about the plan, advisors who have an economic interest in the well-being of the plan, but whose economic interest is best served when the plan does well, not when the plan simply buys what they're selling.

For a half century, plan sponsors have been seeking the right structure to achieve this, and the Fiduciary Manager approach may well be the answer. It combines expertise with commitment to the plan. It puts a premium on dispassionate advice and aligns the interests of the advisor and the plan. It ensures that the advisor does well when the plan does well. Investors may never be able to square the circle when it comes to getting both low risks and high returns at the same time. But it is possible to square the circle in advice, to get both knowledge and objective advice at the same time.

CHAPTER 4

Shaping the Fundamental Investment Policies

O nce a plan sponsor has examined its assets and liabilities, it then needs to consider the risks and returns associated with various investment approaches. As has been noted, its principal goal is to avoid a situation in which the pension fund will not have enough money in the fund to pay its pension obligations, requiring the plan sponsor to have to make a large and unexpected contribution to the fund.

The plan sponsor's concern is somewhat different from the broader society's concern, which is that the plan sponsor will be unable to meet its obligations, and as a result, the pension benefits will not be paid, the retirees will not have the income they anticipated, and this group may become a responsibility of the state. If the plan sponsor cannot pay, it means the plan has run out of money, so neither legal actions nor moral suasion can result in the payment of its obligations.

In the United States the notorious failures of Studebaker, an automobile manufacturer, as well as LTV, a steel company, left behind pension plans that could not deliver the benefits they had promised. One result of this debacle was the creation of the Pension Benefit Guaranty Corporation. This government-owned insurance company requires companies to pay a premium based on the number of employees in their pension plans, and in return it ensures the benefits offered by those plans up to a certain limit. In some other countries, legislation requires pension funds to buy insurance on their liabilities from insurance companies.

For most plan sponsors, going out of business is, hopefully, not an issue. For businesses, and for public employee pension plans, the most fundamental concern is that inappropriate funding and investing will require the plan sponsor to inject additional money into the pension plan, and the need for these contributions may come at a time when the plan sponsor is not eager to use funds to make pension contributions.

The underfunding risk requires focusing on the basic strategy for the pension fund's investment portfolio. Since the creation of funded pension plans, there have been two contending investment philosophies. One view is that the assets and liabilities can and should be matched so that the pension fund is always fully funded, and there is no question about its ability to meet its obligations. Despite the uncertainties associated with pension liabilities, it is fairly simple to *immunize* a pension portfolio by buying a sufficient quantity of bonds to ensure that they will generate enough of a return to meet the pension fund's obligations. Indeed, the interest rates on bonds are related to the interest rates used in calculating the discounted present value of the liabilities, so it is not at all impossible to have the right amount of money available.

In any case, putting extra sums in bonds increases the certainty. This calls to mind the remark of comedian Groucho Marx, who had his substantial wealth invested entirely in bonds. He once visited the floor of the New York Stock Exchange, and when he said he avoided stocks in favor of bonds, he was told "You can't make any money in bonds," Groucho is said to have replied, "You can if you have enough of them." Indeed, a pension fund can immunize itself if it has enough bonds.[1]

But there is a contending school that says this is a costly and inefficient way to fund liabilities. For a recently created company with a relatively small number of employees and a high level of revenues, pension costs are a minimal part of the overall costs of operating the company. For a company with a long history, a large labor force, and a substantial number of retirees, however, the costs of operating a pension fund are significant. Two comments put this in perspective. The American automobile manufacturers complain that they are unable to compete with imported cars because each car produced in the United States contains more than $1000 in pension and health care costs. Secondly, British Airways is frequently described as a pension fund with an airline attached to it because the pension funds' assets are worth eight times the value of the company. This reflects the high level of pension costs in relation to the rest of the company's costs.

In short, pensions are a substantial cost at many companies and at many government agencies as well, and it behooves their managements to attempt to limit these costs. By focusing on bonds, the investor is consigned to a lower return than the stock market has provided, on average, over long periods of history. And while it is true that a short-term investor should not be exposed to the vagaries of the stock market, pension funds, like endowments and philanthropic foundations, are long-term investors. They can and should accept the fluctuations of the stock market in return for the higher long-run returns it can offer.

This view of the two schools is hotly debated. One of the most articulate defenders of the view that long-term investments in stocks are far better than any other alternative is Professor Jeremy Siegel of the University of Pennsylvania's Wharton School. But Professor Zvi Bodie of Boston University disputes this view. He argues that the certainty of better returns being derived by long-term investment in the stock market is illusory. In fact, Bodie argues, at the end of a long period of investments in shares, the investor may well find that his or her portfolio has not done all that well.[2]

This statement contradicts the generally accepted principle that equities will generate a risk premium over bonds to compensate the investor for the greater risks involved in equity investing. Data on long-term investment results generally shows that there is an equity premium, but those results are, of course, on average, and over the long term.

If a nonimmunized investment portfolio succeeds in generating high returns, it can save the plan sponsor vast sums of money. By earning returns far in excess of the growth of liabilities, a strong investment strategy may make it possible for the plan sponsor to sharply decrease contributions. Boender and van Lieshout have calculated that a lifelong 1 percent increase in portfolio returns in a pension fund implies 30 percent lower pension costs.[3] But, there is no guarantee that a search for high investment returns will be successful. If it is not, the plan sponsor would have to make contributions to cover the shortfall. If investments actually lost money, the contributions would have to cover that loss as well.

Over the years, pension executives have vacillated between the objectives of eliminating uncertainty by locking in a return that matches the growth of liabilities versus seeking to reduce costs through the pursuit of high investments returns. At General Mills, the large cereal company, financial officers once calculated that each 1 percent decrease in contributions to the pension fund would bring a 4 percent increase in earnings per share. Indeed, during the heady days of the 1960s, there were corporate pension plan officers who argued that they could turn their company's pension plan into a profit center. Investment performance could be so good that the company would not only cease having to make contributions, it could take excess funds from the pension fund.[4] As another example, during the 1990s, the Dutch government contemplated measures to siphon off the so-called over-reserves of pension funds, which resulted from pension funds having large amounts of rapidly appreciating equity in their portfolios.

In the early part of this century, Boots the Chemist, the British drug store chain, got out of the equities markets completely and invested all of its pension assets in fixed income securities. The timing of this move was excellent: stock prices fell, bond prices surged, and the pension fund benefited enormously by being in bonds. But John Ralfe, the pension officer at Boots who spearheaded this move, repeatedly said the step was not an exercise in market timing. Rather, Ralfe argued that Boots as a company ought to take its risks in its basic business, not in its pension fund.[5]

For many other plan sponsors, the sharp decline in equity prices after the spring of 2002 meant a steep fall in the value of their pension assets, and this reminded them of the risks of stepping away from a match between assets and liabilities. As a result, by 2004 there was growing talk about the need to achieve a closer relationship between the two sides of the pension fund balance sheet. Assets and liabilities need not be matched completely, many said, but they did have to be aligned fairly closely.

Some observers suggested that the first sign of a sharply rising stock market would inevitably put an end to that talk, and at least in the case of the Anglo-Saxon pension funds, they would once again be chasing returns in the stock market.

But there are other factors that have come to shape the investment policies of many pension funds: these include accounting and regulatory provisions.

Accounting rules have been altered in a number of countries so that a plan sponsor's pension assets and liabilities are more visible in reading the plan sponsor's accounts. Once consigned to a footnote in the annual report, corporate pension funds are now on the balance sheet for all to see. If the company's pension fund is substantially underfunded, at some future date the company may have to take substantial sums of money out of its business operations and put this money into the pension fund. That could be viewed as a negative by current and potential investors in the company's shares.

This heightened visibility is enhanced by requirements to mark investments to market at the end of each year. In the past various *smoothing* techniques were used. Companies argued, quite reasonably, that pension funds represented a set of long-term assets and liabilities, and it was inappropriate to focus too closely at a snapshot of these assets and liabilities at any single point in time. By showing average values, they said, those analyzing the company's accounts could get a more accurate reading of the pension fund's true status. There may well be merit to that argument, but the accounting profession and regulators have become increasingly insistent that plan sponsors publish year-end, unsmoothed, marked-to-market figures about the assets and liabilities of their pension funds.

In addition, the bond rating agencies have displayed a growing interest in examining the funding of pension liabilities and including this in their evaluation of the overall financial strength of the company in its role as an issuer of bonds.

Thus, there are powerful external forces that are exerting an impact on the overall approach to risk and reward that underpin a pension fund's investment strategy.

LIABILITY-DRIVEN INVESTMENTS

Starting around 2005, these forces resulted in an intense discussion in the financial press about the advantages and disadvantages of liability-driven investing (LDI). More importantly they led to an intense review of the investment strategy at many European pension funds. In these reviews, LDI has turned out to be a rather flexible notion, meaning different things to different people. But what is paramount, of course, is the idea that liabilities play the major role in determining the investment strategy. Narrowly defined, LDI means working towards the goal of cash flow matching. All assets generating a regular income stream (meaning especially bonds, but infrastructure investments and rent from real estate investments, might in theory fit as well) are framed against the future cash outflows.

In a broad sense, LDI means taking liabilities into account when defining the investment strategy of the fund and in that sense it is not a new phenomenon. What is clear is that almost all asset managers and banks have taken advantage of this heightened attention by supplying a swath of new products, many of which are decidedly pricey, that appear to fit the dictates of LDI, including long-duration bonds, swaps, swaptions, inflation swaps, and swap overlay programs. It is also clear that the use of these products and the narrow interpretation of LDI have not been very successful so far. Increasing the duration of the bond portfolio directly, by purchasing very long-term bonds or, indirectly, by using derivatives, is not likely to pay off in terms of reasonable future pension levels when long-term interest rates are at levels around 3 percent.

A more enduring aspect of LDI is the increased awareness of the liabilities as a beacon for investments. One example of this can be seen in the advice Fiduciary Managers give in the field of portfolio construction. Rather often, Fiduciary Managers recommend dividing the overall investment portfolio into two sub-portfolios: a more-or-less liability-driven portfolio and a more traditional portfolio that seeks to maximize returns within certain risk parameters. In this way the fund is explicitly dealing with the issue of matching its liabilities and the risks associated with any mismatch, but at the same time there is awareness that liability matching is only one of the tasks a pension fund faces. This division of the investment portfolio does not mean that risk management is divided as well; the two sub-portfolios go hand in hand with risk measurement and risk allocation in terms of the overall portfolio.

With or without the recent enthusiasm for LDI, the basic dichotomy in pension fund investment objectives is an enduring one. Should a pension fund immunize its balance sheet by locking in investment returns that will ensure that the pension plan is well-funded? Or should it seek the best possible returns in the hopes of limiting plan sponsor contributions and generating more money that would then be available for increases in benefits? Or is there some point on the spectrum between these two alternatives that is right for a particular pension plan?

These are complex issues, and there is no single right answer that is applicable to every plan sponsor. The Fiduciary Manager can play an important role in helping a pension fund decide what it wants. These issues require advice and analysis that is informed, on the one hand, and dispassionate, on the other. And decisions are not necessarily impervious to market conditions. For example, as the twenty-first century began, interest rates were at the lowest levels in four decades. At such a moment, choosing immunization would mean the plan would be funded at a level that would not offer the promise of very attractive benefits in the future. During periods of high interest rates, the calculus might yield very different conclusions.

CHOOSING AN ACTIVE INVESTMENT POLICY

The decision to employ a mixed portfolio without immunizing assets and liabilities is an important strategic decision, but there is more. An institution that decides that it does not simply want to match assets and liabilities may invest its assets in a way that passively seeks to match the performance of a major market index, or it may try to beat the markets in which it is operating. There is a whole array of managers claiming to be able to outperform specific markets consistently and to deliver net extra returns after deducting the higher active management fees that they receive.

The Fiduciary Manager can help to integrate this so-called active investment policy in an overall portfolio by finding managers who can be expected to generate these extra returns. There are thousands of investment managers, and many of them have approaches and strategies that are worth consideration by major institutional investors. By digging deep into the organizations of these managers and by reviewing the process through which their investment results are obtained, the Fiduciary Manager can improve the probability that a chosen manager will indeed generate what he promises.

The second contribution from the Fiduciary is integrating the portfolios run by these active managers in the overall portfolio. In reviewing a portfolio's risk elements, it may be demonstrated that adding active, or alpha, risk does not add much, if any, risk to the existing portfolio where market risk, or beta risk, is overwhelmingly present. As long as the active bets of the manager have a very low correlation to market risk and return, the portfolio's total risk and return profile may not change very much while creating opportunities for a higher return.

In managing the risk level of the overall portfolio, the Fiduciary may advise employing several active asset managers in a certain market when the risk/reward profile of this mix of managers is better than the profile of a single active manager. The same is true for the question of whether or not to make use of an overlay manager who seeks to exploit the risks and returns of numerous markets and sub-markets without the confinement of a specific market or asset class. Here again, diversification effects can play a role.

In thinking about investment policies, there are several players with different goals. The actuaries want precision and consistency in returns along with all the other variables. The plan sponsors, for whom operating a pension plan is peripheral to their main business or activity, want to know how much they must contribute to their pension plan now, and in the future, in order to have the company's accounts, and the company's true financial position, be in the best possible condition. The investment managers typically want to seek opportunities rather than just immunize liabilities. Those overseeing a pension fund must decide how to harness these contending views and aspirations. And all of these issues are tied together by the issue of risk.

Recently, the growing role of Fiduciary Management structures has helped alter the framework for viewing risk. A growing number of institutions are thinking in terms of having a risk budget. The job of the plan sponsor's management is to work with this budget in the proper fashion, to allocate the risks being taken, and ensure that they are commensurate with the potential rewards and do not aggregate into a level of risk that endangers the plan.

Since the bursting of the technology bubble at the turn of this century, major equity markets have regained some strength, but equity risk premiums seem to have diminished. Moreover, bonds generate a very low return, as interest rates have hovered at low levels not seen for many decades and spreads between government bonds and higher yielding nongovernment bonds have diminished dramatically in many markets. Meanwhile, new legislation has come into effect in several countries requiring pension funds to be more fully funded and to close or diminish gaps between the duration of their liabilities and the duration of their fixed income portfolio.

This conjunction of events suggests that pension funds, like other institutional investors, face years of moderate returns. And in the case of pension funds, this development is occurring at the same time the graying of society is demanding huge future sums to be available.

Institutional investors are therefore more interested than ever in seeking extra returns. There are several ways of pursuing these additional returns. They include the use of nonimmunized portfolios and active managers as well as investments in new asset classes and investment instruments. This pursuit of incremental returns explains the growing popularity of hedge funds, inflation-linked bonds, private equity, infrastructural investments, and other investments that were once unthinkable in institutional portfolios.

Before considering new instruments and asset classes, a plan sponsor first has to come to grips with the issue of active investment policy. This can be described as an investment policy that seeks to achieve higher returns from an asset class than those of the strategic norm portfolio. It is easy and cheap to earn the risk-free rate of return or to earn a market return through a passively managed, indexed portfolio. When interest rates are higher than 5 percent and there is an equity premium of some three percentage points, market returns may be sufficient to meet future liabilities. But these kinds of returns have not generally been obtained by many investors in recent years, and many believe there is good reason to expect modest returns in the years ahead, so active investment policies must become more prominent.

However, achieving excess return or alpha (as compared to beta, referring to the return of the passive portfolio that simply seeks to match the returns of a market) requires insights that are better than those of the competitors and the skill to put these insights to work in an investment portfolio. In the aggregate, active policy is a zero-sum game. If one investor outperforms the index, other parties, by definition, must earn a return lower than that of the index.

In addition to generating extra returns, another advantage of an active investment policy is that the risks associated with it are to a large extent uncorrelated with the risks of the strategic portfolio. Thus, adding active risk to a strategic portfolio improves the risk-return characteristic of the overall investment portfolio.

The Fiduciary Manager's task is to establish the right prerequisites to be able to engage active investment managers who can deliver superior results in the long run. But Fiduciary Management is also an excellent platform to integrate active policy in the overall construction and monitoring of the total portfolio. The Fiduciary can pursue answers to such questions as: How much active policy is to be added to the overall portfolio? Which active managers are to be chosen? How much money should be allocated to these individual managers and how high should their individual risk budget be? What combination of active managers will be employed in a certain market?

INTEGRATING ACTIVE POLICY IN THE OVERALL PORTFOLIO

In practice, many institutional investors often undertake or abandon an active investment policy for the wrong reasons. When active policy falls behind passive results for an extended period, some institutions choose to go to the cheaper passive portfolio management. It should be noted that the definition of an "extended period" is far from clear cut. The period after which a decision to change or not is taken is often too long for the pension fund that suffers disappointing returns, and it is often too short for the active manager to prove his skills. There are some who are convinced of the benefits of active policy for the overall portfolio, and they would argue for using it all the time, while there is another group that would never take this approach, and a third group that would re-examine the decision regularly.

Changes in approach, it should be noted, incur high transition costs in moving from one portfolio to the other. The choice of whether or not to engage in active policy, and, if so, to what extent, requires a consistent decision-making process that operates at three levels:[6]

- *The asset mix policy level*. The asset-liability study provides guidance on optimal asset mix, and if the fund management decides not to implement some of the recommendations with respect to this optimum, this decision should be considered an example of active policy. In most cases, this deviation will take the form of a so-called tactical asset allocation, which is the deliberate but temporary departure from the strategic asset mix in order to generate extra return and/or to adjust the risk profile in response to current market conditions.
- *Within the asset class*. A broad asset class consists of several segments, such as small and large cap stocks in the equity portfolio or government bonds and corporate bonds in the fixed income portfolio. When a fund decides to change the weights of these segments, strategically or tactically, that is an example of active policy as well.
- *Within asset class segments*. Here the choices that specific asset managers make regarding specific securities within each segment are undertaken in pursuit of extra returns.

The evaluation of active policy risks and returns can only be performed when the strategic asset mix does not imply any active bet.

Therefore, the strategic mix should only consist of benchmark portfolios. No considerations of undervaluation of securities should play a role here. The assumption is that assets are priced efficiently (whether or not that is the case in practice is a matter to be decided by an expert). Every deviation from the passive portfolio should be measured as an active bet against the passive portfolio and should not be part of that portfolio. The level of detail used in spelling out this portfolio varies among plan sponsors. Funds seeking the most far-reaching benefits of the Fiduciary's expertise should devise a broad strategic portfolio.

Active management changes the portfolio's expected return and the variability of returns in comparison with the strategic portfolio. The additional variability is the active management risk, and that variable should guide the decisions that have to be made. It is limited by definition—which is why a fund should decide to make many small bets instead of a fewer larger ones. Given the same return distribution of bets, combinations of bets result in lower uncertainty at the overall portfolio level. Unrelated bets are to be preferred as random returns cancel each other out, leading to a more stable overall outcome. Grinold and Kahn[7] refer to this as the "fundamental law of active management."

Another reason to be engaged in many smaller bets is risk control. No active manager can boast a 100 percent success rate in picking the best investments. If experience indicates a manager has a 55 percent chance to make a good bet, while a bad result is likely 45 percent of the time, the probability of a bad result will be almost 10 percent when this manager makes only three bets (45 percent times a power of 3). But the probability of bad choices declines as the number of decisions increases.

Since active management does not add much risk to the overall portfolio when there is diversification and noncorrelation with the underlying strategic passive portfolio in general, funds may well decide to use active management for 100 percent of the portfolio.

A mixture of active and passive management is only appropriate when the volatility of excess returns is high (which can be the case when a manager's excess returns are highly correlated), or when the segment in which active management is considered constitutes a large part of the overall portfolio. Another reason to consider passive management is when managers of the fund are afraid of the inevitable periods during which active management does not deliver the expected results. That fear will be affected by the funding ratio of the pension fund as well as the investment returns that have been earned recently and the financial health of the plan sponsor as well.

Giving active management a prominent place does not necessarily mean hiring a large number of managers. An institution needs to hire enough managers to capture the benefits of relying on specialists for each asset class. But there are reasons for hiring only a restricted number of active managers:

- Just a limited number of managers can produce positive net excess returns.
- Having more active managers brings a higher probability that active bets will cancel each other out. Here, the thin line between diversification, which is good, and overdiversification, which is expensive and counterproductive, may be breached: too much diversification in the end can lead to a return approaching that of the benchmark, while paying large active fees to the investment managers. Net returns will easily fall below benchmark returns in this case.
- The costs (active management fees) are high, especially when relatively small amounts of money are allocated.
- When more managers are hired, there is often an inclination to reallocate amounts from one manager to another more often. But this is a costly practice because the overall implementation shortfall of a transition can be huge (implementation shortfall is the addition of transaction costs, market impact of buying and selling securities, and missed opportunities because of temporarily being out of the market etc.). These costs come on top of the chances that managers are terminated because of bad results at precisely the moment when their strategy is beginning to pay off. Experience shows that replacing managers most of the time does not lead to higher excess return and/or risk reduction.

The extent to which active management should be introduced next to the passive strategic portfolio can be derived from the fund's preference for the risk-return trade-off as it was expressed in the choice of the asset mix. The strategic asset mix is decided upon by choosing the best risk-return combination, often depicted as a specific point on the efficient frontier of risk-return combinations. The impact of different combinations of active management bets can be reflected in the same way. Combinations with higher expected returns at a given level of risk or with lower risks given a certain level of return are an improvement in the overall picture. Combinations with higher expected returns and accompanying extra risk should be weighed against other alternatives, using the risk penalty revealed in the former choice. (In graphical terms this is the slope of the efficient frontier at the chosen point.)

COMPLETION ACCOUNT AS A NECESSARY ADJUNCT TO ACTIVE POLICY

Calculating the extra risks and returns of active management and combining these figures with the risk appetite of the fund management determines the size of the optimal active portfolio and its distribution among the different managers, but there is one aspect still to be analyzed. This concerns the possible structural biases of the active managers. Sometimes they tend to make structural bets against their respective benchmarks or against segments of these benchmarks instead of tactical bets. In addition, the whole array of active managers can place several bets in different areas, and these individual bets may turn out to be related and to accumulate risk in certain specific areas. Another possibility is that the portfolio will drift away from its strategic asset mix. When an asset class tends to have a higher return than others, that asset class grows in relative importance in the portfolio. It is not easy or inexpensive to rebalance between managers, especially in situations that may involve a dozen or more managers. This is particularly true when ordering a manager to rebalance would increase his operating costs and, more important, disturb his normal investment procedure. After all, the manager's carefully chosen active positions would have to be trimmed one by one, which is exactly the opposite of what he is naturally doing as a manager and what he was hired for in the first place.

Nonetheless, there is a need to rebalance periodically because the risks associated with this *drift* can be substantial. Litterman[8] speaks of a level of unintended risk in this respect of more than 50 percent of total active risk, which can easily dwarf the intentional active risk of security selection. His view on this is clear: every deviation from the index portfolio should be an intended deviation.

To eliminate the correlation and tracking errors these situations create, the fund should introduce a completion account and avoid unintended risks by redressing the overweighted areas and increasing stakes in the underweighted areas of the strategic portfolio. The most efficient way to run a completion account is to use derivatives. Then, for example, an underweight in fixed income or equity reflecting high returns from active management in those areas can easily be dealt with by buying futures or other derivative instruments. The implicit leverage that is connected with the use of derivatives avoids setting aside a passive completion fund, allowing more assets to be managed actively.

The completion account can also play a supportive role in a general overlay policy using tactical bets. A special form of overlay policy is the so-called portable alpha strategy, a rather new phenomenon in the area of active management.

A basic portable alpha strategy[9] is used to replace active policy in the bond portfolio as the means of generating excess returns. Using derivates to manage exposure to an asset class reduces the amount of capital that would otherwise be needed. The balance of the bonds sold and derivatives bought can be used to buy derivatives in another asset class. In this way, the strategy *transports* alpha from the fixed income part to the equity part of the overall portfolio, thus making it an overlay policy.

Recent developments make it possible to use whatever sources of alpha there are and to finance them by selling part of the strategic portfolio, buying derivatives to compensate, and using the balance of the capital to engage in the active policy advocated. The completion account can take care of the rebalancing that is necessary when there is the desire to generate more alpha in a certain area without increasing the strategic weighting of that area.

It is hard to overstate the importance of the completion portfolio. It indicates the actual and normative positions and compensates when differences become too large. This way it avoids strategic misallocations, which can result from stressing short-term tactical considerations in investment policy. These misallocations not only produce too much risk, they can also easily wipe out extra returns sought by the tactical policy. Moreover, the completion account ensures that all of the fund's assets are invested all the time. Reality shows that a large part of a periodic return on equity is realized in only a few very positive daily market movements. This suggests that an investor cannot afford to be out of the market even for the shortest period of time, and the completion manager takes care of that. A completion account receives daily information about cash balances and securitizes excess cash pools. By using cheap derivatives, this can be carried out regularly. Scheduled and unexpected cash flows can be dealt with in the same way.

Table 4.1 is an example of a completion account summarizes the setting.

THE FIDUCIARY PLATFORM TO INTEGRATE ACTIVE POLICY IN THE OVERALL INVESTMENT PORTFOLIO

The starting point of the whole process of executing active investment policy is the selection of the right managers. In seeking extra returns above its benchmark, a fund should begin by defining the framework: Will active policy be exploited in all asset classes? Or should a core-satellite approach be used? In the latter case, the choice of passive managers or their slightly more active competitors, the so-called enhanced managers (who make only small deviations from their benchmark in the hopes of achieving modest additional returns) is not too difficult. The search for active managers is

TABLE 4.1 Completion Account of Pension Fund X as per January 31, 2007

Asset Class Breakdown

Portfolio					Benchmark		Difference	
Asset class	Market Value	Physicals	Overlay	Total	Static	Drift	vs static	vs drift
Equity								
EMU Equity	229,427,267	13.31%	8.49%	21.79%	22.00%		−0.21%	
World ex EMU equity	166,096,117	26.58%	−10.80%	15.78%	16.00%		−0.22%	
Fixed income	580,362,845	41.43%	13.70%	55.13%	55.00%		0.13%	
Cash	37,866,997	14.97%	−11.39%	3.59%	3.50%		0.09%	
Global real estate	30,032,408	3.71%	0.00%	3.71%	3.50%		0.21%	
Total	1,052,785,635	100.00%	0.00%	100.00%	100.00%	0.00%	0.00%	

Currency Exposure

Currency	Physicals	Overlay	Totals	Benchmark	Difference
AUD	0.87%	−0.89%	−0.02%	−	−0.02%
CAD	0.15%	−0.15%	−	−	−
CHF	2.84%	−2.84%	−	−	−
DKK	0.33%	−0.32%	−	−	−
EUR	66.17%	33.79%	99.96%	100.00%	−0.04%
HKD	0.43%	−	0.43%	−	0.43%
JPY	2.39%	−2.36%	0.03%	−	0.03%

| | Exposure | | | | |
	Portfolio	Overlay	Net	Benchmark	Difference
NOK	0.35%	−0.34%	–	–	–
NZD	0.02%	–	0.02%	–	0.02%
SEK	1.03%	−1.03%	–	–	–
SGD	0.16%	–	0.16%	–	0.16%
UKS	9.88%	−9.91%	−0.02%	–	−0.02%
USD	15.39%	−15.95%	−0.55%	–	−0.55%
Total	100.00%	0.00%	100.00%	100.00%	–
EUR	66.17%	33.79%	99.96%	100.00%	–
Non-EUR developed	33.83%	−33.79%	0.04%	–	0.04%

Cash Balance Summary

| | | Exposure | | | | |
Cash	Market Value	Portfolio	Overlay	Net	Benchmark	Difference
GTAA manager X	48,884,645					
GTAA manager Y	39,075,183					
Hedge fund	33,634,713					
Cash manager	4,311,004					
Completion overlay	31,747,080					
Total	157,652,626	14.97%	−11.39%	3.59%	3.50%	0.09%

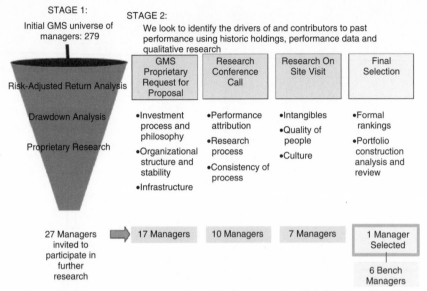

The information contained herein with respect to the number of managers reviewed is for illustrative purpose only.

FIGURE 4.1   Choosing Managers

Source: © Goldman Sachs Asset Management International 2007.

more complex. The universe of active managers is very substantial, so only Fiduciary Managers with their large pools of research capabilities and in-house experience will be able to identify managers with expected excess returns and to combine them in an efficient portfolio. The vast majority of institutions do not have the resources for this task, and they can benefit from the Fiduciary structure.

Figure 4.1 shows how a Fiduciary Manager reduces the universe of managers to the ultimate choice. It emphasizes that certain characteristics in the organization of the active manager are important in helping the Fiduciary choose a manager. Of course, past performance plays a role, but emphasizing these results creates a risk of picking yesterday's winners for the portfolio of tomorrow. Organizational characteristics can shed some light on how these results have been achieved and, herewith, offer some indication of whether or not a process that has brought good results can be reproduced in the future amid continuously changing market circumstances.

Another way to investigate the characteristics of portfolios and how they could be used to satisfy the needs of an investor is shown in Figure 4.2. It stresses the different angles from which these characteristics are evaluated.

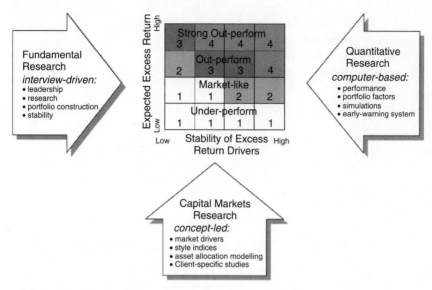

FIGURE 4.2 Manager Rating Methodology
Source: Russell Investment Group.

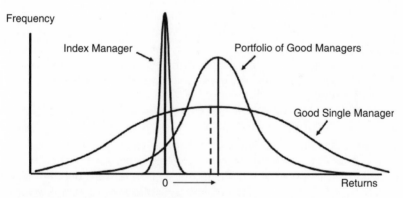

FIGURE 4.3 Benefits of Multi-Manager Investing
Source: Goldman Sachs Asset Management.

Figure 4.3 shows the difference between index and active managers and shows the advantages of combining active managers.

The theoretical approach above needs to be translated into real portfolios, where different characteristics of managers and their portfolios are made explicit (Figure 4.4).

2006: Total Bond and Equity Managers Globally

MONITOR TOTAL UNIVERSE OF MANAGERS — 6,465 Manager products monitored

RESEARCH MANAGERS OF INTEREST — 3,717 Manager products researched

FACE TO FACE INTERVIEWS — 2,541 Manager evaluation sessions held

SOUNDING BOARD — Associate peer review to verify 501 "Hire" rankings

INVESTMENT STRATEGY COMMITTEE — Senior management review to authorize final manager selections and portfolio construction

Notes:

The Sounding Board is a peer review process whereby all ranks are scrutinized and verified.

Investment Strategy Committee provides sign off by senior investment professionals.

The number of managers shown above in each category is an illustrative approximation since the manager universe and rankings are dynamic.

FIGURE 4.4 Reducing the Universe of Managers
Source: Russell Investment Group.

As indicated earlier, managers often show drift in the course of their actions over time. Figures 4.5 and 4.6 show how an advisor discerns this in the case of managers focused ostensibly on companies exhibiting certain market capitalizations and price-to-book ratios as well as managers focused on value and growth.

Over time, many of the aggregate factor risk exposures of the managers will change. While the increased exposure to some risks may be acceptable or even desirable, the Fiduciary Manager needs to monitor these positions, and assess whether changes in the manager weighting scheme might be necessary. While style drift in the sense of a significant departure from the approach originally sought when devising the overall portfolio is unacceptable, some drift can and should be tolerated. The changes in risk profile accompanying any drift determines whether or not action should be undertaken.

The value of the Fiduciary platform with respect to active management is threefold:

- The Fiduciary uses his or her experience to identify and engage the right active managers.
- The Fiduciary undertakes the necessary calculations to construct the optimal combination of these managers. "Optimal" in this context

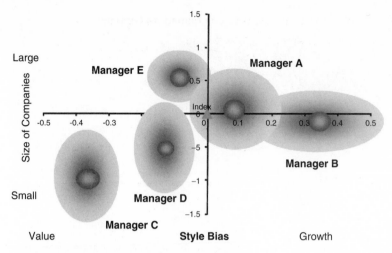

Note: Circle Size reflects target weighting of portfolio in the fund.

FIGURE 4.5 Sample Manager Size/Style Chart
Source: Russell Investment Group.

refers to the situation in which the *ex ante* returns cannot be enhanced further within the same risk budget, and specific restrictions can be accommodated. These restrictions may originate with the regulatory authorities, or they may come from the fund itself, such as decisions to exclude commodities or hedge funds.

■ The Fiduciary aggregates the sub-portfolios to ensure that the overall portfolio shows signs of diversification effects: that is, the overall level of risk is less than the sum of the risks of the individual portfolios. Of course, this aggregation should reveal that the overall targeted level of risk is in accord with the wishes of the fund: no risks beyond the budget, but not too few for too long either.

Monitoring the actual level of risk is one of the Fiduciary's main tasks, and in order to perform this duty a state-of-the-art model is used to see what managers are doing and why. This model indicates what returns and risks are associated with various behaviors and determines whether the guidelines on the level of sub-portfolios and overall portfolio are being adhered to.

In the context of active management this is especially important because the investment managers typically use large portions of the risk budget, and it is important to ascertain whether or not they are delivering what they have promised. This requires vigilant risk control, while monitoring the excess returns ensures that they are greater than the active management fee

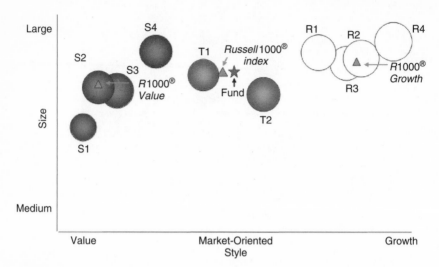

FIGURE 4.6 Manager Positions versus MSCI EAFE Composite Period Ending 12/31/04
Source: Russell Investment Group.

being paid. In short, monitoring should answer the questions of whether risk budgets are being adhered to and whether the bets taken actually do pay off.

The Fiduciary platform is well-suited to avoid the normal pitfalls that go along with active management. A few examples can illustrate this:

- Risk can only be managed when it is measured well. The Fiduciary should be capable of applying more advanced tools to measure risk and to reap the benefits of diversification than the plan sponsor could ever employ by itself.
- Most active managers depict their abilities to add value by specifying benchmarks and excess returns. Using tracking error as the primary guide for risk budgeting is useful, but there should be more. The Fiduciary can examine a broader picture, including diversification effects, and he or she can specify other risk measures, such as value at risk, as well. Within the Value at Risk calculations, the Fiduciary can split the budget into the volume originating from the strategic asset allocation (most of the time some 80 to 95%) and that coming from active policy (5 to 20%).
- Predictive tracking errors are the only way to fill in the risk budget. But funds should be aware that predictions can easily go astray. A huge difference can occur between *ex ante* and *ex post* tracking errors

(and excess returns), so there is a need to monitor the actual situation continuously and to compare actual risk with historic data on volatility.

- When comparing several active managers, *ex ante* tracking errors and excess returns are only two of the relevant criteria. There are many more characteristics to be used in evaluating the desired managers, including style analysis, adherence to style in the past, organizational data, and so forth. These are characteristics that a Fiduciary can take into account when proposing managers.
- Continuous and vigilant risk control by the Fiduciary permits working with ranges of tracking errors per manager. Using ranges instead of fixed numbers avoids constant corrective actions, which would increase costs.
- Finally, the Fiduciary Manager could put results in perspective. When an (expensive) active manager does not perform in the short term, clients tend to be disappointed and to micromanage the portfolio in question, reducing the manager's appetite to add value through adding risk. The Fiduciary should be able to bring some comfort to this situation by sharing his experience with unavoidable disappointments and placing them in the context of overall uncertainty.

A SPECIAL CASE: BRIDGING THE DURATION GAP

The Fiduciary Manager can play a special role in situations in which it becomes necessary to completely overhaul a fund's investment policy. In an environment characterized by low interest rates and more intense regulatory scrutiny, for example, pension funds need to re-examine the duration gap. The risk of a declining funding ratio is present because low interest rates raise the compounded value of the liabilities more than they raise the value of the shorter dated and smaller bond portfolio. This may lead a fund to conclude that bridging the duration gap is a wise course. The Fiduciary platform is especially suited for reviewing all the options attached to that change in policy.

The Fiduciary as an advisor can put the extension of the duration of the fixed income portfolio in perspective by indicating that this bridging of the duration gap will dampen the risk profile of the fund. More important, he or she can calculate the benefits of using the amount of risk saved by this operation in other areas. In short, a narrowing of the duration gap can be used to allocate more money to more risk-bearing assets and to active strategies, resulting in a better return-risk profile of the overall investment portfolio (see Table 4.2).

Figure 4.7 (see page 69) shows two portfolios. The upper one is the existing portfolio, which has a large duration gap. In the lower pie chart,

TABLE 4.2 Simple Overview of Active Managers with Their Weights, Means, and Targets

	Current Portfolio		Active Alpha Portfolio	
	Gross of Fees	Net of Fees	Gross	Net
Total Return	6.8%	6.0%	7.9%	7.1%
of which, risk free	3.25%	3.25%	3.25%	3.25%
of which, benchmark exposure	1.5%	1.5%	1.4%	1.4%
of which, active management	2.0%	1.3%	3.3%	2.5%
Portfolio Volatility	6.8%	6.8%	7.6%	7.6%
Passive Volatility	6.6%	6.6%	6.9%	7.1%
Tracking Error	1.5%	1.5%	3.0%	3.0%
Total Sharpe Ratio	0.52	0.41	0.62	0.51
95% Value-At-Risk (VaR) After 1 Year	−4.4%	−5.1%	−4.5%	−5.3%
95% VaR After 5 Years	9.0%	5.3%	11.8%	7.7%
Surplus Volatility	8.1%	8.1%	6.4%	6.4%
Liability-Adjusted Sharpe Ratio	0.42	0.32	0.70	0.57
95% VaR (of surplus excess return) After 1 Year	−9.9%	−10.7%	−6.1%	−6.9%
95% VaR (of surplus excess return) After 5 Years	−12.9%	−16.6%	−1.1%	−5.2%
Correlation of Assets with Liabilities	0.24	0.24	0.59	0.59

lower risk is achieved by narrowing this duration gap and adding more active elements to the portfolio.

WHAT A FIDUCIARY MANAGER'S REPORT LOOKS LIKE

This chapter will conclude with some examples of reporting. Table 4.3 is a clear indication of risk measurement connected with active policy.

Figures 4.8 and 4.9 show how the report can zoom in on specific topics if so desired or if required in certain market circumstances.

Finally, Tables 4.4 and 4.5 are examples of how a Fiduciary can periodically report on return and risk. The tables refer to a situation in which the Fiduciary is responsible for about half the overall investment portfolio, while two balanced managers are hired for the rest.

Current Portfolio
Expected Total Net Return: 6.0%
Expected Volatility: 6.8%
Expected Volatility of Surplus : 8.1%

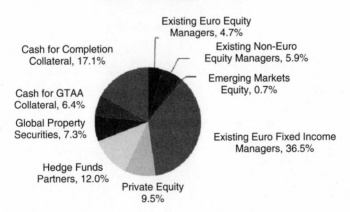

Completion Strategy, 3.2%

Cash for GTAA, 5.0%

Euro ex-Gov. Bond Manager 19.1%

Euro Gov. Bond Manager 29.0%

Euro Equity Manager, 5.4%

Euro Equity Manager, 5.8%

Large Cap Growth Equity Manager, 14.4%

Large Cap Value Equity Manager, 15.2%

Pacific Equity Manager, 2.9%

Proposed Active Alpha Portfolio
Expected Total Net Return: 7.1%
Expected Volatility: 7.6%
Expected Volatility of Surplus : 6.4%

Cash for Completion Collateral, 17.1%

Cash for GTAA Collateral, 6.4%

Global Property Securities, 7.3%

Hedge Funds Partners, 12.0%

Private Equity 9.5%

Existing Euro Equity Managers, 4.7%

Existing Non-Euro Equity Managers, 5.9%

Emerging Markets Equity, 0.7%

Existing Euro Fixed Income Managers, 36.5%

FIGURE 4.7 Simple Manager Size/Style Chart 2

TABLE 4.3 Simple Overview of Active Managers with Their Weights, Means, and Targets

Asset Class	% of Plan	Target Excess Return	Target Tracking Error	Target Information Ratio	Contribution to Active Plan Risk
Regional Equity I	6.7%	3.00%	6.00%	0.50	10.5%
Regional Equity II	6.7%	2.50%	5.00%	0.50	8.1%
Regional Equity III	8.8%	2.45%	2.65%	0.92	4.9%
Regional Equity IV	4.1%	3.50%	7.00%	0.50	6.4%
Regional Equity V	3.2%	2.00%	4.00%	0.50	2.3%
Global Equity (active)	5.4%	1.50%	3.00%	0.50	3.1%
Global Equity (passive)	6.6%	0.00%	0.50%	0.00	0.5%
Global Fixed Income I (Active)	16.2%	1.00%	2.00%	0.50	6.7%
Global Fixed Income II (Active)	16.5%	1.00%	2.00%	0.50	6.7%
Global Fixed Income III (Passive)	15.5%	0.00%	0.50%	0.00	1.0%
GTAA (cash)*	8.3%				
GTAA (overlay)	Overlay	0.75%	1.50%	0.50	49.8%
Completion Account	2.1%				
Total Portfolio	100.0%	1.43%	1.65%	0.86	100.0%

*Cash outlay required for the settlement of the overlay

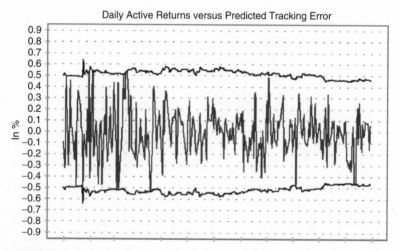

Daily Active Returns versus Predicted Tracking Error

FIGURE 4.8 Daily Movements in the Active Return (in Percentage of Capital Invested) of an Investment Portfolio
Source: © Goldman Sachs Asset Management International 2007.

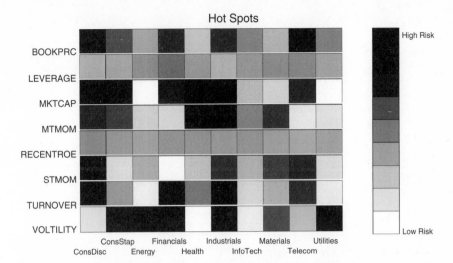

FIGURE 4.9 Risks of Industries Compared to the Benchmark
Source: © Goldman Sachs Asset Management International 2007.

TABLE 4.4 Manager Performance Summary

Manager Performance Summary

Portfolio	Benchmark	Total Gross Return Performance						Target	Total Market Value		∈ Alpha
		YTD			Since Inception					% of	YTD
		P (%)	B (%)	ER (bp)	P (%)	B (%)	ER (bp)	ER (bp)	(∈mm)	Fund	(∈mm)
Equity											
European											
Total European	Europe index	10,85	9,02	183	8,42	9,80	(138)	267	100,0	10,0%	1,8
North America											
Total North America	NA index	(0,47)	(0,87)	39	4,45	3,33	112	288	150,0	15,0%	0,6
Japan											
Total Japan	Japan index	1,89	4,02	(213)	12,60	11,13	146	350	50,0	5,0%	(1,1)
Pacific Rim ex Jpn											
Total Pacific Rim ex Jpn	Pac Rim index	1,89	4,02	(213)	12,60	11,13	146	350	50,0	5,0%	(1,1)
Emerging											
Total Emerging	EM index	15,40	12,36	304	25,05	23,85	120	200	50,0	5,0%	1,5
Total Equity	Weighted Bmk	5,14	4,51	63	9,22	9,04	18	195	400,0	40,0%	2,5
Fixed Income											
Euro Fixed Income	euro fixed income index							60	250,0	25,0%	
Global Fixed Income	fixed income index							100	300,0	30,0%	
Total Fixed Income	Weighted Bmk	(1,87)	(2,27)	40	5,62	4,25	137	85	550,0	55,0%	2,2
Total Fund prior to overlay & rebalancing	Blended Benchmark	1,62	1,23	39	6,56	5,82	74	74	950,0	95,0%	3,7
Total Fund prior to overlay after rebalancing	Blended Benchmark	1,98	1,70	28	8,81	8,11	70	113	950,0	95,0%	2,7
Total Overlay		0,23	(0,59)	82	3,20	0,64	257	44	50,0	5,0%	0,4
Total Active Fund	Blended Benchmark	2,21	1,11	110	12,02	8,74	327	237	1.000,0	100,0%	11,0
Total Liablity Matching Portfolio		0,18	0,16	2	1,00	0,95	5	0	500,0		0,1
Total Fund	Blended Benchmark	1,53	0,79	74	8,34	6,15	220	158	1.500,0		11,1

TABLE 4.5 Manager Risk/Return Summary

Manager Risk / Return Summary

Portfolio	Benchmark	AUM (€MM)	Risk adjusted Return (IR) YTD	SI	Actual TE (bp)	Target TE (bp)	Target Risk Budget (%)	Total Return Since Inception P (%)	B (%)	ER (bp)	Annualized Gross Targets ER (bp)	TE (bp)	IR	VaR 5% (€MM)
Equity														
European														
Total European	Europe index	100,0	1.38	(0.74)	262	444	3,7	8,42	9,80	(138)	267	444	0,60	3,2
North America														
Total North America	NA index	150,0	0.33	0.51	208	310	4,9	4,45	3,33	112	288	310	0,93	7,6
Japan														
Total Japan	Japan index	50,0	(0.88)	0.43	410	700	2,1	12,60	11,13	146	350	700	0,50	0,8
Pacific Rim ex Jpn														
Total Pacifi Rim ex Jpn	Pac Rim index	50,0	(0.88)	0.43	410	700	2,1	12,60	11,13	146	350	700	0,50	0,8
Emerging														
Total Emerging	EM index	50,0	1.83	0.44	286	400	0,3	25,05	23,85	120	200	400	0,50	0,9
Total Equity	Weighted Bmk	400,0	0.63	0.13	126	172	12,5	9,22	9,04	18	195	172	1,13	49,6
Fixed Income														
Euro Fixed Income	euro fixed income index	250,0												
Global Fixed Income	fixed income index	300,0												
Total Fixed Income	Weighted Bmk	550,0	0.79	1.62	88	119	2,5	5,62	4,25	137	85	119	0,71	6,9
Total Fixed prior to overlay after rebalancing	Blended Benchmark	950,0	0.56	1.26	82	88	15,1	8,81	8,11	70	113	88	1,28	94,9
Total overlay		50,0	0,49	1,00	266	100	84,9	3,20	0,64	257	44	218	0,20	2,6
Total Active Fund	Blended Benchmark	1.000,0	0.70	1.59	220	235	100,0	12,02	8,74	327	237	235	1,01	€100,0
Total Liablity Matching Portfolio		500,0	-	-	10	10	84,9	1,00	0,95	5	5	10	0,50	5,0
Total Fund	Blended Benchmark	1.500,0	0.47	1.06	150	160	95,0	8,34	6,15	220	160	160	1,00	€105,0

Asset-Liability Modeling and the Fiduciary Manager

Once a Fiduciary Manager has been hired by a pension fund, as has been briefly noted in Chapter 3, one of the first and most important tasks that the Fiduciary must oversee is the asset-liability study that describes the framework within which an institution's assets are invested. An asset-liability model (ALM) provides a roadmap that clarifies the range of investment mixtures that an institution can and should pursue, given its unique set of liabilities.

The ALM essentially links the two sides of the balance sheet of an institutional investor: the liabilities, and the assets which should cover them. The balance between the two, the funding ratio, is in many ways the most important compass of the fund. The relationship between assets and liabilities helps determine the overall tone of a pension fund's investment policies.

Investment managers do not manage every portfolio in the same way, nor do they always seek to achieve the highest possible return. They must not only be mindful of *risk* but also of *purpose*. It should be clear that the expenditures that an institution makes—the pensions it pays or the insurance benefits it provides—are liabilities, which can only be provided if there are enough assets. But beyond that, while it is important that the assets be invested in a manner that generates a sufficiently high return, it is also important that the manner in which the assets are invested permit meeting the liabilities in a timely fashion. For example, a pension fund with a number of retired workers collecting benefits and a large group of middle-aged workers on the cusp of retirement needs more liquid investments and more current income than the pension plan of a high tech company whose employees are all in their twenties and thirties.

That does not necessarily mean that an institution needs a precise match between assets and liabilities. However, it does mean that there needs to be some relationship between the two. There is a need to study the nature of the assets and liabilities and establish an investment strategy that provides the right relationship between the two sides of the balance sheet, the assets and liabilities.

Following the burst of the tech bubble at the beginning of this century, many commentators called for a reappraisal of the asset-liability relationship at pension funds. There was a growing emphasis on matching assets and liabilities, and a movement in support of liability-driven investing.

This debate was, in fact, a new manifestation of a recurring debate in pension fund management. From the earliest days of funded pension plans, there were those who argued that plan sponsors should turn the pension assets over to an insurance company, which would guarantee the returns and shoulder all exposure to investment risks; that way, the plan sponsor could concentrate on managing the risks it was prepared to manage—the risks associated with running its business. However, there has always been another school of thought, which has taken the view that the riskless approach to pension management is too expensive: The plan sponsor can and should seek to maximize long-run investment returns because the additional funds contributed by investment returns would reduce the cost of operating a pension plan. Over the years, the plan sponsor community has wavered between these poles.

What this debate reflects is the broader reality that there is a spectrum of relationships that can occur between assets and liabilities, a spectrum that extends from a complete match to a complete lack of any relationships, as investment managers seek to maximize total return without caring, or perhaps without even knowing, anything about the liabilities. This last situation has to be avoided, and that is why asset-liability modeling has gained a prominent place in the management of pension funds.

THE ROLE OF THE FIDUCIARY MANAGER

While the ALM should be one of the first tasks for a Fiduciary Manager, he or she does not necessarily have to personally carry out this study. The Fiduciary Manager's principal role is to ensure that the study is undertaken and that it utilizes reasonable assumptions and methodologies. For example, any ALM inevitably contains assumptions about future rates of return on various asset classes. By utilizing high future rates of return, the ALM will show that the plan sponsor need make limited contributions. But if those rates of return are not achieved, the sponsor would, in fact, have to make enormous contributions in later years to make up for the shortfall in assets.

Conversely, utilizing projected rates of return that are too low will saddle the plan sponsor with unnecessarily high contribution requirements.

The problem, of course, is that no one knows for sure what future rates of return will be. Because the Fiduciary Manager has knowledge of both financial markets and ALM estimation processes, however, he or she can ensure that the assumptions used regarding future rates of return are reasonable. By the same token, the Fiduciary can examine and/or propose the remainder of the assumptions that go into an asset-liability model.

Another major task facing the Fiduciary Manager is to help the pension plan determine where it should be on the spectrum that, at least in theory, runs from absolutely matching assets and liabilities to investing in a manner that absolutely ignores liabilities. In practice, of course, the range of alternatives is more limited, but the principle is the same—to determine how the pension fund's assets and liabilities will be interrelated. In order to shape that determination, the Fiduciary Manager oversees the development of an asset-liability model (ALM) that clarifies the relationship between assets and liabilities and the implications that various developments would have on each side of the pension fund's balance sheet.

THE ASSET-LIABILITY MODEL (ALM)

An asset-liability model is essentially the set of calculations in which the interaction of liabilities and investment policy is examined. The model consists of several basic ingredients:

- *Liabilities.* In the case of a pension fund or insurance company, these are the benefits that it can expect to pay out. Actuarial mathematics can determine with a good degree of accuracy how long people will live, on average, and therefore how much needs to be available to pay their pensions. This calculation often includes some kind of indexation or assumption about inflation to reflect the fact that beneficiaries may be entitled to receive more than their current nominal level of proposed benefits.
- *The range of potential investment policies.* This reflects the kinds of assets that a fund is permitted to invest in. In some countries, for example, life insurance companies are only permitted to invest in bonds that are rated investment grade by major rating agencies. Thus, there is no point in examining the returns that might be available for investments in lower-rated bonds or equities. Other institutions may limit the percentage of the portfolio that can be invested in a particular asset class.

- *The contribution policy.* The level of contributions that the plan sponsor makes is the balance wheel in many pension fund analyses. The willingness to raise that level if and when required is the simplest way to resolve any financial issues. It can also be the most expensive.
- *The economic and social context.* The ALM must incorporate estimations of data relating to the economic surroundings in which the investments and benefit payments are going to be carried out. For example, the model needs to reflect demographic developments (such as a continuation of the trend toward increasing longevity), patterns of wage increases, and their implications for pension benefits, inflation, and returns on assets.
- *The probabilities.* In addition to laying out the range of things that *could* happen, the ALM also needs to take a position on the probability that any of them *will* happen. Monte Carlo simulations and other statistical techniques can be used to develop a picture of the range of outcomes and the likelihood of their occurrence. For example, the asset-liability model incorporates expected asset and liability returns and volatilities. Assumptions are made with respect to the correlation between assets and liabilities and between the different asset classes that are reviewed. If 10,000 simulations are run, this procedure yields a series of simulated values for assets and liabilities after a specified number of years, which lead to a series of funding ratios.

The *raison d'être* of asset-liability modeling is threefold: to provide the best possible picture to stakeholders regarding the financial health of the pension plan; to calculate the impact of various alternative strategies; and to demonstrate to regulators that the plan is unlikely to be underfunded, which is forbidden in many countries. The interplay of the various factors shapes the thinking of a pension fund's managers and trustees regarding such issues as future benefits, funding requirements, and investment strategies. The goal is to achieve a meaningful integration of asset management strategies and liabilities in the context of a universe of possible assets.

If it is well executed, an asset-liability study should help a plan sponsor to:

- Gain insight into the current financial health of a plan and provide a picture of the funding ratio, costs, prospective returns, and risks for all stakeholders over the next few years.
- Gain insight into the effects of various policy decisions. The examination of investment returns should be restricted to strategic or long-term

returns. In case active policy is considered, the fund should be very careful to pencil in the expected extra returns that the data material might reveal. Volatility and uncertainty associated with these returns can be so great, and the level of excess return so large, that using these returns in the optimization process might tilt the outcome toward active policy too much. Active policy might then take the upper hand compared to strategic mixes.

- Explicitly spell out the risk tolerance of all stakeholders and the price imposed by this level of risk tolerance in terms of opportunity costs. Risk tolerance is typically compared to several risk measures that are simulated, such as tracking errors and value at risk. The latter is an absolute measure of risk, defined as the amount of money that can be lost due to unfortunate market circumstances. It can be calculated at a 95 or 99 percent confidence level, typically on the basis of a normal distribution of returns.[1] The value at risk approach is particularly useful for deciding on the best risk-return trade-off.

The ALM provides the framework for reaching the best *ex ante* risk-adjusted returns for the pension fund or insurance company. But in these calculations, as noted, future returns and risks are, by their nature, inevitably uncertain, and that can create problems in meeting regulatory demands to be fully funded at all times. It is very difficult and very expensive to devise and execute a policy in which the chances of underfunding will be zero all the time. Volatility in the markets and the uncertainty of economic life in general make absolute certainty impossible. The asset-liability framework helps to bridge that gap between adverse developments in the real world and the desire for security by interpreting the certainty of future payments so as to indicate a limited possibility that there will be some degree of underfunding. But the fund has to be able to make it clear that it is seeking to minimize the chances of being underfunded and that it has invested in instruments that have a high probability of helping it to remain adequately funded.

Low risk levels in investing are not the same as low risk levels in the overall asset-liability context. Higher risks in the fixed income portfolio realized by increasing the duration of this portfolio will go together with lower risks at the overall level when the duration of the investment portfolio is brought closer to the duration of the liabilities. The same holds for adding active risk to the equity and fixed-income portfolio: when this active risk is not closely and positively correlated with the market risk of the existing equity and fixed-income portfolio, active elements can lead to a lower level of overall risk because of increased diversification.

POLICY INSTRUMENTS USED IN ASSET-LIABILITY MODELING

There are four policy instruments that can be used in the asset-liability context in order to reach the fund's goals. These are

1. Contributions or premium policy. What fees are levied on insurance policyholders or what contributions are required of pension plan sponsors, and which maximum level of volatility in these amounts is regarded as acceptable?
2. Investment policy. What asset classes are used, and what investment strategies are pursued?
3. Benefits policy. While existing benefits may be fixed by collective bargaining agreements, a plan sponsor can negotiate changes in the formula used to determine benefit increases and cost-of-living allowances.
4. Insurance. A pension plan can purchase insurance to make up any shortfall in its ability to meet future liabilities.

Changes in the level of contributions or *premiums* are the most common ways to react to changing financial conditions at the fund. In most countries with funded pension plans, regulations require premiums to be set at a level that covers the costs of the future benefits. And these future benefits are calculated to include not only the likely cost of existing benefit levels but also the likely additional costs generated by increases in benefits based on indexation or negotiated increases granted by management.

Regulations often distinguish between various types of premiums, which reflect the different goals set by the fund and vary substantially between countries because of the existence of different accounting rules. For instance in the Netherlands, the actuarial premium should cover some nominal future benefit, supplemented by an additional premium to finance the ambition to raise benefit levels in response to increases in the cost of living. In addition, an additional premium should be paid in order to maintain the funding ratio, and, finally, operational costs should be provided for by a premium. Similar rules in other countries acknowledge the idea that no new liability should be recognized without contributions that are responsive to its fair value.

In the case of a start-up situation, premiums have to be levied that enable the pension fund to achieve full funding within a predefined period of time.[2] Moreover, in the Netherlands, the funding ratio should always be at least 105 percent of liabilities, and if there is any underfunding, it must be eradicated within three years. That typically means that higher premiums or employer contributions must be imposed, since this is the only certain way of improving a pension fund's financial picture. To be sure, superior investment results might eliminate underfunding, but no pension fund manager can guarantee that such results will be achieved. Meanwhile, if investment results are good, it may be possible later to reduce premiums or employer contributions. A bull market in stocks, for example, has often resulted in premium holidays for plan sponsors.

There has been a debate in many countries about the flexibility that employers can and should have in making contributions and in managing pension surpluses. While it is tempting to reduce contributions when returns are strong, it is clear with the benefit of hindsight that many pension funds laid the groundwork for the funding problems they felt in recent years by reducing contributions when equity returns were strong and being slow to restore them when the equity bubble burst.

A *change in the investment policy* is another way of coping with developments in the relationship between assets and liabilities, although this alternative should be used less frequently than the premium instrument. A pension fund or other institutional investor is supposed to develop a long-term investment strategy on the basis of such factors as long-term statistical evidence of the returns on various assets. A few years of favorable above-average investment results should not lead to changes in the asset mix. In adverse situations, by contrast, looming financial difficulties might force a change in strategy on short notice; this so-called poverty trap cannot be ruled out.

Changing liabilities is yet another alternative that should be seen even more rarely than changing the asset mix or the investment policy. In most cases, changes in liabilities take the form of a reduction of current or future cost-of-living adjustments or indexation of benefits to wage increases in order to reduce the rate of increase in benefits. It is inevitably easier to reduce the rate of increase in future benefits than to reduce the benefits themselves. In some cases, however, benefit indexation or cost-of-living adjustments can be deleted or postponed for a certain period, and even existing nominal benefit levels can be reduced. This, however, must be viewed as an instrument of last resort, to be imposed only in dire financial circumstances, when other alternatives cannot be expected to offer enough relief of the difficult funding situation.

Institutions may also choose to respond to a favorable funding situation by offering more generous future payments to employees by increasing the level of benefits or changing the formula for increasing them. This situation does not occur often, as the sponsor is usually eager to retain the benefits of a favorable funding status. If such increases are offered, however, then the pension plan must undertake careful and complex calculations to determine the impact of these increases on future liabilities as the long-term impact of these increases can be far greater than might be foreseen at the moment of the decision to grant the improvement.

Insurance is the fourth mechanism for changing the asset-liability mix. It will not be discussed here, because, in essence, it means the end of a funded pension plan. In the case of an insured pension plan, the plan sponsor merely collects premiums or contributions and hands them over to the insurer, who takes full responsibility for future payments.

CALCULATIONS TO COPE WITH UNCERTAINTY

The asset-liability picture can be fleshed out by calculating the effects of various changes in economic circumstances, such as new developments in economic growth, wages, and inflation rates to name the most important variables, as well as by changes in premium policy, benefits, and investment returns. Correlations between financial markets also change. The inherent uncertainty is dealt with by means of simulations with respect to the possible levels of these variables. Many combinations of different asset mixes and different levels of premium volatility generate a whole range of possible future solvency ratios. In addition, scenarios are calculated with respect to possible changes in the set of plan participants and their future claims, which are generally dependent on longevity, career patterns and wage rate developments. In this way, all the possible endogenous and exogenous developments are incorporated into a coherent model, and this produces pictures of present and future asset-liability ratios.[3]

The Fiduciary Manager uses this analysis as a basis for suggesting to the fund's management the most attractive combination of future returns (which may be translated into future premium levels) and uncertainty (chances of underfunding to a certain degree). This procedure comes down to choosing the optimal asset mix. This mix is dependent on such variables as the initial solvency ratio of the fund, the maturity of its liabilities, the statistical properties of the assets, and the interaction of those assets.

A specific asset mix will produce some level of value at risk and will also indicate the possible volatility of premiums to be paid. These last variables are to be compared to the risk appetite of the decision makers, which turns out to be a major factor in the whole decision process. It should be stressed that the Fiduciary Manager, and other consultants as well, typically only "advise" the board in this matter. The ultimate decision regarding which combination of risk and return will be chosen can only be taken by the board of the fund. This responsibility cannot be delegated to any other party. Even if a board chooses to let others make these decisions, under the laws of most developed countries, the board retains ultimate responsibility for those decisions.

Because these calculations are based on uncertainties and the outcome will constantly be impacted by unforeseen events, the Fiduciary Manager needs to evaluate the asset-liability context on an ongoing basis. If the profile of the labor force does not change significantly, and markets do not exhibit large fluctuations, intervals of some two to three years are adequate. Of course, if regulations change or the population of plan participants is disrupted (by, for example, a takeover of another company and the integration of its pension plan and plan participants into the acquiring company's pension plan), new calculations are necessary (in fact, these are obligatory under European regulation). Quick scans are advisable in case some major event causes disruptions in assets or liabilities. The relevant criteria are maximizing returns within the constraints of a risk tolerance level and minimizing insolvency risks.

The all-embracing word to capture the issues at stake is *risk*, which is of relevance for two parties: the members or clients of the plan and the plan sponsor. The Fiduciary Manager needs to find an answer to two basic questions: To what extent are the members' future benefits secure, and to what extent are the employer's and employee's financial contributions limited? All across the financial world the second question is so critical that employers are taking drastic measures to curb the risks associated with their pension plans.

THE CRUCIAL ROLE OF ALM

The importance of asset-liability studies cannot be overestimated. A pension fund can use this tool to obtain a better view of its long-term financial situation and to devise a set of policy instruments enabling it to cope with potentially detrimental developments in the future. This is essential to securing the long-term health—and survival—of a pension fund or other institutional investor. But in addition, pension funds closely tied to a corporate plan sponsor derive important benefits from an appropriate asset-liability framework. The implementation of new accounting rules is reshaping corporate financial statements, making unfunded pension liabilities a much more visible part of a company's financial reports.

As a result, potential changes in the relation between assets and liabilities are very important for a corporate plan sponsor, and it should be very interested in undertaking a thorough analysis of the factors that could change the pension plan's funded status. Because most companies would go to great lengths to avoid negative financial influences on their balance sheet caused by their pension fund, it can be argued that the asset-liability study is even more important for corporate pension funds than it is for public employee pension funds or pension funds covering a number of employers or industries. For insurance companies, meanwhile, the asset-liability framework delivers insight into future reserve positions, which can be the basis for fundamental strategic decisions to be taken by the company.

One way to mitigate the influence of pensions on the financial health of the sponsoring company is to manage the rate of increase in benefits. Instead of integrating indexation of benefits or cost-of-living increases in the schedule of benefits, for instance, employers can make this kind of indexation dependent on investment returns. (Note that this policy implies a shift from defined benefit toward defined contribution.) The effects of this change in benefit policy can be calculated in an asset-liability context. This can be a powerful instrument because regulators in some countries insist that the required funding ratio must be a function of the ambitions of the fund in this field.

A looser commitment to cost-of-living adjustments reduces the required ratio compared to the situation in which the fund has a strong commitment to indexation. This ruling implicitly leads to the conclusion that, on average and over the long run, members of a pension fund can be better off with limited aspirations regarding the indexation of future benefits. This lower ambition raises the possibility of taking more investment risk in the portfolio, thus creating, on average, higher investment returns and more room to pay for higher benefits in the future. Although it may seem like a contradiction, it can be said that future retirees should welcome some uncertainty in future indexation.

Of course, an employer's ultimate protection against rising benefit levels is to close down the defined benefit plan and create a defined contribution plan. These plans are increasingly appealing to employers precisely because the risk of underfunding is eliminated. The employer makes contributions to the DC plan, the employee chooses how those contributions are invested, and at retirement the employee gets whatever money has accumulated in his or her defined contribution account. Regulation in this area abundantly lags in several countries, as for instance in the United Kingdom, where DC plans are set up at one third the cost of a DB plan. This compares to Iceland, where a switch to DC requires the sponsor to pay as much premium as in the DB plan, or at least 10 percent of salaries.

ASSET-LIABILITY MODELING IN PRACTICE

What follows is an illustration of the basic calculations and decision-making processes involved in developing an asset-liability model and using it to guide the management of a pension fund. The example embodies the principles generally used in many countries, although the specific figures used generally

TABLE 5.1 Balance Sheet of Pension Fund X as per December 31st 2004

Balance sheet per December 31 2004 (€ 1.000)

Investments	851,000	Provisions	785,000
Cash	9,000	General reserve	49,000
Other assets	4,000	Investment reserve	30,000
		Other liabilities	0
Total assets	864,000	Total liabilities	864,000
Funding ratio		= (provisions + general reserve + investment reserve)/ provisions	
		= (785,000 + 49,000 + 30,000)/(785,000)	
		= 110%	

Source: Ortec, presentation for pension fund X, 2005.[4]

reflect the regulations issued by the Dutch authorities. All calculations, graphs, and tables refer to an actual Dutch pension fund, which is not identified for reasons of privacy. The tables and graphs are derived from calculations carried out for this fund.

The first step in the ALM process is to describe the initial status of the fund in terms of its fundamental characteristics, such as

- The number and status of all plan members or participants.
- The complete set of benefit contracts.
- The mechanisms for financing liabilities (premium policy next to investment income) and the explicit indexation goals of the fund (these include the conditions under which the fund will maintain the relationship between benefits and price or wage levels and the triggers that will change that relationship).
- The current financial position, including the funding ratio.

The funding ratio at this starting point can be derived from the balance sheet. See Table 5.1.

The long-term development of the number and status of plan members is calculated on the basis of the plan sponsor's estimates of employment trends combined with general demographic trends, such as longevity. In addition, a base scenario is calculated based on the estimated members, grouped according to the nature of their contracts, the economic data, investment policy, premium policy, and indexation policy. In addition, possible new arrangements can be taken into account. (See Figure 5.1, where a new agreement between employer and employees has led to substantial savings in the long run.)

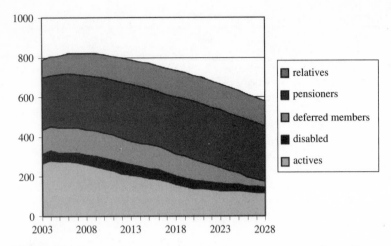

FIGURE 5.1 Prognosis of non-indexed reserves (amounts × € 1 million)
Source: Ortec, internal document.

TABLE 5.2 Economic Data as Provided by the ALM Specialist

Data as of January 1ˢᵗ 2005.	Mean	Volatility
Price inflation	2.5%	2.0%
Wage inflation	3.25%	2.25%
Return on bonds	5.0%	4.5%
Return on equity	8.0%	18.8%
Return on real estate	6.5%	5.0%
Return on hedge funds of funds	7.0%	6.0%
Return on cash	3.75%	2.0%

Source: Ortec, presentation to pension fund X, May 2005.

The economic data are provided by asset-liability specialists. This data should be plausible in the eyes of the fund as well as in accordance with the views of the regulator in that area (Table 5.2). In the example, the initial calculations are based on a fixed compounding rate of 4 percent with respect to the liabilities.

Prognosis of Future Reserves without Policy Changes

Initial population data, career lines, and economic data give an indication of the nonindexed reserves of the pension fund. These reserves are defined as the provisions for future cash outflows, plus general and investment reserves, all calculated on the assumption that no indexation will be provided during the entire future of this graying fund.

Total provisions decline shortly as a result of less expensive arrangements between the pension fund and its members, arranged in the overall revision of agreements between employer and employees.

The underlying basics of financing can be summarized as follows:

- Initial funding ratio: 110 percent.
- Premium policy:
  - 100 percent single premium or lump sum, including back service of indexation (lump sum is the sum needed at a certain time to finance the pension rights in the future of new participants).
  - indexation of non-actives.
  - when general reserve + investment reserve < 5 percent, transfer from employer to maximum 0.5 percent of provisions.
  - when funding ratio < 100.5 percent, transfer from employer to 100.5 percent.
  - refund to sponsor when funding ratio is higher than 105 percent (excluding investment reserve).
- Indexation:
  - non-actives receive actual indexation of inflation minus 1.2 percentage points during the period 2004–2008; afterwards indexation is conditional on funding ratio.
  - indexation of actives is unconditional.
  - all indexations are 3 percent maximum.
- A possible extra provision can be calculated with respect to longevity risk. Some funds create reserves in order to be able to smoothly convert toward the expected new life expectancy tables (probably indicating longer average lives).

These data are accompanied by an example of a strategic asset mix. See Table 5.3.

Future Financial Situation with Flexible Premium Levels under the Regime of a Fixed Compound Rate

The grey area in Figure 5.2 represents all 10,000 Monte Carlo simulations of different scenarios with respect to all the relevant variables. The solid smooth line denotes the development of the average funding ratio, while the dotted line represents one random path of development.

TABLE 5.3 Strategic Asset Mix in the Base Scenario

Bonds (specified according to currency)	60%
Equity (regional mix)	40%
Real estate	0%
Funds of hedge funds	0%
Cash	0%
Currencies	Hedged

A dynamic asset mix may result when lower funding ratios induce more bonds at the expense of equity (with, for instance, steps of five percentage points when the funding ratio declines from 135% to 120% and 105%) and with increasing weights of equities in case the funding ratio rises.

Source: Ortec, presentation to pension fund X, May 2005.

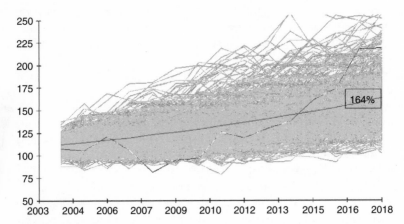

FIGURE 5.2 Results base policy in 4 percent world: funding ratio (investment reserve included)

The most important conclusion is that the average development of the funding ratio as in line with standard policy (in the 4 percent world) comes up to the regulations in place. See Table 5.4.

The interpretation of this table can be summarized as follows.

With respect to solvency:

- There is a strong restoration of the funding ratio in times of underfunding.
- The probability of short-term underfunding is high (7.7 percent).
- Periods of underfunding do not last long because the sponsor increases contributions in those situations.

TABLE 5.4 Numerical Results Base Policy with Fixed Compounding Rate of 4%

Time period under investigation	(1/5)*	(1/15)**	(15/15)***
Average funding ratio incl. investment reserves	117.3%	134.5%	163.3%
Probability of funding ratio < 105 percent	17.2%	8.9%	0.2%
Probability of funding ratio < 100 percent	7.7%	3.8%	0.0%
Probability of funding ratio < 90 percent	0.7%	0.3%	0.0%
Surplus at risk (97.5 percent reliability)	95.0%	97.6%	116.4%
Average gross base premium	24.7%	27.4%	26.3%
Average net premium	29.5%	31.4%	28.9%
Value at risk net premium 1 year (95 percent reliability)	39.1%	42.9%	38.5%
Value at risk net premium 1 year (99 percent)	84.8%	81.0%	39.6%
Probability of indexation less than 100 percent	98.4%	32.8%	0.0%
Average indexation for non-actives	0.7%	1.4%	1.8%

*(1/5) indicates that only the first five years are analyzed. So 17.2% depicts the probability that the funding ratio will be below 105% during one of those five years.
**(1/15) indicates that the full fifteen years are analyzed.
***(15/15) indicates values in the fifteenth year, the end of the period of prognosis.

- The surplus at risk (SaR) is the level of the funding ratio, which will be met with a probability of 97.5 percent. So, in the first five years, the funding ratio will be 95 percent or higher with a probability of 97.5 percent. When a pension fund should be solvent all of the time at this level of probability, the value of SaR would have to be 100 (percent).

With respect to premium risks:

- The gross premium is the single premium (in percentages of the wage sum) calculated for future pension rights including indexation of the active and non-active populations. Net premium is gross premium including restitution or cash call, depending on the financial situation of the fund.
- The premium level (as a percentage of the wage sum) is very volatile, inducing a high probability of very high premiums. This is caused by unconditional transfers in times of underfunding.
- The level of average net premium is higher than that of average gross base premiums, because the sponsor has to supplement in case the base premium does not suffice to pay for indexation of actives.
- With a probability of 95 percent, the level of premiums will not be higher than 39.1 percent of the wage sum in the first five years.

In the course of later years, this level does not decline very much. At a probability level of 99 percent, possible premium levels may be much higher, however.

With respect to indexation risks:

- There is no indexation risk for active employees (by agreement).
- Nonactives receive 40 percent of price inflation on average until the end of 2008; from 2008 onwards, on average, they receive 90 percent of price inflation.

Future Financial Situation with Flexible Premium Levels under the Regime of Compound Rates Equal to Market Interest Rates

Things can change dramatically when the fixed compounding rate of 4 percent is replaced by market interest rates. In this instance, it is assumed that all fixed income investments are made in securities denominated in Euros, so there is no foreign exchange risk and that the following yield curve (most of the time the so-called swap curve is used) prevailed in the market (see Figure 5.3):

It is important to note that if long-term interest rates are higher than the compounding rate of 4 percent (as is the case in the graph), then using market rates has beneficial effects on the funding ratio. Based on market value, the reserves and liabilities change, and this leads to a totally different financial situation. For instance, in a forecast for the ensuing 12 months, note the differences: The fixed compound rate: reserves are 820 million and the funding ratio is 112 percent. The nominal market value (based on the

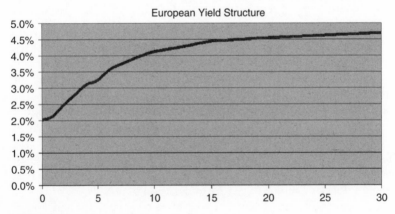

FIGURE 5.3 European yield structure

yield curve above): reserves are 793 million, the funding ratio is 116 percent, and the duration of liabilities is 12.

The same is true for the situation in which the real value of the funding ratio is defined. This is the financial status of the fund expressed as the value of the investment portfolio divided by the liabilities, with full indexation. In this example, future liabilities are calculated using a compounding rate equal to the nominal interest rate minus the expected inflation. As a result, reserves are 1,007 million, the funding ratio is 91%, and the duration of liabilities is 15. In this calculation all nominal values are reduced by the expected level of inflation.

Comparison of this market value situation with the 4 percent case reveals that the market value funding ratio is not hugely different because market interest rates at the duration level are not far from 4 percent, but, more important, the ratio is more volatile. The use of four percent and the use of market value funding cause ratios to move in opposite directions. For instance, a rise in interest rates has no effect on the value of the liabilities as they are compounded with a fixed four percent rate, while at the same time the fixed income portfolio declines in market value. Both results taken together, of course, lower the funding ratio. With nominal market value however, higher interest rates raise the funding ratio as liabilities decline to a larger extent than the value of the fixed income portfolio. This is because the duration of liabilities is higher than the duration of the fixed income portfolio and because liabilities are larger than the fixed income portfolio. Other "killer" scenarios become evident: Declines in interest rates, for example, are much more important because the duration of the fixed income investments is far lower than the duration of the liabilities. The interest rate level replaces equity prices and inflation as the most important determinant of the funding ratio. Table 5.5 summarizes these findings.

TABLE 5.5 Summary of Impact of Various Scenarios

Scenario	Liabilities	
	4%	Nominal Market Value
Interest rates increase	Value of fixed income portfolio decreases, present value of liabilities is constant.	Value of fixed income portfolio decreases, present value of liabilities decreases stronger.
Interest rates decrease	Value of fixed income portfolio rises, present value of liabilities is constant.	Value of fixed income portfolio increases, present value of liabilities increases more strongly.

When premium policy and investment policy are not changed, the following distribution of funding ratios occurs, going from 4 percent to nominal market value and to real market value. See Figure 5.4.

Because the actual nominal interest rate is higher than 4 percent, the probability of the funding ratio being lower than 105 percent decreases going from fixed rates to nominal market rates. In real terms, however, the chances are much higher. At the 97.5 percent reliability level for surplus at risk (SaR), this surplus rises with the higher interest rate, but declines strongly with real interest rates. The average funding ratio rises in time in all three cases, but this movement is more pronounced in the case of nominal market value. The higher long-term interest is beneficial for the present value of the longer-term liabilities.

The third picture reveals the variables when assets and liabilities are compared to each other in the real world. In that situation, all liabilities are indexed; that is, all future liabilities are compounded by the real interest rate, which is the nominal interest rate minus the expected inflation rate. Of course, future liabilities rise significantly compared to the nominal world, and therefore the probability of a low funding ratio and a low level of surplus at risk increases. The lower (real) compounding rate works its way through the liability side because of the huge difference between the duration of the liabilities and the duration of the fixed income portfolio and because the fixed income portfolio is much smaller than the amount of the liabilities.

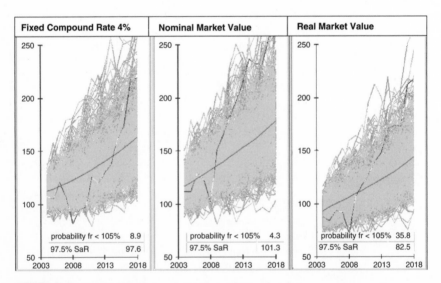

FIGURE 5.4 Funding ratio results with unchanged policies

This substantial deterioration of the financial situation clearly indicates the power of the indexing mechanism. Building in the possibility of not completely indexing future pensions is a powerful tool to improve the funding ratio.

Meanwhile, because premium policy is unchanged, premium levels change, going from fixed rate to market rate. Figure 5.5 illustrates this.

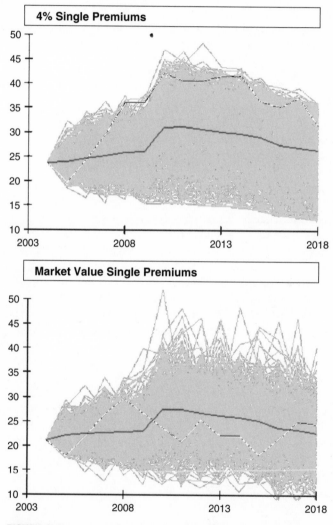

FIGURE 5.5 Single premiums at 4 percent and market value interest rate

- Market value single premiums are lower on average than 4 percent sums.
- Single premiums in the 4 percent world are volatile because of price inflation; volatility in market value single premiums is higher because of the effects of both interest and price inflation.
- Until the end of 2008 single premiums are lower because of indexation restriction (actual price inflation minus 1.2 percent).

Net premium levels are also lower when moving from a 4 percent discounting factor to market interest rates (Figure 5.6). The reason for this is that with the interest rates higher than 4 percent, future liabilities are lower, making it possible to return part of the premiums paid because of the better financial position of the fund.

This change, of course, influences both lump sums and yearly premiums:

- Single premiums are calculated at market value.
- Extra premiums depend on market value funding ratio: extra premiums are due when the funding ratio falls below 105 percent.
- Market value net premium is lower than 4 percent net premium on average.
- The probability of high net premiums occurring is smaller.

The effects of single premiums and net premiums based on market interest rates instead of 4 percent on the funding ratio can be seen in Figure 5.7.

With nominal interest rates higher than 4 percent, the average funding ratio is somewhat higher on average, and the frequency of low funding ratios is reduced. This is clearly reflected in the lower probability of having a funding ratio lower than 105 percent. By the same token, the surplus at risk at the 97.5 percent reliability level is higher. Making these calculations using real rates yield results that are quite the opposite—a very high probability of having a funding ratio lower than 105 percent and the surplus at risk is some 20 percent lower than in the nominal case.

Regulatory authorities can be specific in determining the required level of premiums and the appropriate investment policy, prescribing the minimum level of funding. The Dutch case, overhauling the whole scene, can be summarized in the following steps defining the required premium levels:

Step 1:
    a. Market value single premiums:
        Future employee service.
        Back service indexation (actives).
        Risk premium (for insurance against disability).

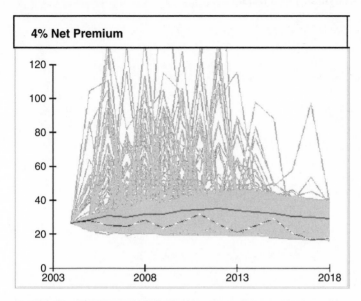

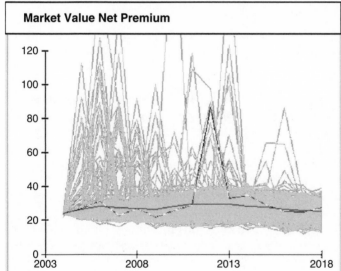

FIGURE 5.6 Net premium level in 4 percent discount case and at market value

Average net premium	31.4	Average net premium	27.4
Probability net premium ⟩30%	46.7	Probability net premium ⟩ 30%	23.6
Probability net premium ⟩4−%	10.3	Probability net premium ⟩ 4−%	2.0

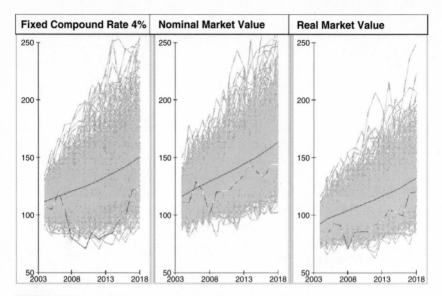

FIGURE 5.7   Results base policy 4percent versus market value: funding ratios

Fixed Compound Rate 4%		Nominal Market Value		Real Market Value	
Probability < 105%	15.1	Probability < 105%	5.3	Probability < 105%	43.8
97.5% SaR	91.1	97.5% SaR	100.2	97.5% SaR	80.4

Extra premium for longevity (in case new longevity tables show increases in longevity requiring the payment of additional benefits).

b. Extra premium over the single premium as a buffer.

c. Extra premium as in 4 percent policy, based on nominal market value funding ratio:

When general reserve < 5 percent, transfer from investment reserve.

When general reserve + investment reserve < 5 percent, transfer with a maximum of 0.5 percent of provisions by employer.

When nominal market value funding ratio < 100.5 percent, transfer until 100.5 percent by employer.

Extra premium for longevity.

Step 2: Extra premium to be paid by the employer until nominal market value funding ratio is 105 percent (in connection with minimum reserves requirement).

Step 3: Extra premium for restoration of required buffers in 15 years.

Step 4: Restitution when real market value funding ratio > 100 percent + buffers. Figure 5.8 shows the effects of these steps on net premiums and probability of underfunding.

The single premiums and premium levels in adherence with the regulations show the pattern exhibited in Figure 5.9.

Definition regulatory premium:

- Market value single premiums (coming service, back service, risk premium, extra premium longevity).
- Extra premium over net cash flow (the regulator defines the cost price of future pension rights, and this includes a buffer for calamities; when future rights are paid actually, this buffer is no longer necessary and will be translated into lower net premiums).
- Unconditional extra premiums for required reserves.
- Extra premium for restoration (lack of buffer restored in 15 years).

Table 5.6 summarizes the four steps in both regions.

The extreme volatility in net premium levels is not caused by the volatility of single premiums but by the volatility of the funding ratio because extra premiums are required when this ratio becomes too low. The difference between the minimum contribution and the cost covering premium therefore is less relevant here.

The differences between market value policy and the regulator's view can be summarized as follows:

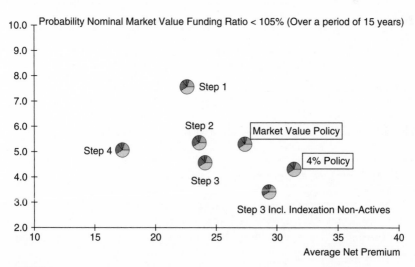

FIGURE 5.8 Single premiums and premium levels in regulatory policy

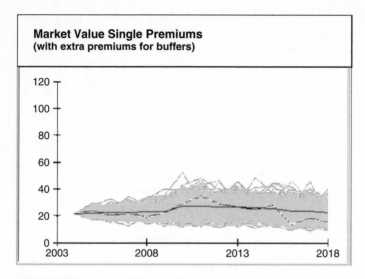

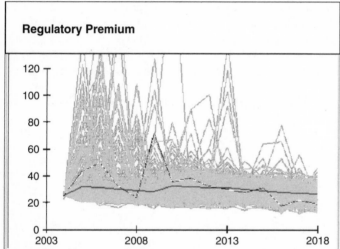

FIGURE 5.9   Net premium level in 4 percent discount case and at market value

Definition market value policy:
- Premium:
  - Single premiums at nominal market value (coming service, risk premium, indexation actives and non-actives).
  - Transfer as in 4 percent policy, based on nominal market value funding ratio.

TABLE 5.6 Numerical Summary (Steps 1 through 4 Refer to the Steps Elaborated in the Previous Pages)

Horizon 15 years	4% Policy	Market Value Policy	Step 1	Step 2	Step 3	Step 4
Average funding ratio at market value	145.3%	138.6%	132.7%	134.8%	136.2%	130.8%
Probability of market value funding ratio < 105 percent	4.3%	5.3%	7.5%	5.3%	4.5%	5.0%
Probability of market value funding ratio < 100 percent	2.0%	2.3%	3.5%	2.3%	1.9%	2.1%
Probability of market value funding ratio < 90 percent	0.3%	0.2%	0.3%	0.1%	0.1%	0.2%
Market value surplus at risk (97.5% reliability)*	101.2%	100.2%	98.3%	100.3%	101.1%	100.6%
Probability of market value funding ratio < 105 percent after extra premium	1.9%	2.2%	4.2%	0.0%	0.0%	0.0%
Average gross base premium (percent of wage sum)**	27.4%	24.2%	18.3%	18.3%	18.3%	18.3%
Average net premium**	31.4%	27.4%	22.6%	23.6%	24.1%	17.3%
Value at risk net premium 1 year (95 percent reliability)***	42.9%	35.5%	29.0%	32.8%	33.4%	33.8%
Value at risk net premium 1 year (99 percent reliability)***	80.8%	59.6%	67.3%	88.5%	78.0%	83.1%
Probability of indexation lower than 100 percent	32.8%	32.8%	32.8%	32.8%	32.8%	32.8%
Average indexation nonactives	1.4%	1.4%	1.4%	1.4%	1.4%	1.4%

Horizon 5 years	4% Policy	Market Value Policy	Step 1	Step 2	Step 3	Step 4
Average funding ratio at market value	124.3%	122.8%	121.5%	122.3%	123.1%	122.9%

(*continued*)

TABLE 5.6   (*Continued*)

Horizon 5 years	4% Policy	Market Value Policy	Step 1	Step 2	Step 3	Step 4
Probability of market value funding ratio < 105 percent	10.3%	11.3%	12.6%	10.1%	9.3%	9.3%
Probability of market value funding ratio < 100 percent	4.7%	5.2%	6.2%	5.0%	4.3%	4.3%
Probability of market value funding ratio < 90 percent	0.6%	0.5%	0.6%	0.4%	0.4%	0.4%
Market value surplus at risk (97.5 percent reliability)*	96.8%	96.0%	95.1%	96.8%	97.5%	97.5%
Probability of market value funding ratio < 105 percent after extra premium	4.2%	4.8%	6.4%	0.0%	0.0%	0.0%
Average gross base premium (percent of wage sum)**	24.7%	22.2%	19.5%	19.5%	19.5%	19.5%
Average net premium**	29.5%	26.6%	24.3%	26.0%	27.1%	26.4%
Value at risk net premium 1 year (95 percent reliability)***	39.1%	32.8%	31.6%	54.3%	51.0%	50.8%
Value at risk net premium 1 year (99 percent reliability)***	84.4%	78.9%	84.9%	104.0%	103.1%	102.9%
Probability of indexation lower than 100 percent	98.4%	98.4%	98.4%	98.4%	98.4%	98.4%
Average indexation nonactives	0.7%	0.7%	0.7%	0.7%	0.7%	0.7%

*Percentages indicate the level below which the funding ratio will not decline with a probability of 97.5 percent.

**Net premiums in general differ from gross (both in percentages of the wage sum) because in the course of years developments in all variables can lead to positive or negative influences on the funding ratio, making it necessary to raise the net premium level or making it possible to lower it.

***Net premiums will be below the percentages of the wage sum shown in the table with a probability of 95 or 99 percent.

- When general reserve < 5 percent, transfer from investment reserve
- When general reserve + investment reserve < 5 percent, transfer with a maximum of 0.5 percent of nominal market value provisions by employer.
- When nominal market value of funding ratio < 100.5 percent, transfer up to 100.5 percent by employer.
- Indexation as in 4 percent policy.

Definition regulatory policy:
- Premium:
  - Single premiums at market value.
  - Extra premiums over net cash flow.
  - Required transfer when reserves are insufficient.
  - Recuperation premium.
- Indexation as in 4 percent policy.

In the examples used here, investment policy is fixed (as represented by the pies, indicating strategic mixes of fixed income, equities, real estate, hedge funds and cash, whereby equities and real estate are supposed to appear in a fixed proportion to each other). The differences between 4 percent policy, market value policy, and regulatory policy with respect to the surplus at risk are summarized in Figure 5.10.

Calculation of the buffers, required by the regulator in the so-called standard test, encompasses six sorts of risks:

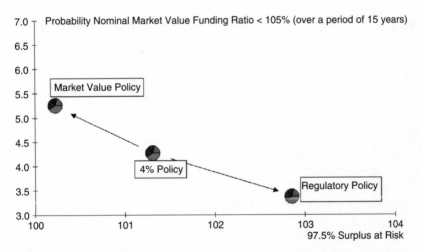

FIGURE 5.10 Results base policy 4 percent versus market value: funding ratios with market value lump sums and net premiums

- Interest rate risk (S1): the effect of the most unfavorable change in the yield curve: 8 percent, caused by the difference between the duration of the provisions (13.7) and the duration of the fixed income portfolio (6.7)
- Equity risk (S2): 13.3 percent
- Currency risk (S3): 3.2 percent
- Commodity risk (S4): 0 percent (not invested in)
- Credit risk (S5): 3.1 percent
- Insurance risk (S6): 0.3 percent

The effects of the risks have to be summarized by the following calculation rule:

$$\sqrt{(S_1^2 + S_2^2 + 2{*}0,65{*}S_1{*}S_2 + S_3^2 + S_4^2 + S_5^2 + S_6^2)}$$

= 19.8 percent of the market value of the liabilities (rounded figures).

The first conclusion is that the funding ratio (110 percent, as indicated in Table 5.1) is insufficient. The implication is that if there are developments that would reduce the funding ratio to 105 percent or lower, the fund must come up with a plan to provide for a restoration to 105 percent within three years.

Future Financial Situation with Changes in Investment Policy

In this example, modifications have so far been restricted to premium policy. Investment policy, of course, is another way to cope with changes in the financial environment and in the regulations. Consider the implications of the following variations in investment policy:

Base scenario (required buffer: 17.8 percent):

Equity and real estate: 40 percent
Fixed income: 60 percent
Duration fixed income portfolio: 5

Equity proportion 30 percent (required buffer: 14.8 percent):

Equity and real estate: 30 percent
Fixed income: 70 percent
Duration fixed income portfolio: 5

Longer duration fixed income portfolio (required buffer: 14.5 percent):

Equity and real estate: 40 percent
Fixed income: 60 percent
Duration fixed income portfolio: 12

Figure 5.11 supplements Figure 5.8 by including two new policy alternatives.

As we have seen in Figure 5.8, in order to facilitate the choice of asset mix and premium level, the scenarios can be summarized in pie charts in which each pie represents a certain strategic mix. For reasons of simplicity, the mix used is reduced to bonds (white) and equity (grey tints referring to certain regional equity markets). The pies are set in a diagram indicating expected premium levels and risk of underfunding. These two variables are the most important ones for the plan sponsor: What is the tolerable level of risk that the plan may become underfunded and which level of premiums is acceptable? In one figure, the two major policy instruments are indicated: investment policy (asset mix) and premium policy (level of premiums in terms of the wage bill). In case none of the combinations is acceptable, the whole process has to be restarted using another aspiration level with respect to such variables as the level of indexation of benefits.

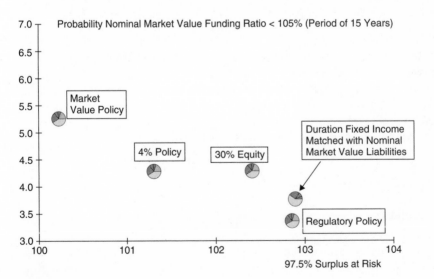

FIGURE 5.11 Chances of nominal market value funding ratio being lower than 105 percent (over a period of 15 years)

Of course, these figures have to be compared to the requirements of the regulator. For instance, the probability of underfunding should be lower than 2.5 percent in the first year, and the funding ratio should be 105 percent or higher. If that level is not reached, however, improvement will be required within a well-defined period of time.

POLICY CHANGES

If the figures result in an outcome that meets the wishes of the board and comply with regulations, the policy with respect to premiums and investment policy is set. If, however, the board or the regulator is not satisfied with the prospective future funding ratio or with the chances of underfunding, the whole process has to be recalculated. Changes in policies have to be defined in order to achieve better results. The whole spectrum of changes in premiums and investment policy as well as the potential to redefine intentions or aspirations regarding increases in benefit levels has to be used to generate these improved results.

This reframing of the whole situation could also be triggered by major developments in the financial markets. Since all calculations have as their starting point "normal" conditions, which are by definition the most probable conditions, departures from the range of normal conditions will inevitably result in significant changes in asset-liability studies. Indeed, it is to be expected that in one way or another, the future never looks like the past, and "normal" conditions, levels, and rate of changes will not characterize every variable. As a result, there is good reason to expect that future developments will show a different pattern from what has been modeled.

That is not an argument against asset-liability studies; quite the contrary. Precisely because things change, it is important for those overseeing an institutional portfolio to understand the impact of various changes on their assets and on their liabilities and to know what steps they can take to counteract that impact in order to maintain funding ratios and meet their obligations.

WHERE DOES FIDUCIARY MANAGEMENT FIT IN?

As indicated at the outset of this chapter, the Fiduciary Manager can and should play a vital role in the calculations of liabilities and the determination of asset-liability issues. The Fiduciary Manager generally has much greater capability than the plan sponsor to formulate liability scenarios, to judge their probability, and to evaluate investment alternatives. Fiduciary and asset-liability specialists speak the same language with respect to risk and statistical analyses, and both parties together can give a fund's managers and trustees a sense of comfort that all the alternatives are being evaluated and plans are in place to deal with a wide range of contingencies.

CHAPTER 6

Fiduciary Management in Practice — Portfolio Construction

O ne of the major tenets of contemporary approaches to investing is that the portfolio is more than an accretion of good ideas. In the past, perhaps, an astute investor was one who accumulated an array of investments, each one of which was thought to be, and hopefully turned out to be, a good idea. For the past few decades, however, the sophisticated view of investing has been that the right way to put together an investment portfolio is to begin with a broad-gauged asset allocation approach, and then, within that framework, the investor should create a series of sub-allocations. Then, and only then, investment managers within each of the realms that have been defined would be mandated to pick specific securities.

The Fiduciary Manager works with the plan sponsor to define the risk-reward principles that should guide the fund. After establishing the basic objectives of the fund in terms of acceptable risks and desired returns, and after thinking through the risk budget, the Fiduciary Manager can then turn to the task of portfolio construction. That task has several components:

- Defining the allocation and sub-allocation of assets
- Defining benchmarks for measuring the managers
- Formulating the mandates for managers

After this work is completed, then, as we will see, the Fiduciary turns to the process of selecting and monitoring investment managers.

DEFINING APPROPRIATE ASSET CLASSES

The process of asset allocation is spelled out in Modern Portfolio Theory. An investor formulates his or her views of the expected returns for the asset classes to be invested in and then constructs an efficient frontier, which indicates the expected risks and returns associated with various combinations of asset classes. This is used to identify the combination of investments that seems to offer the highest potential return at a given level of risk and the lowest potential risk at a given return level.

There are two problems with this formulation. One is the issue of expected returns. The investor does not know for sure what returns various markets may provide, so this construct is built on decidedly shifting sands.

The second issue is that the range of acceptable assets must be determined. Originally, most pension assets were invested in high grade fixed income securities. Not until the 1950s, and later in many cases, were equities viewed as acceptable institutional assets. They quickly moved from acceptable to predominant among Anglo-Saxon investors, and by the 1980s it was not uncommon for UK pension funds to have upwards of 70 or 80 percent of their assets in equities, while fixed income securities were reduced to 10 or 20 percent or even less.

While equities have been the most prominent addition to the array of acceptable asset classes, several other asset classes have also entered this select circle.

Property came early to European pension funds, and more recently to U.S. plans. Continental pension plans typically have substantial holdings of real estate in their home countries and beyond. Indeed, vast swaths of office blocks and hotels in many major cities are owned by pension funds.

In more recent years, alternative investments have generated substantial interest, although allocations to them remain rather modest. This is a somewhat loosely defined category that can include a variety of investments whose common bond is chiefly that they are "alternatives" to stocks and bonds and that they are generally less liquid than publicly traded securities. Alternative investments include private equity, venture capital, natural resources, and hedge funds or absolute return strategies.

HEDGE FUNDS: WEIGHING THE "NEW" ALTERNATIVE

Hedge funds are the most prominent addition to the list of accepted institutional asset classes, and in many respects they are also the most controversial. Many investors regard hedge funds as highly aggressive, even speculative, investment vehicles and sometimes this is true. Long Term

Capital Management failed some years ago because of highly speculative currency positions, while more recently Amaranth went the same way as a consequence of huge positions in a very specific part of a sub-class in the commodity market. But in fact, many hedge funds actually pursue very conservative arbitrage strategies that enable them to eke out small but consistently positive returns month after month. By the early part of 2007, there were some 10,000 hedge funds worldwide with well over a 1.5 trillion euros in assets under management.

Hedge funds are confusing vehicles because their name has ceased to explain anything about their investments. When A.W. Jones, a former financial magazine writer, created his "hedged" fund in the early 1950s, he took a pioneering step in creating a fund that combined long and short positions in equities; that is, this fund not only bought stocks, it also sold shares it did not own, hoping to buy these stocks when the prices fell and cover its short position. This hedged portfolio was designed to generate a return regardless of whether the stock market rose or fell. It also sought to capitalize on Jones's insight that astute investment managers should not only be able to pick stocks that were destined to go up but also those poised to fall, and they should be permitted to act on these ideas.

Following Jones's success, a variety of other investors created hedge funds, but in many cases, these funds did not, in fact, hedge at all. Moreover, they began to invest in a wide range of instruments and markets. The so-called global macro funds, such as those created by legendary hedge fund investor George Soros, roamed the world, investing wherever they saw opportunities.

As a result, hedge funds have come to be defined by their structure and their compensation system rather than by the instruments in which they invest. Hedge funds are typically organized as limited partnerships in the United States, although in other countries some hedge funds have publicly traded shares. The most distinct attribute of hedge funds is their compensation structure: They typically charge "two and 20." That means the fund manager receives a fee equal to 2 percent of the assets under management plus 20 percent of the returns generated above some previously determined benchmark.

Many hedge funds seek to provide consistently positive returns, month after month, with no down months (although not too many manage to actually achieve this). This approach stands in contrast to traditional managers, who measure themselves in relative terms and are prepared to accept declines in value if those declines are less than those of the markets that constitute their benchmarks. In fact, the objective of achieving consistent, positive returns is one of the main attractions of hedge funds. Many institutions, like many individual investors, have concluded that they would like to be assured that they can maintain what they have and generate a steady return. This is sometimes more attractive than having the opportunity of generating high returns, but at the risk of having low returns. The promise of consistent absolute returns clearly has an appeal to pension funds; after all, retirees cannot eat relative returns.

Hedge funds raise a number of issues for a Fiduciary Manager and a plan sponsor. One is whether or not they fit into the portfolio's risk parameters. That requires understanding the hedge fund's investment strategy. Some hedge funds, particularly those involved in various forms of arbitrage, are, in fact, low risk investments. However, other hedge fund strategies emphasize highly concentrated portfolios and invest in very volatile markets and instruments. The question issues for pension funds are is how risky these strategies are and how appropriate they are for the plan. It is important for pension funds to understand and monitor the strategies used by any hedge funds they invest in, because time and again institutional investors have been unpleasantly surprised to learn that their hedge fund investments had exposed them to troubled markets.

Another question is where do these funds fit into an asset allocation: Are they an asset class in themselves, or should they be considered part of other assets classes—that is, should a hedge fund that invests in equities be considered part of the equities allocation, while a fixed income hedge fund is part of the fixed income allocation? Or should all hedge funds be grouped together into a hedge fund allocation that stands apart from allocations to equities and fixed income securities?

A third question is how to access the hedge fund market: Investing in a single hedge fund may create substantial risk, but this risk can be modulated by investing in a diversified portfolio of hedge funds. However, examining scores of hedge funds and then finding a dozen or two dozen in which to invest can be a time-consuming and expensive process. This is particularly true because hedge funds are generally more secretive about their policies than are traditional asset managers. Some hedge funds argue that they invest in niche markets and their operations can only thrive when their strategies are little known. Because information on hedge funds is limited and difficult to obtain the substantial costs involved in analyzing hedge funds may be prohibitive if these hedge funds are, in the aggregate, going to constitute no more than 5 percent of the portfolio.

However, as in many other markets, commingled pools of hedge fund investments have been created. They are useful for investors whose allocations to hedge funds are too small to implement the desired diversification and for those who want to outsource the task of putting together and monitoring a diversified portfolio of hedge fund investments. There is an assortment of funds of funds that make it possible to buy into a diversified and managed portfolio of hedge funds. Of course, these funds of funds impose another layer of fees on investors. Fund of funds managers frequently charge a fee of one and ten—1 percent of the assets under management and 10 percent of the (excess) returns. This may not necessarily add up to total fees of three and 30 because a fund of funds may obtain a fee rebate from hedge funds eager to attract large-scale investors. Nonetheless, the fees involved in accessing the hedge fund market through funds of funds can be hefty, and these fees mean that an investment in hedge funds must provide very sizable returns in order to outperform traditional markets. That does not mean that the fee level should be the most important criterion for inclusion in the portfolio. As long as a hedge fund's risk characteristics differ from the more traditional assets, the hedge fund does not compete with the traditional assets in the risk budget, and the principal consideration should be the net returns that it might provide.

There is a third way of accessing the hedge fund market—multistrategy funds. These are hedge funds that employ several strategies, all housed within a single fund. In theory, the hedge fund manager allocates funds among the various strategies, based on his or her expectations for these strategies. To be effective, such funds need to be able to forecast where the best opportunities will be found, and they must also be able to take funds away from one of their own managers and give it to another. These assumptions can be questioned, and it often requires third-party advice to assess whether the indicated strategy has indeed been carried out and, if so, whether this was successful.

For the plan sponsor, meanwhile, these multistrategy funds raise the question of how to assess the risks involved. When investing in equities, fixed income, or real estate, there is some basis for estimating prospective returns, and this is an important element in the asset allocation process. In the case of a multistrategy hedge fund, however, it is much more difficult to assess prospective risks or returns. Indeed, these funds shift a portion of the asset allocation decision away from the plan sponsor.

All of these issues need to be addressed before a plan sponsor can determine what role, if any, hedge funds are to play in the portfolio.

BURROWING IN: DEFINING SUB-ALLOCATIONS

In addition to choosing asset classes, the Fiduciary Manager and the plan sponsor need to drill deeper into the investment firmament and make several sub-allocations, based on two dimensions of the asset classes.

In the case of equities, there is first of all, the question of market capitalization. Should the fund invest only in large cap stocks? Should it also invest in mid-cap? And what about small cap? Or even micro-cap? The market for smaller cap stocks is generally considered less efficient, and therefore the opportunities for finding undervalued investments is greater. But so is the risk of getting it wrong. And liquidity is limited in the case of many small cap stocks.

There is also the issue of investing internationally. For many European plans, this issue was settled years ago. First of all, large plan sponsors, like the ABP in the Netherlands, or some of the Scandinavian plans, found their domestic markets too small to permit them to stay within them; they had to go abroad lest they end up owning too large a share of their domestic market, leaving them no room for adjusting their portfolios. For U.S. plan sponsors, their vast internal market was sufficient until the last decade or two. Even now, many American investors believe they can gain a significant international exposure by investing in American companies that are themselves deeply involved internationally. "American" companies like Coca Cola and McDonalds derive half or more of their revenues outside the United States.

For all investors based in industrial countries, there is also the question of whether or not to invest in emerging market equities. These are relatively inefficient markets offering the prospect of substantial returns but also the risk of substantial problems. As such, they represent the classic expression of the views on risk associated with in Modern Portfolio Theory: Are you willing and able to construct a portfolio of emerging market equities, in which some companies and countries will inevitably face major problems, but others may perform so well that the aggregate results will be better than what could be achieved in more developed markets?

One of the latest developments in equity investing is the introduction of leveraged portfolios in certain markets, often referred to as 130/30 products. Instead of having long positions only, the managers of these types of portfolios combine long positions in equities they expect to outperform with short positions in equities they regard as laggards. These short positions, which may total as much as 30 percent of the value of the portfolio, generate funds that enable the managers to add money to the long position, so they can invest 130 percent of the portfolio budget in those shares, and the combination gives the portfolio a 100 percent exposure to this market. In this way they have a leveraged position in the equities they like, and they also have a potential hedge against a certain bias that may accompany the leveraged positions in the preferred shares.

Large parts of many major stock market indexes consist of a number of small stocks, where a long position essentially restricts the managers to a zero weighting when they do not like the stocks. This does not add much to the return of the overall portfolio. Even the Standard & Poors 500 Stock

Index consists of 251 names, which represent individual weights of less than 0.1 percent, giving more than 50 percent of the index names only 13.3 percent of the index weight. Similarly, the Morgan Stanley Capital Markets International Index for Europe, North America and the Far East (MSCI EAFE) consists of 1,697 names, with more than 80 percent of them having a weight of less than the same 0.1 percent (numbers as of September 2006). So there is a vast area where expert managers can increase their efficiency by turning positive expectations into a leveraged investment, while exploiting their negative views more strongly than simply maintaining a zero weighting as required by a long-only constraint.

The Fiduciary Manager should be able to advise the fund what to do with this type of product. The Fiduciary might, for example, highlight the differences (and similarities) among hedge funds and provide detailed data on risks and returns.

THINKING ABOUT STYLE

Besides defining the characteristics of a portfolio in terms of the markets to be addressed, the instruments to be used, and such distinctions as large and small capitalizations, there is also the question of investment style. In equities markets that translates into two alternatives: growth and value.

Growth stock investing involves investing in the shares of companies that are expected to grow faster than other companies, and because of that growth, the investor expects the company's share price will appreciate faster than the rest of the market. Value investing means investing in shares that are undervalued relative to some measure of typical valuation in the market. The investor buys undervalued shares in the expectation that the market will ultimately recognize the mispricing and elevate the price of the shares.

There are variations on these two approaches, such as "GARP," investing in Growth At a Reasonable Price (although critics would say, "Who would want to buy growth companies at unreasonable prices?"). And there is a substantial body of research attempting to determine which approach yields better risk-adjusted returns. The research, alas, is ambiguous, demonstrating that one approach works better at certain points in time and the other outperforms at other times.

As this debate suggests, the Fiduciary Manager and the plan sponsor need not only to confront the broad question of what portion of the portfolio should be invested in equities, but also the more specific question of how the equity portfolio should be divided and allocated among the various segments and approaches to the market.

APPORTIONING THE FIXED INCOME PORTFOLIO

Some of the same issues apply to the fixed income market. Historically, many institutions invested only in government bonds. As corporate bonds became more plentiful, and as the level of credit risk they entailed came to be regarded as acceptable by many institutions, particularly in a diversified portfolio (again, thanks to Modern Portfolio Theory), many pension funds have moved into that arena.

But two developments have added complexity to bond portfolios. One is the development of the high yield bond market. Three decades ago, Michael Milken and the investment banking firm he was associated with, Drexel Burnham Lambert, led the way in convincing investors that a diversified portfolio of lower rated bonds offered the prospect of higher overall returns than so-called investment grade bonds. Yes, some of these *high yield* or *junk* bonds would inevitably default, but the others would offer such attractive returns that they would compensate for those that didn't pay interest or principal on time or even at all.

Though Mr. Milken would eventually run afoul of the law in the United States, the American high yield market has grown to enormous size. Efforts to create a corporate high yield market in Europe have proceeded more slowly, but it has clearly been developing. Moreover, there is a government equivalent of the corporate high yield market in the form of developing country or emerging market bonds. In all of these cases, the question is the same: Will a collection of lower-rated bonds paying high yields ultimately produce greater overall returns—even though some of these bonds will inevitably default—than a portfolio of bonds with higher ratings and, hence, far lower probability of any defaults, but with lower coupons?

In addition to defining the acceptable range of quality in a bond portfolio, an institution also has to determine the range of bonds open to specific fixed income managers. Are narrowly defined mandates the right approach? That might mean different specialized fixed income managers for domestic and international bond portfolios and for investment grade and high yield portfolios, with perhaps a specialized manager for emerging market debt or structured investment products, such as Collaterized Debt Obligations (CDOs). Instead of narrow mandates, however, in recent years some institutions have been turning to a broadly defined *core plus* approach, which gives managers the opportunity to invest across a wider swath of the market.

MEASURE FOR MEASURE

As the efforts to define the investment choices and the investment mandates go forward, the Fiduciary Manager must also assist the plan sponsor in developing appropriate benchmarks. At first glance, measuring investment results seems much easier than measuring achievements in other realms. Publicly traded securities have publicly known prices, prices that are published in the newspapers every day. There are well established and agreed upon methodologies for calculating rates of return.

The real question, however, is what to make of those returns. To know that a portfolio has done better than some "risk free rate," such as the interest rate paid on U.S. Treasury securities or the bonds of another major government is helpful. To know that a portfolio has done better than some broad stock market index is also helpful. But this is not enough because additional benchmarks are required to determine more precisely both how the investor is doing and how the investment manager is doing.

A plan sponsor typically disaggregates its portfolio and mandates various managers to invest in specific segments of the market. The sponsor needs to know how well each segment has done, and that requires very specialized yardsticks. One approach is simply relative return: How has that portfolio done against others, particularly others from similar institutions? How did your small cap portfolio do compared to other small cap portfolios at pension funds in your country?

But there is also a need to know how a portfolio did versus the overall market in which it is invested. This requires developing benchmarks for each market. They need to be broad enough to have meaning yet specific enough to measure things of interest to a particular plan sponsor.

Ultimately, the Fiduciary Manager must ensure that each mandate and each manager is matched with a benchmark that provides an accurate and fair assessment of how well that asset class or set of instruments did and how well the manager did in that arena. These benchmarks need to be agreed upon and accepted by the manager.

It should be noted that benchmarking inevitably creates the risk of closet indexing. There is an adage that what gets measured gets managed. If an investment manager is measured against a specific benchmark, the manager may well hew closely to that benchmark, slightly overweighting some securities and slightly underweighting others, but never straying too far from the benchmark. While there is a risk of being accused of closet benchmarking, that may well be a smaller risk than the risk of having a manager place a large bet on some exotic strategy in the hopes of generating good performance.

Good benchmarks not only help assess how well the various components of a portfolio are doing, they also help investors and plan sponsors understand that performance. The Fiduciary Manager can work with the plan sponsor in examining performance by probing beneath the surface and seeing how the manager has departed from the benchmark and what the results of that deviation have been.

In addition to helping develop benchmarks, the Fiduciary Manager can also help with the development of attribution analyses. This mode of analysis provides a comprehensive explanation of precisely what contributed to a portfolio's performance. Which securities and which transactions served the portfolio well, and which ones didn't? This kind of analysis makes it possible for the plan sponsor—and the investment manager—to determine on a systematic basis what was done right and what was done wrong. Perhaps the manager frequently sold shares before their prices peaked or moved down the quality spectrum of the bond market just as yield spreads were narrowing. Good managers can learn from this kind of analysis of their actions, and astute investors can learn a great deal about their managers.

FORMULATING MANDATES FOR MANAGERS

After due consideration of asset classes and styles, and after thinking about appropriate benchmarks, it is time for the Fiduciary Manager to help the plan sponsor formulate and promulgate mandates for managers. This process is designed to capitalize on one of the most important insights of modern portfolio theory: specialized managers tend to do better in many markets than do generalists who are dabbling in that market.

The Fiduciary Manager's task is to identify the scope of work that needs to be done with regard to various markets, securities, and instruments, and styles, and then seek to select the managers to work within the framework that has been developed.

CHAPTER 7

Horses for Courses— Selecting and Overseeing Investment Managers

F or those not familiar with modern investment ideas and practices, the selection of an investment manager might appear to be the first and most important step in the investment process. It is not. Getting the risk budget right and defining a fitting strategy are far more important in terms of both risk and return than choosing the right managers. In fact, as has been indicated, the task of choosing investment managers comes well down the line; it should be undertaken only at the end of a long process of defining investment objectives and risk parameters. The process of selecting investment managers is an ongoing one. Obviously, if and when a new pool of capital is created and its overseers decide not to manage the assets internally, there is a need to pick managers. But once an institution is up and running, the manager selection process continues to occur in three circumstances: The institution may choose to enter a new investment arena, and consequently it may wish to engage an investment manager who specializes in that area. The institution's assets may increase significantly, and as a result, it may decide to add additional managers to its roster. This makes it possible to sample other managers and to hold down the risks associated with having too much money with any single manager. The third reason an institution may be seeking a new manager is, obviously, because it has chosen to terminate one of its current investment managers, and it needs to hire a replacement.

Terminations typically take place for three reasons: A manager has provided poor investment results for an extended period of time; the manager has deviated, consciously or unconsciously, from its designated investment mandate—for instance, a small cap manager is suddenly investing in large cap stocks—or third, the management firm has suffered some setback, such as the departure of key staff members, and the institution may decide its best interests require it to choose another manager.

In all of these cases, the broad parameters of the process of selecting an investment manager are similar. The key elements of this process should be established in advance, and they should be transparent so that all of the parties involved in the process can see how it is unfolding.

CREATING THE BEAUTY PARADE

The first step in the process is to make sure there is a clearly defined mandate that the investment manager is being asked to meet. When a manager is terminated, the Fiduciary Manager and the plan need to determine whether they want to hire a new manager to do the same job—or whether this might be an opportune moment to change the definitions and boundaries of the mandate. This may, in fact, be the moment to reappraise the path that is being followed.

Once the mandate is clear, then the Fiduciary Manager must develop a list of candidates for the mandate. There is no shortage of investment managers; indeed, there are thousands of them in countries around the world. And there are few shortages of managers within any specific asset class or style. Thus, the Fiduciary Manager and plan sponsor will find there is not going to be any dearth of candidates for positions that are to be filled.

There are well-established mechanisms for publicizing searches and generating applicants. Any hint that a sizable pension fund is seeking an investment manager will bring a flood of applicants knocking at the door. In more rarified asset classes, however, the Fiduciary Manager may wish to go beyond these efforts and draw in additional applicants. This may be the case in asset classes where there are only smaller managers who are not equipped to scan the markets and ferret out opportunities. In a few settings in the United States and elsewhere, the plan sponsor may choose to encourage applications from investment management firms run by women or members of minority groups.

Whatever the setting, the goal is to bring forward a substantial number of applicants in order to have a broad range from which to make a choice. In this process, the Fiduciary Manager's role is to be the eyes and ears of the plan sponsor. The Fiduciary Manager must thoroughly investigate the applicants and assess their abilities.

Marketing has become a well-developed skill at most sizable investment management firms. These firms are well-equipped to fill out the questionnaires and answer questions in ways that show them in the best light and make them sound like precisely what the plan sponsor is looking for.

The Fiduciary Manager must look beyond the questionnaires. In fact, a Fiduciary must have a well-developed proprietary process for assessing the strengths and weaknesses of asset managers.

Different commentators encapsulate the process in different ways, summing it up with three or four or five attributes. But they all come back to the same basic ingredients: investment performance, investment philosophy and process, and investment personnel.

INVESTMENT PERFORMANCE

Surprisingly, perhaps, a firm's *investment performance* cannot be decisive because, as every investment document inevitably notes, past performance is not necessarily a good predictor of future performance. On the other hand, past performance is not to be ignored. There is no guarantee that those who have done well in the past will do well in the future, but those who have never done well do not seem particularly likely to do well in the future.

One of the crucial issues in understanding performance is assessing whose performance it is. Is the team that produced attractive results still intact? Or has the primary source of that good record since moved elsewhere, suggesting that perhaps his or her current firm ought to be the candidate, rather than the previous employer. But attributing performance can be difficult. Each member of an investment management team may say—and in their heart of hearts they may believe—that they are single-handedly responsible for the good results that have been achieved, while the other team members functioned largely as sounding boards, amen corners, or coffee deliverers.

While sorting out who did what is difficult, there are some standards developed by self-regulatory organizations. These specify under what conditions a firm or team can claim performance as theirs. But this remains a tricky area. Nonetheless, this is precisely the kind of area where the Fiduciary Manager can and should become involved in sorting out who has achieved what.

INVESTMENT PROCESS AND PHILOSOPHY

Precisely because past performance is not a guide to future results, any analysis of a potential manager must rely on a careful examination of that firm's investment philosophy and process. It is an article of faith that contemporary investment managers cannot do a good job simply by arbitrarily making investments. Their decision making must be grounded in a philosophy and a process that helps identify investment ideas. Otherwise, the good decisions that they make cannot be replicated, the bad ones cannot be avoided, and there is little hope of achieving consistent results.

The investment philosophy, the somewhat grandiose term for the basic strategy a manager is pursuing, needs to make sense. It needs to reflect market realities and be internally consistent. It needs to provide a broad framework for decision making so that the manager is not deciding everything on an ad hoc basis.

But in addition to having an investment philosophy, a prospective manager needs to have a well-defined investment process. The Fiduciary Manager's first task is to make sure there really is a process, and not an elaborate description of something that looks good in a presentation but is not followed in practice. The second task is to understand and evaluate the process. Does it have the potential to produce good results? Is it scalable, so that if the assets under management increase, the process is still workable?

One important question is whether the process is balanced by the resources that the firm has devoted to that process. A firm that purports to mount a *qualitative* analysis of all listed stocks in the UK, and has only one analyst working on the task part time raises alarm bells. A firm that has a *quantitative* screening process for looking at bonds may need only one person overseeing what may be a highly computerized process. But if the screening methodology is highly complex, and the firm has delegated oversight of this process to a young person who has recently earned a degree in renaissance literature, this should raise concern.

The investment process needs to cover many aspects of investing. It should not only be about buying one security, for example, but about constructing a portfolio of securities. If the process has only a few dimensions, how can the firm build a diversified portfolio? Similarly, the process should not only be about buying but also about selling. Are price goals in place to indicate when it is time to sell a security? Are these mechanisms automatic, or is there room for human judgment about whether to sell or hold? Many investment managers have fared poorly because they knew a great deal about how to buy securities but not about how and when to sell them.

INVESTMENT PEOPLE

There are a number of so-called black box investment strategies in which models or algorithms or equations of one sort or another determine which securities to buy and sell. However, most investment approaches depend heavily on the judgment of individuals. Even the black boxes are ultimately constructed by individuals who have applied their interpretation of reality to the development of these automated approaches. As a result, it is imperative to take a close look at the people who compose an investment management firm.

The Fiduciary Manager must examine their backgrounds, including not only their education and training but, most important, their previous experience. The Fiduciary must also examine the organization to see how the individuals interact. What is the structure of the organization and the hierarchy? Is the firm really the lengthened shadow of one man? Or is it a team? How much turnover has there been at the firm, and what reason is there to believe there will not be turnover going forward?

In the case of larger firms, the Fiduciary Manager may expect there is ample depth of personnel to ensure a smooth transition in the case of anyone's departure. In the case of smaller firms, however, the Fiduciary must decide whether the firm is excessively dependent on one individual, so that if something were to happen to that individual, the firm would essentially be out of business. The financial arrangements among team members are important because they can provide assurances that the team members have a strong incentive to continue working together.

Analyzing the strength and weaknesses of people is a difficult task. But it is precisely the kind of task that a Fiduciary Manager can undertake on behalf of a plan sponsor. It is a task that needs to be done, and it needs to be done by someone with a depth of knowledge regarding the investment management industry. The Fiduciary Manager who has evaluated many investment processes and talked to many investment managers is as well-positioned as anyone can be to evaluate yet another process and manager.

OPERATIONAL RISK

The work of an investment management firm essentially consists of making decisions about the purchase and sale of securities. Those decisions are executed by others, and the securities themselves—or the computerized records of those securities—are also kept by external custodians. Nonetheless, there are operational issues associated with an investment manager that must be evaluated by the Fiduciary Manager.

The manager must have the technological resources to maintain consistent and rapid communications with the markets and the custodians so that its investment decisions and record-keeping tasks can be maintained on an efficient and timely basis. It must have business continuity and disaster recovery plans and resources so that it can maintain its operations in the event of a wide range of calamities. A plan sponsor needs to know that its portfolio will not be ignored for three days because a water pipe broke in an investment manager's office, or the head of IT had the flu, or the telephone connections with major brokerage houses were severed by an errant carpenter.

Some believe that larger firms have an advantage in managing operational risks because they can afford to have redundancy in their systems and resources. If their computer goes down, there is likely to be a sophisticated back up system that goes online while an IT team quickly begins to repair the main computer apparatus. If there is a legal question, there are a number of in-house lawyers who can focus on it.

Smaller firms don't have these resources. The founder may be the chief investment officer and also the chief executive. He or she is picking stocks but also picking health insurance plans for employees. One of the four major partners may be analyzing oil stocks but also analyzing floor plans for the new office. If things go wrong at smaller firms, they may not have the resources to quickly fix them.

This problem is particularly visible at hedge funds that have been attracting investor interest in recent years. Hedge funds may be major forces in the market for various securities, but they are small businesses by most operational measures. They may have no more than two or three dozen employees. If the computers go down, who is there to fix them? If there is a back office problem, how fast can they solve it?

In fact, there are many small firms that are very well equipped to deal with a wide range of operational issues, and there are also large firms that are operating with systems and processes that are stretched to the breaking point. These are the kinds of issues that the Fiduciary Manager must focus on when evaluating an investment management firm.

How is this to be done? Clearly the Fiduciary Manager must visit any and all prospective managers in their offices. Much can be seen on such a visit. There is not only the issue of whether people seem to be working in an organized fashion, but also the question of whether everything is as it is said to be: Most fundamentally, does the firm have a real office at the address they have offered, or is it a mail-drop or rent-by-the-hour office space? Are there, in fact, all those people mentioned in questionnaires? Are people working on something that seems to have form and process? Are the offices so lavish and ornate as to call into question the judgment of the firm's managers? Are they so threadbare as to raise questions about the viability of the firm? Do the senior executives seem to know their employees and their resources well? Or is the office almost as new to them as it is to the visiting Fiduciary Manager? In short, much can be learned by going to the manager's office rather than having the manager come to the offices of the Fiduciary Manager or the plan sponsor.

Meanwhile, there is a new and important device for evaluating managers: the Internet search. To Google someone has become a part of the language in several countries, and it should be part of any due diligence process. It can be very useful to surf the Internet to see what information can be gleaned about a firm and its principal staff members.

For better or worse, an enormous amount of information about individuals, from a variety of sources, is now available on the Internet. Enter someone's name, and who knows what may come up. One may learn that a manager has been arrested several times for drunken driving. Or that he is going through a messy and expensive divorce. Or that her previous firm went bankrupt. Perhaps he is a party to a regulatory matter. Or she is involved in a law suit.

Maybe the manager will be quick to mention all this. Or maybe not. All of this needs to be explored. Many people have the same name, and the Fiduciary Manager must make sure that information, good or bad, is about the person and the firm being reviewed, and not some namesake. Moreover, many people have had problems that have good explanations and are not as negative as they may seem at first glance. And many people do things that do not turn up in an Internet search. Nonetheless, this kind of search process helps identify questions that need to be asked and issues that may need to be resolved.

MANAGING THE BEAUTY PARADE

Once all the due diligence has been completed, the Fiduciary Manager can offer the plan sponsor an array of candidates who have all been vetted. The Fiduciary should do more than certify that all of the candidates are reasonable choices. He can also play a significant role in *guiding* the choice. But he should not simply *make* the choice. One element of a successful relationship with a fund manager is being comfortable with him or her. The plan sponsor's feeling about a manager needs to be taken into account, and if the plan sponsor's board and staff are more comfortable with one manager than another, this is worth taking into consideration.

After the winning candidate has been identified, the Fiduciary Manager also needs to negotiate the asset management agreement with the manager. While there is much that is standardized in investment management contracts, there is also much that is not. The Fiduciary has the expertise to pursue the plan sponsor's best advantage in structuring the contract. The would-be manager may ask for the sun and the moon, but the experienced and knowledgeable Fiduciary Manager knows what is usual and customary and may be granted, and what is excessive and can be safely resisted.

It is advisable that the plan sponsor sign the contracts with the external asset managers that are chosen. Although the Fiduciary may negotiate all of the contract's components, including fees, the plan sponsor must be the counter-party. If not, a crisis in the relationship between the plan sponsor and the Fiduciary Manager could result in the investment portfolio being left without a manager. When the external manager contracts with the plan sponsor, this means that asset management goes on if and when there are problems between the plan sponsor and the Fiduciary. If the fiduciary agreement is terminated, the fund may want to build a new roster of external managers, but the existing portfolio will continue to be managed.

In drafting the asset management agreements, it is advisable to use specialist lawyers, as is the case with the fiduciary agreement. Most sizable asset management firms have an internal legal department familiar with the drafting of management agreements. It is imperative that the institutional investor be advised by equally experienced legal counsel. In these contracts, the parties should also agree on which court should be involved when the parties cannot resolve their problems through negotiations. Often this will be the court in the institution's home country, but it may be advisable to propose American or English courts because of their experience with investment matters.

MANAGING THE TRANSITION

Once a new investment manager is signed up, the next step is to provide the firm with assets to manage. The manager would like to start with a blank slate—with cash that can be invested within the confines of the manager's mandate. When there is new money flowing into an institution, it is relatively easy to marshal it and turn it over to a new manager. When the money to give to a new manager is already invested, perhaps because there has been a previous manager who has been terminated, it is the Fiduciary Manager's job to organize a smooth transition. This entails selling the existing portfolio in a fashion that does not depress prices or exert a sizable market impact. And this task can be made more difficult if there is a disgruntled departing manager who is not going to go out of his or her way to assist the process.

It is possible to sell the securities in a portfolio, one by one, over a period of time, or even quickly. But that is expensive and time consuming. Selling large quantities of a security in a short period of time can significantly depress its price.

One avenue the Fiduciary Manager has to explore is the use of a transition management team. These are groups lodged within the confines of major securities firms. Their services can take various forms. Most of these managers begin by inventorying the existing or legacy portfolio and collecting information on the wish list from the new manager. Then, they transfer the securities that the new manager wants and sell the others as efficiently as possible. The costs of the transition, which not only include brokerage commission and other transaction expenses, but also the market impact that can occur if large amounts of a security are sold all at once, are borne by the plan sponsor. However, some transition managers are prepared to make a bid for the entire portfolio, making it possible to go from the fully invested legacy portfolio to the fully invested new portfolio in a matter of days at a limited cost. In these cases, the transition manager takes in all the risks of market developments as well as all of the other transition costs, but these costs and risks are priced into the bid made by the transition manager. The competing transition managers are given an overview of the portfolio: they are not told the names of the securities in the portfolio, but they are given the portfolio's most important parameters (e.g., 30% large cap U.S. listed stocks, 10% small cap US listed stocks, etc.), and they make a bid on the entire portfolio.

The fiduciary must be able to contract with the cheapest or the most efficient transition manager by knowing all relevant players in the arena and by organizing a competitive environment. Once again, this specialized activity is precisely the place where an experienced Fiduciary Manager can provide the expertise that a plan sponsor lacks and ensure that a delicate transition is completed in the most cost-effective and least disruptive way. As a result, a new manager can start out with a clean slate, and there is no interval during which the portfolio is not being managed.

OVERSEEING THE MANAGERS

The work of the Fiduciary Manager is not completed after overseeing the selection of managers. The Fiduciary also has an important ongoing role in monitoring the managers. This role has several dimensions. Obviously, the Fiduciary Manager must monitor performance on behalf of the plan sponsor. And this goes beyond simply reading quarterly performance numbers. He or she scrutinizes the investment performance to understand the source of whatever returns have been attained.

One important component of this process is being on the lookout for *style drift*. Managers are not simply hired to do well; they are hired to perform a certain role in the portfolio. And, surprisingly perhaps, good performance achieved by departing from their role may not be acceptable. A symphony derives its sound by organizing people playing various instruments, and the orchestra suffers if the second violinist decides to play the clarinet. Similarly, a small cap stock manager may find his or her arena out of favor and—consciously or unconsciously—this manager may move into large cap stocks. But that is not what he or she was hired to do, and the Fiduciary Manager must make sure managers are adhering to their assigned roles.

Another component of the oversight process is keeping track of people. People are important resources at investment management firms, and their comings and goings are highly relevant bits of information. Some turnover is inevitable in any professional services firm, particularly in a field such as investment management, where people are highly paid and therefore have the economic freedom to act on their aspirations and discontent. But it is important to know when changes of personnel occur at a management firm. Many firms are well aware of this and manage the communications process, taking care to inform clients and the market if there are changes in personnel. But they are likely to put the best possible light on these changes. (Do all of those executives really resign solely because they wish to "pursue personal interests"?)

The Fiduciary Manager must monitor personnel changes at the investment management firms and make sure he or she understands what is behind any changes. Is this an important loss of personnel, or is this a nonevent? Were these changes planned well in advance, or is something brewing? Does this departure represent the first public signs of a festering feud in which more people will leave and the team may be eviscerated? Is the departing manager going to attempt to attract other people from the firm to join him or her in a new venture? Only those with their pulse on the investment management industry can decipher personnel shifts and understand what is really going on at a firm.

In short, the Fiduciary Manager is the Early Warning System for problems at an investment management firm. The Fiduciary must know if the strategy isn't working, if key people leave, if there is dissention in the ranks, or if people are facing problems—or opportunities—that may cause them to lose focus on their responsibilities to the plan sponsor.

In the case of alternative investments with limited liquidity, these tasks have additional dimensions. The Fiduciary Manager needs to know what other investors are doing. Hedge funds in particular can find that weak performance may lead to a run on the bank phenomenon. At the point at which investors can seek liquidity, a number of them may want to get out of the fund, requiring the fund to sell investments at unattractive prices in order to raise cash for their investors. They must often sell their best investments because these are the most marketable, leaving them with the least marketable and least attractive investments, and this leads to even worse performance. No one wants to be the last investor left in such a downward spiral. So the Fiduciary Manager must deploy his or her expertise in order to know not only what is going on at the fund, but also what other investors are doing.

In short, the Fiduciary Manager not only guides the plan sponsor through the development of a team of managers, he or she also keeps a close eye on the team so that the plan sponsor is aware of any developments that can affect the manager and the manager's relationship with the plan sponsor.

CHAPTER 8

Performance Measurement and Benchmarking

One of the critical roles that a Fiduciary Manager can play is to ensure that the investment results being obtained are properly measured and analyzed. Performance measurement is a critical part of the management process in almost every sophisticated organization, and it is particularly important in the investment world.

One of the fundamental attributes of modern management is that whatever can be measured inevitably will be measured, and investments are described by a variety of very specific numbers that lend themselves to regular and accurate measurement. In many organizational settings, it is not clear when there have been changes or why and which effects they produced. But it is perfectly clear what it cost to buy a publicly traded security, and it is equally clear what price was received upon selling it. The rate of return can be measured to several decimal points, after which there are well-established protocols for calculating returns in various settings and circumstances. Even when normal transparent pricing is not possible, such as in thinly traded or nonpublicly traded securities, there are still a range of pricing services and conventions that permit a substantial degree of accuracy in measuring results.

The Fiduciary Manager's role is not only to ensure that results are measured carefully but also to make certain that these results are analyzed carefully. Precisely because investment returns can be measured so precisely, they are subject to a variety of comparisons. One crucial question for any investment portfolio or manager is whether the results obtained are better or worse than the market as a whole. It is all well and good to be up 16 percent, but if the overall market is up 18 percent, those results are less impressive. Similarly, if a portfolio is down 16 percent, but most of the others in its class—all of the other similarly sized pension funds or insurance companies or university endowments—are down 19 percent, the results may seem at least somewhat less disturbing. While investment performance in terms of returns is easily compared to other investors, it is equally important—but much more difficult—to assess investment performance in terms of risk. Risk and return are inextricably related. It is possible to achieve high returns at certain points in time by shouldering enormous risks, but that is not the equation most institutional investors want. The goal is to obtain the highest possible returns within specific risk parameters.

Institutional investors are frequently involved in benchmarking themselves, and benchmarking others as well, most notably the investment management firms they employ. And they are also subject to being measured or benchmarked by others. These measurements are focused on the investment returns a portfolio generates, the risk/return ratio associated with these investment results, and the costs associated with the management of that portfolio.[1]

While there are various measurements seeking to ascertain whether a pension fund is efficient or cost-effective in many aspects of its administrative operations, this chapter will focus only on benchmarking with regard to investment results. The performance of a fund, with respect to such matters as the timeliness and accuracy of paying benefits and the like, however important for the ultimate well-being of retirees, falls beyond the scope of this book.

By the same token, there are a variety of established conventions and methods for calculating returns, such as the GIPS/AIMR (Global Investment Performance Standards, endorsed by the Association for Investment Management and Research). We shall accept such methods as a given.

WHY HAS BENCHMARKING GROWN MORE IMPORTANT?

Assessing the achievements of pension funds and insurance companies has become increasingly important in more recent years because performance is now subject to increasing scrutiny from an assortment of stakeholders, including a pension plan's active members and retirees and, of course, the plan sponsor, as well as regulators, securities analysts, and debt rating agencies. And last, but not least, the financial press is showing a keen interest in performances.

There are several reasons why evaluating institutions by their figures has gained so much importance.

- At all levels in society, decision makers are increasingly expected to take responsibility and to report more frequently on their activities and processes.

- Financial institutions take decisions that involve huge amounts of money and affect the well-being of many people.
- The results achieved by institutional investors have macroeconomic consequences.
- The investment results of corporate pension funds have a direct impact on the competitiveness of the plan sponsors and their ability to generate jobs and capital investment in an economy.

Regulators have become increasingly interested in measuring and assessing various aspects of the investment results achieved by pension funds. There are examples of this throughout Western Europe.

During the years 2001 to 2003:

- Denmark introduced resilience testing and fair value accounting.
- The UK introduced FRS 17 and announced risk-based capital adequacy standards.
- Germany suspended prudent value accounting.
- The Netherlands imposed resilience tests and a 5 percent general risk reserve requirement.
- Switzerland lowered the statutory guarantees to 3.25 percent.
- Sweden lowered the discount rate to 3.25 percent for insurers.

During 2004 and 2005 a number of additional changes were made:

- Switzerland lowered the statutory guarantees to 2 percent.
- Germany lowered the statutory guarantees to 2.75 percent.
- The UK implemented more realistic accounting for insurers and pension funds.
- France, Sweden, and the Netherlands proposed the introduction of fair value accounting.

In many countries, these developments have been accompanied by the introduction of the so-called IFRS-rules, which specify that pension fund surpluses or deficits must be included in the financial statements of the plan sponsor. This has created the concern that large swings in a pension fund's surplus or deficit can produce substantial changes in the plan sponsor's reported earnings. Corporations have been seeking ways to shelter their earnings from the impact of pension funds, and some have even considered selling off the pension fund to a third party, such as an insurance company or other provider of securities.

There is another important accounting change that is being implemented in the Netherlands. This involves marking pension fund holdings to market.

Instead of compounding future liabilities at a fixed interest rate of 4 percent, and leaving it up to the funds to value their fixed income assets on the basis of market value or historical value, Dutch regulators have changed the compounding rate to the actual long-term interest rate. Starting in 2004, Dutch institutional investors had the option of using this compounding rate, and on January 1, 2007, this became compulsory.

Two important developments result from this move. The first is that the actual long-term interest rate could be lower than the formerly fixed 4 percent rate. Liabilities rise with this lower rate because pension fund liabilities are long term in nature. Most funds have fixed income assets with durations shorter than the life of the liabilities; in fact the difference in duration can be as high as eight to ten years. Since most pension funds invest in other assets besides fixed income securities (and regulators are not willing to consider the duration of real estate or equities as sources of coverage), the lower value of the fixed income assets compared to liabilities works its way through as well. The lower interest rate level decreases the value of the balance of the assets minus the liabilities. This puts pressure on premiums and can even lead to renegotiations of promised levels of future benefits.

The second effect, which is even more severe, results from the change of the fixed compounding rate of 4 percent to a variable rate that is linked to market interest rates. Changing interest rate levels immediately changes the long-term liabilities, so the balance of assets and liabilities can fluctuate widely. This is especially true when there is a large duration gap between fixed income assets and liabilities and when the portfolio contains more assets than just fixed income, which is typically the case.

For corporate pension plans in particular, this second effect is extremely important because with new international accounting principles coming into force, the fluctuations in the funding ratio are translated on a one-to-one basis to the corporate financial statements. In effect, this means that a company finds a portion of its financial results is influenced by developments that are essentially outside the operations of the business and in many ways beyond the control of its management.

As a result of this array of regulatory and accounting changes in a number of countries, institutional investors are pressed to publish more information than ever before, to be more open with respect to the processes involved, and to enable more people to judge the performance of institutions. One of the results of this change was demonstrated in the Netherlands. After huge losses as a result of the technology bubble, combined with various accounting scandals, pension funds and insurance companies found themselves under the spotlight. Employees, employers, regulators, and, in the end, the Dutch central bank have all sought to become more informed about the economic health of these investment institutions.

Pension funds in Holland and elsewhere now not only have to provide general reports on their activities, they also have to reveal their relative performance. For instance, Dutch industry-wide pension funds are compared with each other with respect to their risk-adjusted returns in a so-called Z-score.[2] If a fund is underperforming for several years in a row, members are entitled to leave the plan and take their savings to a better-performing competitor in the sector. Moreover, pension funds that are underfunded have to put forward a plan for recovery. Depending on how severe the underfunding is, the institutions' plans have to be able to restore sufficient funding within a certain period. Detailed changes in premium and investment policy have to be revealed in order to be able to continue operating as an independent fund.

All these examples of regulatory involvement ultimately rely on timely and accurate benchmarking of a portfolio's results.

THE USE OF DIFFERENT TYPES OF BENCHMARKS

In the context of Fiduciary Management, there are three levels of benchmarking: liability driven, strategic, and detailed benchmarking. The distinction between these three originates from the planning cycle of an institutional investor, which encompasses the stages as depicted in Figure 8.1.

These three benchmarks can help illuminate the performance at the respective levels in this framework.

Liability-driven benchmarks are used in order to assess the investment policy in relation to the liabilities of the fund. In this context, returns on investments and the risks inevitably attached to them, are not the ultimate goal. They are only means to reach the real objective, which is securing liabilities as far as reasonably possible and providing for the highest attainable future levels of benefits. The time horizon involved is lengthy, and the ultimate goal is evaluating the performance of the board or the trustees in the light of the fundamental mission of the fund—being able to pay the promised benefits. Their prudence is not really judged by the risk-adjusted returns as such—in the end, nobody can be held responsible for erratic market movements—but by the care with which the entire process has been established and carried out. Has there been an asset-liability study, and was it carried out properly? Have other essential tasks, such as risk budgeting, portfolio construction, and manager selection been delegated properly? Was the monitoring and reporting of investment results, as performed by the Fiduciary Manager, timely and accurate?

Strategic benchmarks are used to measure the effectiveness of the responsible managers of the fund. If these managers hire a Fiduciary, the

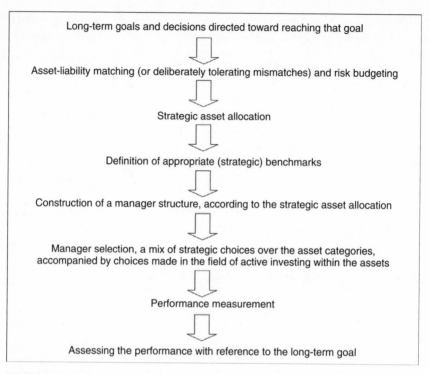

FIGURE 8.1 Stages of the Institutional Investor's Planning Cycle

value-added of the Fiduciary Manager can also be measured in this way. The Fiduciary Manager has the task of structuring the investment process in the best possible way. His or her contribution should be measured along the lines of the long-term investment policy.

Detailed benchmarks are used in order to judge the value-added of the specialized internal and/or external investment managers that are being employed. Active management in this context can serve two purposes: attaining extra returns or obtaining temporary changes in the risk profile. Active management can take the form of

- Deliberately deviating from the weights of the strategic asset allocation.
- Introducing special products (with a relevant benchmark).
- Changing the degree of discretion an asset manager has in a specific market. Within the framework of the strategic policy, several assets and markets are specified in which active management is tolerated. Each active manager operating in these markets is benchmarked against a relevant index.

An active manager adds value when his returns are higher than the average market return or when he realizes the same return with lower risk levels. This relative return or alpha (actual return minus benchmark return or beta) was very important until the 1990s, when equity markets were performing very well. After the downturn in early 2001, absolute returns became more and more important to many investors. The term *absolute returns* refer to the actual level of returns earned without comparison to what the overall market was doing or what other investors were earning. The adage that "you can't eat relative returns" became increasingly salient to many institutions following the bursting of the technology bubble. Hedge funds and other managers seeking consistently positive returns have come to the fore in recent years precisely because of these concerns.

Benchmarks clearly indicate the extent to which managers add value. When evaluating the managers' contribution, it is important to measure risk as well as return. In fact, only the risk-adjusted net return of managers should be relevant to the fund. A net excess return is nice, but if that has been achieved with a large amount of risk, the fund might be better off with another manager.

LIABILITY-DRIVEN BENCHMARKS

Integrating assets and liabilities into the benchmarking process requires a mathematical model in order to assimilate the dynamics of both financial markets and the economic variables that determine liabilities. An asset-liability modeling framework is generally required for this task. This kind of modeling can be defined as "the systematic structuring of financial risks, attached to the asset and liability portfolios of financial institutions, with the aim of creating an efficient risk return profile for the entire institution."[3] This approach enables a fund's management to gain insight into various possible scenarios and to react to them with appropriate instruments. The developments that may affect a fund can originate in the financial markets, but they can also be set in motion by new arrangements with respect to pension rights and premium levels, which are periodically changed during wage negotiations between employers and employees.

As has been noted, in principle, a fund has four instruments to cope with outside influences on its financial situation: investment policy, premium policy, benefits policy, and insurance of benefits.

The latter two can be described as instruments of last resort: they are explored only when liabilities can no longer be met, or the sponsor is not able to cope with the uncertainties and transfers this uncertainty to an insurance company. The other two instruments, investment policy and premium policy, can be judged and benchmarked. Within the asset-liability framework, the board chooses the best combination of investment policy and premium levels, and it is responsible for the effects of that decision on the relevant variables.

The easiest and most comprehensive way to evaluate the performance of a board and a fund is by examining the surplus or funding ratio in relation to the premium level. In this approach, all of the actual inflows (premiums and investment returns) and outflows (benefits and administrative costs) come together. This information, together with an exploration of demographic tendencies in the relevant population, provides an updated picture of the assets and liabilities.

A comparison of the ratio and accompanying premium level with the figures of the year before and with the figures of peers provide clear criteria to judge the board (and its advisors). That is in line with the ultimate responsibility the board has for the financial situation. The premium level can, of course, blur the actual achievements in terms of surplus or funding ratio. Therefore, overall returns per period and relative risk-adjusted returns may also be useful indicators of the performance of the board.

STRATEGIC BENCHMARKS

The strategic policy should be defined in a medium-term framework. The optimal asset mix that has been decided upon is translated into a strategic policy, which is stated in the form of permissible bandwidths for each asset class. For example, a strategy can call for having 40 percent of assets invested in fixed income securities, but the policy may stipulate that this allocation can go as low as 35 percent and as high as 45 percent. By providing this band, the fund is freed from having to rebalance its portfolio too frequently in response to day-to-day fluctuations in the relative value of different assets classes.

Within each asset class, detailed mandates can be formulated with respect to the geographic regions and specific markets as well as to the kind of strategies and securities that are acceptable within those markets (e.g. large cap and small cap equities, high yield and investment grade bonds, etc.). In this part of the decision process, the fund also determines whether or not there is room for tactical policy.[4] The exact contents of this policy are determined in the next phase, but the decision regarding whether or not to take such an approach is a strategic issue.

Table 8.1 provides an example of a broad strategic asset mix and the benchmarks that are to be used to measure the results of each asset class in the strategic asset mix.

TABLE 8.1 Benchmarks for a Broad Asset Mix

Assets	Broad Benchmark	Weight
Equity	MSCI World Equity Markets Index	30%
Fixed income	J.P. Morgan World Government Bond Index	50%
Real estate	MSCI World Real Estate Index	10%
Hedge funds	Credit Suisse First Boston Tremont Index LLC	5%
Cash	Euribor 3 months	5%

TABLE 8.2 Example of a More Detailed Strategic Asset Mix and Its Benchmark

Categories	Weight	Bandwidth	Subcategory	Weight	Benchmark
Fixed income	35%	30–40%	Europe	35%	J.P. Morgan European Government Bond Index
High yield bonds	15%	11–19%	a) emerging markets	7.5%	J.P. Morgan EMBI
			b) U.S.	7.5%	J.P. Morgan or Merrill Lynch High Yield Master II Index
Equity mature markets	25%	20–30%	a) Europe	9.8%	MSCI Europe
			b) U.S.	11.0%	MSCI North America
			c) Far East	4.2%	MSCI Pacific Free
Equity emerging markets	5%	2–8%	Worldwide	5.0%	MSCI Emerging Markets Free
Real estate	20%	16–24%	Worldwide	20%	MSCI World Real Estate Index
Currency hedge	0%		Hedge USD	26.0%*	EUR/USD 1 year
			Hedge GBP	7.7%**	EUR/GBP 1 year

*Approximation of the structural U.S. $ exposure in high yield bonds, equity markets and real estate.
**Approximation of the structural GB Pound exposure in fixed income, equity markets and real estate.

This group of broad benchmarks is appropriate for evaluating the value added of the strategic policy choices of the board for the long term. It also can be used to assess the contribution of the Fiduciary Manager.

For the medium term, a more detailed benchmark can be constructed (see Table 8.2), in which (possibly temporary) ingredients of broad markets find their place.

Fixed Income

The fixed income portfolio can be regarded as the "riskless" base of an investment portfolio. A properly chosen portfolio of high grade bonds that is held to maturity has a very high probability of delivering precisely the results anticipated for it (disregarding the reinvestment risk). But the returns will be relatively low. In order to generate higher returns than the bond market might offer, many investors look to equities, real estate, hedge funds, and other assets that have the potential for generating high returns. But these asset classes make the fund very vulnerable to downside volatility. Therefore, some investors choose a middling course, extending the borders of their bond portfolio to include high yield bonds or emerging market bonds, both of which hold the promise of potentially higher returns but at the risk of higher volatility in the value of the portfolio.

Investing in bonds requires decisions to be made regarding several attributes, including

- *Maturity or Duration.* There are two principal appeals of bond invest-ing: the relatively low downside volatility (especially compared to equities) and the close positive correlation between changes in the value of the bonds in a portfolio and changes in the present value of the future liabilities. Changes in both are caused primarily by changes in interest rate levels. The characteristics of bonds make them a natural hedge for the present value of future liabilities. In order to generate higher returns or to reduce portfolio risk, however, the investor deliberately chooses bonds whose absolute volatility is different from the volatility of liabilities. Creating a bond portfolio with a duration other than the duration of the liabilities is the essence of an active bond management policy.
- *Quality.* An investor can choose from among a well-established hier-archy of credit quality in the bond market, ranging from triple A-rated government and corporate bonds to lower rated investment grade bonds to low rated high yield or junk bonds. Many institutions face regulations regarding the ratings or credit quality of the bonds they can buy.
- *Geographic distribution* of bond issuers. As interest rates have become increasingly intertwined around the world, the geographic distribution of a portfolio in terms of the countries and regions where issuers are located has become a less important characteristic. Still, many investors find merit in seeking diversification in terms of the geographic areas represented in their bond portfolios.
- *Currency.* The question of currency can be an important issue in bond investing. Because of the constant fluctuation in exchange rates, the return on a bond generated by its coupon or the price at which it is

bought and sold may be amplified or reduced by the value of the currencies involved. Some argue that investment choice should not be blurred by the question of relative currency values. For long-term investors, some would argue, currency fluctuations cancel out as purchasing power parity takes hold. Others argue that currency is an important question in investing in foreign bonds. The question of whether or not currency changes should be allowed to affect bond and/or other returns and values is a problem to be solved at aggregate portfolio level. A clear hedging policy is necessary because currency can be an important determinant of interest income and valuation of the bond portfolio. If perceived currency movements would be a main contributor to the *ex ante* total return of a bond, the bond at stake should not be bought, as that currency contribution would be wiped out by the strategic hedging taking place at a higher level of portfolio management.

A vast number of bond indices can be used as a measuring rod for evaluating the implied policy. However, one problem with many fixed income benchmarks is that their geographic compositions are a function of market capitalizations, and they are therefore related to the volume of supply from the respective countries. This is a built-in risk factor, because a large weighting coincides with a large volume of debt, and that may be an indication of a less stable financial situation. In Western Europe, for example, Italian government bonds dominate many indices because the government of Italy is such a large borrower. This relative large volume of government bonds, however, reflects the less stringent fiscal policies of the Italian government, which should cause an investor to be reluctant to buy too many of these bonds.

Alternatives exist in the form of indices in which country weightings are related to gross domestic product, but they have their own disadvantages, such as the difficulty of full replication of sub-indices, which, in theory, is an important prerequisite for a benchmark to be used as such. The GDP weighted approach is more widely used in the equity markets.

Equities

In equities markets, as in bond markets, there is a range of sub-markets that need to be recognized in formulating ways of measuring performance. For example, a distinction should be made between equities from developed countries and emerging markets. Equity markets in developing countries generally display higher risk profiles, less liquidity, and less market efficiency. Those characteristics warrant a special allocation. Their weight should represent the balance between tolerated risk (a higher allocation than 10 percent could exceed the budget) and a discernable contribution to the overall return (a weighting smaller than 5 percent would not add enough additional return to be meaningful). Moreover, the additional attention that management has to devote to emerging markets and the higher level of costs should also play a role in determining a minimum level of allocation. It is not worth devoting a great deal of time and attention to an allocation so small that even remarkable returns will not be noticeable in the overall results.

The geographic or regional allocation within the mature markets is the most important policy decision (although allocation based on industry sectors is gaining in importance). Regional weights can be based on market capitalization or on GDP. In addition, equal weighting approaches and some kind of optimization may be used as well. Market cap considerations depart from the idea that financial markets are almost perfect markets, where all information is adequately reflected in equity prices. That is why a cap weighted portfolio should offer the best diversification. Weighting by GDP presupposes that the regional domestic product is a stable and fair indicator of its real economic weight. Weightings can be calculated in a base currency, or they can be specified in purchasing power terms. Equal regional weighting has no real justification, since it is based on the idea that all regions are more or less of equal importance and show a comparable risk profile.

The mean-variance optimization model constructs weightings according to historic data and correlations, enabling efficiency to be reached between risk and return.

Asset managers use different criteria to determine an optimal weight distribution. For instance, one major asset management consulting firm, Mn Services,[5] uses five criteria to come to the best decision:

- *Risk and Return.* The ideal situation is choosing a profile with the highest return and the lowest risk.
- *Significance.* Are the differences found in risk and return significant?
- *Stability of Weightings.* From a practical point of view, a stable weight is preferable to an unstable one. Frequent changes in internal and external asset managers and high transaction costs make it exceedingly difficult to change weightings frequently and dramatically; less change is preferable.
- *Economic Relevance of the Method.* The method used should have a sound economic rationale.

Per factor, rankings can be given according to the scores, with1 indicating the best score, 5 the minimal score. (See Table 8.3.)

TABLE 8.3 Different Criteria and Scores for Factor Ranking

	Risk and Return	Significance	Stability	Economic Relevance
Market capitalization	5	2	4	3
GDP U.S. dollar	3	2	3	2
GDP PPP	2	1	2	1
Equal weighting	4	2	1	4
Optimization	1	2	5	4

Clearly, the GDP weighting at purchasing power parity is the best method. That is not the case because this method is necessarily better in all respects, but rather because other methods sometimes have severe deficiencies.

Equal weighting loses out because it has no economic basis and is not conducive to reaching a good risk/return ratio. Optimization clearly has a good score in the relevant field of risk and return, but its stability constitutes a problem, and its economic relevance is limited. Market cap weighting scores well on significance (in fact, all do), but its low ranking in risk and return and stability is fatal. The main problem is that it leads to procyclical investment behavior—that is, the allocation in a certain region will reach its maximum when that market is at the top. This disadvantage is avoided by choosing GDP weighting, and the purchasing power parity version scores best in all respects compared to GDP by currency. An additional advantage of the use of this weighting is that purchasing power parity GDP is also related to future pension benefits as measured in real terms. It can be related to the idealized situation in which pensions are indexed completely.

Real Estate

Real estate investments need to be divided into direct and indirect real estate. The first category refers to direct purchases of office buildings, retail stores, residential properties, and other categories of buildings.[6] Indirect real estate investment or equity real estate refers to the purchase of shares in real estate companies or funds, which can be listed or not. Diversification, especially in the case of smaller institutions, often demands that real estate investments be restricted to indirect involvement, preferably in the form of investments in listed securities. This approach not only provides diversification but also liquidity. The low correlation that real estate investments usually have with equity and fixed income only hold for nonlisted real estate, however. Shares in real estate companies reflect the movements of the stock market as well as movements in the real estate market.

In the case of real estate investing, strategic risk is far more important than active risk. In fact, active risk is dwarfed by it, since asset allocation decisions can determine up to 90 percent of a plan's performance.[7] The choice of the real estate benchmark depends on the strategic issues pursued by the fund. If the strategy is defined as having a stake in worldwide indirect real estate, the benchmark should reflect that. Active policy benchmarking in this case can be threefold: by regional weighting, by sector weighting (residential properties, offices, retail, etc.), and by type of manager. If this asset class is strategically limited by region, as is often the case, the benchmark is defined more narrowly, and active policy can lose one factor to be used to generate extra return.

When the fund has a stake in direct real estate, the same benchmarks can be used as with indirect interests, whether or not there are geographic constraints. The simple reason being that, in the end, indirect interests also are investments in bricks and mortar. The big advantage of having direct real estate in the portfolio is the substantially lower volatility of the value of the investment. Appraised valuations of properties tend to exhibit much less variation on a year-to-year basis than do the market prices of real estate equity. The big disadvantage of direct real estate is of course, its illiquidity it is far more difficult to sell buildings than to sell shares of stock. This illiquidity, it should be noted, is exactly the reason why the average return on property investments is higher than that on other assets and higher than the returns on indirect investments in real estate. Finally, it should be noted that a really bad investment in securities may end up worthless, but a bad real estate investment can lead to a negative return because a building may not only become worthless but subject to maintenance and demolition costs.

DETAILED BENCHMARKS IN THE CONTEXT OF ACTIVE INVESTMENT POLICY

The actual execution of an investment policy can deviate from the strategic policy because of active management. Managers, if permitted, may deviate from their benchmarks in order to generate excess returns (or limit risk). The normal procedure is to grant the manager an explicit *ex ante* tracking error, related to the benchmark the manager is supposed to use. In addition, special products, such as an overlay mandate, can be introduced as a strategic decision to manage the impact of deviations from benchmarks.

The desired level of active risk is determined by the risk appetite of the fund, the relationship between asset mix risk and active risk, and the fund's belief in the active manager's ability to achieve excess returns (or reduce risk without losing too much expected return). Since strategic risk constitutes the bigger part of the overall risk, the total risk budget is not the main constraint on the active allocation. What is more important is the relationship between the two types of risk. In general, it is assumed that there is no correlation.

Cost Effectiveness Measurement Inc. has found that the average correlation coefficient between strategic return and performance was zero for American pension funds during the period 1998 to 2002.[8] Mn Services has calculated, that a tracking error of 1.5 percent adds a mere 0.15 percentage points of risk (active or alpha) to the existing risk level of 7.1 percent for a specific, but representative portfolio.

The stronger the institution's belief in the expected returns of an asset and the capabilities of an asset manager in that sphere, the larger the allocation to that asset class should be. The information ratio—the ratio of excess return over tracking error—seems to be the best guide in this matter. However, this ratio not only depends on the capabilities of the asset manager and his organization, it also depends on the efficiency of the market in which the excess return has to be realized. In mature markets with large trading volumes, there are numerous buyers and sellers and many analysts doing research and providing information, so it is more difficult to generate an outperformance than it is in less mature markets.

Grinold & Kahn[9] derive an optimal level of active risk for investors by using a quadratic utility function, in which expected excess return is a positive determinant and risk aversion a negative one. On the basis of this theoretical framework, De Ruiter & van As[10] constructed a table of fitting tracking errors (see Table 8.4). They are determined by the risk appetite of the fund and the expected information ratio.

The table indicates that a pension fund that has a risk tolerance at the high end of the "moderate" category (0.15) and that can engage an investment manager capable of an expected information ratio of 0.6 should generate an optimal risk level for the fund in terms of tracking error of 2.00. The manager will use his discretion through tactical asset allocation and security selection. Both forms of decision taking are encompassed by the phrase active policy.

Tactical asset allocation (TAA) seeks to capitalize on short-term fluctuations in returns by shifting funds between asset classes in order to capitalize on brief opportunities. For example, equities have higher returns than bonds over the long term, but during certain shorter periods of time, bonds can outperform equities as a result of macroeconomic developments or market trends. Investors can make use of this temporary event to generate extra returns by allocating more money in bonds at the expense of equities. This overweighting of a certain asset class can represent a deliberate reallocation

TABLE 8.4 Tracking Errors, Fitting Different Attitudes toward Risk

Information Ratio		Risk Aversion*						
Characterization	Level	Low		Moderate			High	
		0.050	0.075	0.100	0.125	0.150	0.175	0.200
Reasonable	0.30	3.00	2.00	1.50	1.20	1.00	0.86	0.75
	0.33	3.30	2.20	1.65	1.32	1.10	0.94	0.83
	0.36	3.60	2.40	1.80	1.44	1.20	1.03	0.90
	0.40	4.00	2.67	2.00	1.60	1.33	1.14	1.00
	0.43	4.30	2.87	2.15	1.72	1.43	1.23	1.08
Good	0.46	4.60	3.07	2.30	1.84	1.53	1.31	1.15
	0.50	5.00	3.33	2.50	2.00	1.67	1.43	1.25
	0.55	5.50	3.67	2.75	2.20	1.83	1.57	1.38
	0.60	6.00	4.00	3.00	2.40	2.00	1.71	1.50
	0.65	6.50	4.33	3.25	2.60	2.17	1.86	1.63
Very good	0.70	7.00	4.67	3.50	2.80	2.33	2.00	1.75

Risk aversion is represented by a subjective parameter λ, indicating the risk tolerance in the function: VA $= \alpha - \lambda^*$
VA = tracking error of the active policy
α = alpha of the active strategy.

of money or active policy, but there can also be a more passive variant in which the manager simply tolerates drift. For example, if bonds yield a higher return than equities, the weight of that asset class will automatically increase at the expense of the lower-yielding assets. The room to let this endogenous process run is restricted to the limits of the bandwidths, which have to be set in advance by the fund.

In addition to making shifts in a portfolio using tactical asset allocation, a manager may also alter a portfolio through security selection. At any point in time, a manager can shift the portfolio by selling some securities while buying others, typically based on research, indicating that some securities are undervalued while others may be overvalued. All this takes place within the confines of a particular mandate and a particular asset class, yet it can bring substantial changes in a portfolio and the results it attains.

By combining several asset managers within a segment of the overall portfolio, it is possible to diversify risks, without causing *ex ante* excess return to deteriorate. Therefore the tracking error per manager can be higher than the tolerated tracking error of the sub-portfolio.

ACTIVE OVERLAY MANAGEMENT

In addition to tactical asset allocation, another way of affecting a portfolio's aggregate exposure to various asset classes is to implement an active overlay management approach. Instead of picking stocks or taking bets on maturity or spreads in fixed income, an overlay manager takes positions in certain segments of asset classes, such as large cap or small cap stocks, or in regional markets, in the asset classes (using derivatives to gain an extra exposure to equities, for instance).

Diversification can be achieved in this area by hiring different tactical asset allocation (TAA) managers. An important advantage of using active overlay policy is the diversification effect it brings with it. The risk generated by this policy has limited (if any) positive correlation with the risks associated with being invested in the equity or fixed income markets. The risk profile of the overall portfolio is therefore ameliorated when this risk is pooled with the so-called beta-risk. This is not to say that TAA does not contribute to the risk budget; in fact, it is contributing more risk to the portfolio than other active strategies. This is logical because, as has been noted, the strategic asset allocation often determines more than 90 percent of overall risk, and TAA uses changes in the asset allocation to add return.

Since TAA is often executed by using derivatives, this form of active policy induces some degree of leverage. Depending on the specific way in which derivatives are used, this leveraged exposure can cause problems. When leverage takes the form of longer duration, this is not viewed as a problem. In fact, it could well be part of the solution for the need to reduce a duration gap, which is a major contributing factor to the overall risk of many funds.

However, many funds do not want to be drawn into a situation in which leverage means that additional money must be added to an initial investment in order to maintain market exposure. In such cases, if prices in that market deteriorate further, losses could exceed the amount invested. Even when using derivatives with inherent leverage, this kind of situation can be avoided by pooling TAA positions in a special-purpose vehicle set up specifically to deal with such a financial structure. Participation in such a pooled fund can limit the downside risk for the fund so that it does not exceed its initial financial participation, enabling the fund to take advantage of the leveraged positions, without an increase of the original commitment during negative market developments.

REBALANCING

When total returns for each of the different asset classes differ—and they always do—the respective weights of the various asset classes begin to depart from their strategic levels. A portfolio may begin a year with a 60–40 mix of stocks and bonds, and if stocks go up more than bonds over the course of the year, the portfolio may end the year with 70 percent stocks and 30 percent bonds. The overall total return may be very good, but the fund now has a much greater exposure to equities than it wants, or at least than it had indicated as being desirable when specifying the strategic policy.

By the same token, when several asset managers all have mandates within the same asset class, their results can mean that certain asset classes become a component of the overall portfolio that is larger or smaller than what is countenanced by the overall risk budget.

In these cases, a strategic decision has to be taken as to whether or not to bring the asset allocation back into line with the strategic mix and, if so, how to proceed. This process of rebalancing makes it possible to avoid drifting into situations in which the actual allocations of assets in the portfolio deviate too much from the strategic allocations. Rebalancing also has to take place in order to prevent individual currency exposures from becoming too large. This can be the case when a fund has chosen to hedge its currency positions on the overall level, but at the same time hired managers who have discretion with regard to currency exposure. Rebalancing then functions as the aggregation of individual currency exposures and intervenes when the aggregate exposure exceeds some limits.

One effective way to maintain the proper asset allocation is to appoint an overlay manager, who is responsible for keeping all the specified assets within the bandwidths agreed upon. The activities of this overlay manager should be summarized in a completion account, which contains all the actions needed to bring the actual portfolio back in line with the strategic allocations.

Financial market theory generally suggests that rebalancing is necessary in order to control the risk profile of the portfolio. The basic argument is that permitting overweighting of the asset classes with higher total returns increases the risk profile of the portfolio above the intended level of the risk budget (this is particularly true if there is mean reversion, when significantly appreciated assets can show huge declines).

There are commentators who advocate tolerating drift in order to generate extra returns and to avoid selling assets when prices are rising. But others would argue that drift should not be tolerated when the risk budget is being exceeded, making rebalancing a necessary part of the investment process. There are two major methods for rebalancing in a disciplined way:

- *Time rebalancing.* Buying and selling of securities (including derivatives) at clearly defined intervals, such as monthly, quarterly, or yearly.
- *Range rebalancing.* Buying and selling programs are executed when the actual weight of an asset in the portfolio exceeds a certain limit or bandwidth. This approach permits responding to rapid changes in relative asset values so that the rebalancing process doesn't have to wait until the end of a quarter, for example.

Finney[11] argues that it is more important to rebalance as such than it is to use a specific method. Depending on the periods, regions, and asset mixes, the outcomes of various research studies on rebalancing provide somewhat different results. It is clear, however, that when time rebalancing is chosen, the frequency should not be too high. Very frequent intervention brings high transaction costs (although those costs can be ameliorated by using derivatives), and this kind of frequent intervention also offsets the merits of being invested in appreciating assets and automatically adding assets at relatively low prices.

From a practical point of view, rebalancing should probably be done using futures and other derivatives because cash rebalancing is much more costly and time consuming, especially when several different external managers are employed. These rebalancing costs can easily offset a large part of the excess returns generated by the active managers.

Time rebalancing is defined clearly, and its execution is clear cut. The disadvantage is its static character. It wipes out the potentially beneficial effects of rising prices in certain asset classes. Range balancing is more reflective of the beneficial effects of rising and falling prices within specified boundaries. As it departs from the notion of mean reversion, however, the rising trend will induce intervention at some level of over- and underweighting.

MEASUREMENT OF ACTIVE POLICY

In assessing the value added by the tactical policy, there is an interesting anomaly that can occur. Theory suggests that the ability of managers to generate outperformance should not be evaluated over the short term. In reality, however, the fund and its overseers often have short-term horizons with respect to the investment returns. In cases in which a manager needs several years to prove he can outperform his benchmark, a complete business cycle should be taken as the relevant period over which to measure the manager. But the fund has to report at least annually, and frequently quarterly or even monthly. The mismatch between the time horizons of the manager and the fund often leads to a situation in which the managers are evaluated over a time horizon that is too short to be truly meaningful. That can lead to untimely decisions to terminate managers because of temporary underperformance.

Table 8.5 is an example of a detailed overall summary of investments, managers and benchmarks, that constitutes a platform which enables the fund to assess performances and their originators.

The overall table can be used to evaluate the value added (actual returns versus benchmark returns and actual risk versus risk budget) of several players:

- The specific manager responsible for a single mandate, such as European equities or North American growth stocks.
- "Manager 1" in European equity, which consists of a pool of several managers. The Fiduciary or another expert who constructed this pool can be evaluated against the same single benchmark.
- The Fiduciary or the fund itself with regard to a combination of mandates; for instance, in the case of North American equities, one manager or the combinations of more managers with specific North American equities mandates.
- The Fiduciary or, in the absence of a manager responsible for tactical weights, the fund itself for the contribution of tactical asset allocation. The performance of the actual (sub-) portfolio is compared with the relevant benchmark (for instance, tailored overall benchmark equity).
- The tactical managers with an overlay mandate.
- The Fiduciary Manager (or the fund itself) with the overall result of the total portfolio.

The intricacies of measuring performance and benchmarking it so that the source and meaning of the investment performance is fully understood make this task as difficult as it is critical. While there are many questions that can be raised about various approaches to evaluating investment results, it is clear that less is not more. Quite the contrary: the more information that can be marshaled and the more analytical tools that can be deployed, the greater the likelihood that an institution can fully grasp the meaning of its investment performance. It can not only understand the results that have been achieved by its investments but also the exact sources of those results and the position that its results hold in the pantheon of results that can and have been achieved by other investors in the same markets.

The role of the Fiduciary Manager is to bring its expertise to bear on the task of measuring results and finding the meaning of those results. By combining technical expertise in measuring results with communication

TABLE 8.5   Example of Relevant Benchmarks in the Most Detailed Portfolio

Portfolio		Benchmark	Performance (%, Excess Return in Basis Points)			Target Excess Return	% of Fund
			Perf.	Bench	ER		
Equity Europe							
	Manager 1	MSCI Europe net unhedged	5.25	4.92	33	300	9.8%
	Manager 2	MSCI Europe net unhedged	5.22	4.92	29	250	6.2%
Total Europe		MSCI Europe net unhedged	5.24	4.92	31	275	16.0%
Equity North America							
Large cap growth	Manager 1	Russell 1000 growth unhedged	10.77	9.61	116	300	3.7%
Large cap value	Manager 2	Russell 1000 value unhedged	8.11	7.07	104	275	4.0%
Total North America		MSCI NA net unhedged	9.32	7.85	146	288	7.7%
Equity Asia-Pacific							
	Manager 1	MSCI Pacific net unhedged	3.93	3.84	9	350	3.4%
Total Asia-Pacific		MSCI Pacific net unhedged	3.93	3.84	9	350	3.4%
Equity Emerging Markets							
	Manager 1	MSCI EMF net unhedged	8.16	8.19	(3)	200	3.6%

(*continued*)

TABLE 8.5   (*Continued*)

Portfolio		Benchmark	Performance (%, Excess Return in Basis Points)			Target Excess Return	% of Fund
			Perf.	Bench	ER		
Total Emerging Markets		MSCI EMF net unhedged	8.16	8.19	(3)	200	3.6%
Global Equity							
	Manager 1	MSCI World net unhedged	6.72	6.41	31	150	5%
			6.72	6.41	31	150	5%
Total Equity		Tailored benchmark	6.40	5.93	46	250	35.7%
Fixed income Global							
	Manager 1	J.P.M GGBI gross hedged	0.70	0.89	(19)	100	20.0%
	Manager 2	J.P.M GGBI gross hedged	0.71	0.89	(19)	100	13.5%
Total Global Fixed Income		J.P.M GGBI gross hedged	0.70	0.89	(19)	100	33.5%
Sub-total		Tailored benchmark	2.82	2.71	11	123	69.2%
Real Estate		MSCI World Real Estate Index	3,80	3,50	30	100	10%
Completion			(0.62)	(0.61)	(1)		4.7%
Tactical Asset Allocation							
	Manager 1	Absolute return benchmark	0.59	0.01	58	80	7.9%
	Manager 2	Absolute return benchmark	0.77	0.37	41	80	8.2%

TABLE 8.5 *(Continued)*

Portfolio	Benchmark	Performance (%, Excess Return in Basis Points)			Target Excess Return	% of Fund
		Perf.	Bench	ER		
Total Tactical Asset Allocation	Absolute return benchmark	1.37	0.38	99	160	16.1%
Total Fund	Tailored benchmark	3.56	2.47	109	244	100%

Legend:
Tailored benchmark:
19.63% MSCI Europe hedged
15.94% MSCI NA hedged
5.96% MSCI Pacific hedged
4.36% MSCI EMF unhedged
54.11% J.P.M GGBI hedged.

skills in helping an institution understand the full meaning of the results, the Fiduciary helps the institution formulate the right questions and move toward the right answers in formulating and modifying its investment policies and approaches. The reports at the end of Chapter 4 are an example of the way a Fiduciary can integrate the benchmarks in an overall picture of the portfolio.

CHAPTER 9

The Fiduciary Manager Experience in the Netherlands and Beyond

Fiduciary Management is more than a theoretical construct. Several Fiduciary Management arrangements have been established in the Netherlands in recent years, and valuable experiences have been amassed at several major pension funds and insurance companies. Examples of these fiduciary relationships include

- The pension funds at such companies as Campina, Interpay, TDV and Océ.
- The industry-wide pension funds covering workers in the transportation industry (Vervoer) and the health insurance sector (SBZ).
- The investment portfolios at such insurance companies as VGZ-IZA, CZ, Yarden, Dela, and ZLM.

VGZ-IZA signed up for this approach in 2002, Campina came on in 2003, and the others have enlisted since then.

The demand created for Fiduciary services since 2002 has led a number of institutions to execute internal organizational changes in order to be able to offer Fiduciary Management services. The Appendix lists a number of Fiduciary Managers and contains a condensed description of what they see as their principal objectives and methods of operating.

Some of the experiences and lessons that have resulted from these fiduciary relationships follow.

CHANGES IN INVESTMENT POLICY

- One area in which the Fiduciary Manager has clearly made an impact, perhaps its biggest impact, is in investment policy. At institutions which have Fiduciary Managers, the investment portfolio not only has become more balanced in terms of the different asset classes and in terms of the different assets within these classes, it also employs far more diversifying asset managers than before. Moreover, in the wake of the changes that were put through and because of the more complicated portfolio structure, pension funds using this approach report that there have been much more intensive and informed discussions among the fund's staff members and with the Fiduciary Manager. The best example of this is the issue of bridging the duration gap. Those discussions, which have taken place within the plan sponsor as well as with the Fiduciary Manager, have focused on such questions. Does the duration gap represent an intended or unintended risk?
- Is reducing or closing the duration gap a strategic or a tactical decision?
- Should market timing play a role if a fund decides to reduce the duration gap? With interest rates rising, for example, it may pay to wait. But then at what level of long-term interest rates does it become acceptable to lengthen the duration of the fixed income portfolio?
- If bridging the duration gap reduces risk, how should this saving in the risk budget be used in other areas?

Examining these kinds of questions has helped several pension funds reach the kind of well-researched and well-balanced decisions that have not always been evident in the decision making at many Dutch pension funds in recent years. Financial markets are always changing, and there is a steady flow of new products, new strategies, and new ways of thinking about problem solving. With the help of a Fiduciary Manager, more institutions are able to capitalize on change instead of being victimized by it.

A good Fiduciary pays close attention to details. For example, Fiduciary Managers have proposed cash sweep vehicles at several funds in order to make sure that the fund's cash is fully invested and earning a return at all times. As a result, the constant leakage of returns resulting from idle cash—however small the amounts—is avoided. Similarly, the level of brokerage commissions is continuously assessed as are the quality of transactions being executed on behalf of the fund, and, in some instances, plan sponsors have initiated commission recapture programs. Transaction costs and the market impact of transactions can add up to sizable sums, and they should not be neglected.

CHANGES IN THE ROLE OF A FUND'S INVESTMENT COMMITTEE

Fiduciary Management requires greater commitment from a fund's investment committee because investment policy generally becomes more complex and more sophisticated when a Fiduciary is involved in advising the process. Similarly, the number of asset classes in which a plan is invested frequently increases in comparison with other management models, and the relationship between these asset classes becomes more intricate.

One of the clearest examples is the array of alpha products that may be combined with the traditional beta, or market exposure, products. When a Fiduciary Manager is involved, the traditional asset mix of equities, bonds, real estate, and cash has, in most cases, been transformed. In its place, there is often a more carefully constructed mix of regional equity portfolios with an active touch. Moreover, the fixed income portfolio is likely to include a mix of government and corporate bonds combined with emerging market debt and high yield bonds. There may also be indirect investments in real estate, an array of alternative investments, an active overlay policy, a completion account, and a cash sweep vehicle. It is obvious that this kind of complex portfolio requires greater involvement of the board and/or the investment committee.

By the same token, monitoring investments and managers has become a continuous matter instead of a periodic review in which investment managers deflect criticism by stressing their long-term track records. The fund should have a structure in place in order to receive documentation from managers on a timely basis and make use of it in the discussions with the Fiduciary and in communications to the fund's various constituencies.

CHANGES IN THE BREADTH AND DEPTH OF DISCUSSIONS WITH ASSET MANAGERS

Management of the portfolio becomes more complicated when the investment policy becomes more complex. That is not seen as a problem however, because the fund is supported by a Fiduciary with professional skills. For most pension funds, the only issue in managing this new level of complexity is getting used to having more frequent and more sophisticated issues and deliberations.

There is intensive coordination between the Fiduciary and the asset-liability experts, with the collaboration of the responsible staff members from the fund. Responsibilities in combining assets and liabilities are clearly separated, as they should be, but the objective is a shared one.

In all policy discussions, risk plays a major role. That is the case both within the funds themselves and in the discussions between funds and their Fiduciary Managers. Fiduciaries seem to have performed an educational function here, enabling more fund executives to think about risks and their relation to returns in greater depth and with more rigor than before fiduciary contracts were introduced.

CHANGES IN THE COMMUNICATION PROCESS

Several aspects of the communications between the plan sponsor and other entities are altered when a Fiduciary Manager enters the picture. For example, communication with the regulatory authorities becomes easier and represents more of a dialogue because the professionalism of the fund's messages is enhanced by Fiduciary support.

Similarly, a level playing field develops between the fund (working in collaboration with the Fiduciary) and the external managers. When a fund's management has a Fiduciary Manager at its side, its conversations with investment managers are no longer conversations between amateurs and professionals but rather between two parties who are peers in terms of the knowledge and information each has at its disposal. Discussions regarding past performance and potential changes in investment policy are more of a two-way street than they were before. Meetings often take on more of a prospective rather than retrospective character when a Fiduciary Manager is involved. The objective is not merely to judge past performance but to learn from past experiences and to improve and refine future policy.

The level of communication within the fund itself is also improved. In general, communications become more consultative than authoritarian.

These days there is also more frequent and intense communication between pension funds and the companies in which they are invested. Active shareholding has become a buzzword, and institutional investors are responding to heightened expectations regarding the role investors should play in making sure that companies pursue appropriate policies with regard to various social as well as economic issues. In many countries, the public wants institutional investors to be more engaged in corporate governance than they were before. The Fiduciary Manager can assist plan sponsors in formulating their contribution to corporate annual meetings and advise them in executing their voting rights.

CHANGES IN THE LEVEL AND STRUCTURE OF COSTS

Portfolio management is likely to become more expensive when a Fiduciary Manager is involved. An additional layer of fees is added by virtue of engaging a Fiduciary. This increase in costs, however, does not mean that the fund is worse off. Instead, investment decisions are taken on the basis of better information, and they involve potentially more effective and more rewarding strategies. In addition, risk management is improved. There is good reason to expect higher returns, in net terms, because the fund is now using its risk budget more effectively and efficiently combining carefully selected asset managers. The sum of these benefits should outweigh the costs of Fiduciary Management and the experiences so far have clearly validated this view. Since higher costs are easier to pay in good times, a plan sponsor may conclude that a performance-related fee structure is advisable. In practice, however, some plan sponsors have found that performance fees can create major problems. If both the Fiduciary's fee and the investment managers' fee are performance-related, the sum of these fees may result in a larger portion of the excess return being paid to managers, leaving less for the fund. However favorable the investment circumstances are, and however high the gross returns are, this turns out to be a problem for some institutions, which find it difficult to explain to their stakeholders why this redistribution is taking place.

This is even more true if incentive fees only have an upside while markets are generating disappointing returns. If portfolio returns are less than market returns—and particularly when returns are negative—the fund experiences this decline while the managers receive their base fee. The investment managers do not earn a large amount of money, but they are not confronted with losses. Some institutions hold the view that market declines should be reflected in management fees as well. The problem in this case, however, is that a fund doesn't want a poorly performing manager penalized so severely that the manager cannot afford to go about its business as effectively as possible.

There have been efforts to avoid some of the concerns associated with performance fees. One is having external managers working for only a flat fee. This can create problems, however, because some managers only want to work under a performance-related regime, and if a plan sponsor does not offer such a fee structure, it may end up with managers who are not the best in their class. Another approach is to offer performance fees, but eliminate the effects of outperformance from the Fiduciary's fee. The problem with this arrangement is that the Fiduciary may feel no incentive to look for the best external manager as this will not enhance the Fiduciary's fee.

The ultimate goal is to ensure that the Fiduciary will still act in the best interests of the client, and only the client, so any possible conflict of interest should be avoided. It is therefore advisable to have a flat fee for external managers if the Fiduciary fee is performance-related (unless the accumulation of performance-related fees stays below an acceptable limit, such as 50 percent of the outperformance).

An efficient performance-related fee is not easy to devise. Recent experience indicates that risk management benefits when performance fees are determined on the basis of the information ratio rather than the excess return. This approach recognizes that markets can be inefficient during certain periods, and when markets do not reward risks appropriately, it would be advisable for the fund to take less risk than normal. However, a Fiduciary being paid on the basis of excess return would be inclined to use all of the risk budget all of the time because that approach would be likely to improve the chances of achieving an excess return and generating a higher fee. The prospect of this detrimental course could be ruled out if the fee is related to the excess return, divided by the actual tracking error—in other words, relating the fee to the information ratio.

Sometimes performance related fees can be determined in stages. The participation rate for the Fiduciary can be substantially higher when the realized information ratio is higher than, for instance 0.5, while below that inflection point the rate falls toward a much lower percentage.

Finally, it makes sense to have a so-called high-water mark in the fee structure. That implies that the Fiduciary Manager only receives a performance-related fee when some underperformance left from former years has been compensated by excess returns in the year at hand. The balance of that sum, if positive, should be the determinant of the current fee level.

CHANGES IN THE IMPORTANCE OF THE CUSTODIAN

A good custodian is essential to the investment process. The complexity of the investment process increases when a Fiduciary Manager is at work, and consequently, the plan sponsor must make sure that its incumbent custodian is up to the job. A Fiduciary and of course, the fund itself, require detailed, reliable, and timely data with respect to all aspects of the investment portfolio in order to monitor risk and return and to evaluate investment managers.

The Fiduciary Manager can advise the fund with respect to the necessary skills required of its custodian, and the Fiduciary can also use its experience to assist in the process of choosing another custodian if the current one is found wanting. Since the Fiduciary depends on the information compiled and provided by the custodian, he or she has an abiding interest in the selection of a custodian who can meet the needs of the fund. The Fiduciary's experience is a good guide to defining the exact role of the custodian and determining whether to use such value-added services as securities lending and voting proxies in response to social responsibility concerns.

OVERSEEING THE FIDUCIARY

While the Fiduciary Manager plays an important role in overseeing most of those who provide services to the plan sponsor, the question arises of how oversight is provided for the Fiduciary. The question of who watches the watchers is, of course, a classic managerial issue. In fact, this presents something of a dilemma in the context of Fiduciary Management. On the one hand, many organizations would be well served by a Fiduciary because they lack sufficient know-how and operational infrastructure, but, on the other hand, the same organizations need to have a substantial degree of expertise and know how to judge whether or not the Fiduciary Manager performs its tasks well enough. How much knowledge, information, and internal expertise are required to properly evaluate a Fiduciary Manager?

This problem, in essence, is not different from the problems attached to evaluating every task that has been delegated by every organization, and in the context of this book, the same questions are relevant for evaluating external asset managers or the asset-liability specialist. They are, after all, being engaged precisely because they have more expertise in their areas of specialization than does the plan sponsor.

The answer to this dilemma is to be found in good reporting and benchmarking, supplemented perhaps by peer group comparison and, of course, a well-drafted Fiduciary Management agreement. Reporting goes back to the delivery of information in a transparent and comprehensible way, and this information should be compared with a benchmark that has been defined before the Fiduciary started his or her job. In addition, the outcome of the whole investment process can be compared with the results of funds that are similar in size, structure, and strategic approach.

The custodian has a place in this process of overseeing the Fiduciary. The custodian's data are the principal inputs to be used in assessing investment results, but there is another dimension as well. Because it is arbiter in the calculation of returns, the custodian's data should also be used in calculating the Fiduciary's fee. The Fiduciary should not calculate his or her own fee; rather an independent third party should deliver the appropriate data for calculating the fee.

To be sure, judging the results of a Fiduciary's activities is a complex task. Budgeting and managing risk in the best possible way are no easy things to do, nor are they easy tasks to measure. The educational aspects of the Fiduciary activities are of vital importance in this context. It is the duty of the Fiduciary, not only to keep the plan sponsor well-informed, but also to see to it that the fund's organization assimilates that information and is able to handle it in such a way that the plan sponsor maintains control. This comes down to informing the sponsor on all the steps that are taken to define and allocate risk in the various markets. How many data and technical characteristics in reporting are appropriate can be learned over time on the basis of experience. While some funds may focus on overall returns and tracking error, others may require in-depth statistical data on all the markets where they are invested.

As in any industrial setting, it is useful when the fund and its advisors regularly visit the factory and meet with the workers in the field. In an investment setting, this kind of contact and dialogue with external service providers offers valuable background information regarding the process through which an efficient portfolio is constructed. It also encourages the plan sponsor and its executives to dig deeper into the issues of investing as an expression of allocating risk.

As a final check, the whole Fiduciary Management process can be judged by the regulator, providing a degree of comfort for the plan sponsor when this body expresses its positive attitude toward the structure. Typically, this kind of assessment is only offered in case of an institutional investor that has to report on a weak financial position, but a plan sponsor can be proactive in this area and seek a regulator's views on its structure.

It should be noted that the education provided by the Fiduciary Manager can be seen as having a positive effect on the degree of work satisfaction felt by the executives of the plan sponsor. The fear is often expressed that choosing a Fiduciary Manager structure would chase away a plan sponsor's best talent as more responsibilities are taken over by the Fiduciary, rendering the remaining duties less interesting. Experience shows the opposite. As the investment process becomes more complex and more professional, the investment department of the fund enjoys the enlarged education and the higher level of professionalism associated with this new sophistication. More importantly, working with a Fiduciary reveals that responsibilities indeed are split, but that important duties and responsibilities, indeed *the* most important ones, are still on the fund's desk. The involvement with the Fiduciary Manager does not mean abdicating these issues but rather tackling them in a more professional environment. Surprisingly, perhaps, this is not clear to all observers. Indeed, some consultants remain convinced that Fiduciary Management situates "governance and control" outside the organization.[1]

FUTURE DEVELOPMENTS OF THE MARKET FOR FIDUCIARY SERVICES

Research undertaken by McKinsey & Company[2] indicates that in the Netherlands the market for Fiduciary Management has grown rapidly from less than €10 billion in 2003 and 2004 to some €30 billion in 2005 and to €50 billion as of the end of August, 2006. And since publication of the McKinsey research, a number of new Fiduciary Management contracts have been agreed upon, leading to a higher volume than anticipated by the end of 2006 (some €90 billion). Therefore, McKinsey's forecast of potential growth in the Dutch market for this service to some €50 to €100 billion in pension fund assets seems to be too conservative. The largest part of this potential market is generated by midsized pension funds, defined as funds with reserves ranging from €100 million to €5 billion.

The development of interest in Fiduciary Management is being stimulated on the demand side by new and stricter regulations as well as the pressing need for higher returns than what are likely to be generated by traditional investment products. In addition, the growing understanding of more sophisticated risk management tools and better manager selection procedures is playing a role. But in addition, growth is also being generated by developments on the supply side. McKinsey found that retail asset management brings in far higher profits than institutional asset management, and one way to improve the business case for the latter area is to broaden the scope of services on offer. Fiduciary Management captures a full relationship with more income-generating potential and more loyalty from the customer attached to it. In October 2006, KPMG asked 100 major Dutch corporate pension funds to offer their views on a number of developments in the pensions market.[3] These questions were put to the chairmen of the funds or, if not available, to another member of the board or to a senior administrator. Table 9.1 provides the questions and answers at the core of this survey.

The growing interest in the concept of Fiduciary Management is likely to be related to the fact that 58 percent of those interviewed in this survey regard governance as the most important item for the year to come. Hiring a Fiduciary strengthens the organization and delegates tasks in an efficient and appropriate way, thus enhancing the quality of governance. Those interviewed view governance as involving such matters as the expertise and integrity of the board, continuity in management, and shared control by retirees and transparency. And all of these issues benefit from a Fiduciary Management environment.

The survey notes that 7 percent of respondents have pondered the survival of their fund, and they have considered such dramatic options as

TABLE 9.1 Selected Questions and Answers from a 2007 KPMG Survey of Pension Funds

Question	Answer	Score
Which are the four most important issues for your pension fund in the coming year?	Pension fund governance	58%
	Communication	33%
	New set of regulations	29%
	Investment policy and ALM	26%
	Pension law	25%
	Administrative organization/ internal control	13%
	Adaptations to or renewal of pension contract	13%
	Indexation of pensions	12%
Are you familiar with concept of fiduciary management?	Yes	60%
	No	39%
Do you think that fiduciary management fits the needs of your fund?	Yes	45%
	No	45%
	Don't know/No answer	10%
Which would be the most relevant reason to enter into a fiduciary contract?	Increased complexity of investment management and accompanying increased need for expertise (without the possibility of hiring this yourself)	53%
	Continuity in the organization	28%
	Regulatory requirements in the area of risk management	28%
	Deliberate focus of the board on strategy and policy (and not on operational aspects)	28%
	Other	8%
	Don't know/No answer	13%
Which are your most important objections to fiduciary management?	No need for a fiduciary manager: my own organization works perfectly.	38%
	Would I still be in control to a sufficient degree as a manager?	30%
	Dependency of one party	27%
	Old wine in new bottles	8%
	Tendency toward foreign asset management of Dutch pension capital	7%
	Costs and cost structure	5%
	Other	8%
	Don't know/No answer	18%

Source: KPMG, De pensioenwereld in 2007, Amstelveen, January 2007, pages 118–123.

a merger with another pension fund, liquidation of the fund, or seeking shelter in an industry-wide pension fund. KPMG sees as the main reasons for this kind of heightened concern a lack of sufficient continuity and expertise among respondents, combined with the growing complexity of the financial issues facing these funds. Other issues, not mentioned in the table, include risk management, contracting out, the review of contracts, and improvement of reporting. All of these items fare well in a Fiduciary context, and concern about these issues could lead to a Fiduciary solution instead of a merger or one of the other more drastic solutions that were mentioned by survey respondents.

One remarkable finding is that 60 percent of the pension funds interviewed are familiar with the concept of Fiduciary Management and that 45 percent of all respondents indicate that this idea would suit their needs. KPMG therefore concludes that a major change seems to be looming in the asset management market. Some 45 percent of respondents indicate that Fiduciary Management does not suit their needs, but some of this may indicate that a number of respondents are simply not familiar with the concept. The survey found that small and midsized pension funds are less familiar with the Fiduciary concept than are their colleagues at larger funds. That is regrettable, since one might presume that the concept could, in fact, be of more relevance to the smaller funds. The differences in the degree of familiarity with the Fiduciary Management concept based on size of fund probably reflects the fact that the smaller the fund, the harder it is to be informed about new developments.

The most often cited reasons why funds would consider using the Fiduciary approach are that it would help them cope with growing complexity, add continuity, and assist them in meeting increasingly complex regulations. Respondents also said that Fiduciary Management would help the board to concentrate on strategy and governance. It is striking that 71 percent of the larger funds cite complexity and expertise as the drivers of fiduciary change while only 37 percent of midsized funds and 43 percent of smaller funds do so.

Some 38 percent of respondents view their organization as working well, and therefore they see no reason to consider a fiduciary structure. If these respondents were to be found in midsized and smaller funds, one might suspect their answer reflects a lack of familiarity with the fiduciary concept. But, of course, many pension fund executives and board members would find it hard to acknowledge that their organization lacks essential attributes.

Some survey respondents also expressed concern that the board's control would be diminished by a Fiduciary Manager. This concern suggests a lack of knowledge regarding the Fiduciary concept. In this context, the board is fully in control, but it has delegated certain duties to the Fiduciary Manager. The concern about responsibility being concentrated in the hands of one party can only refer to risk management and strategic advice. In these areas institutional investors have to realize that it is a perfectly reasonable managerial practice to share important responsibilities. Defining a neutral risk budget and an accompanying strategic benchmark is still the responsibility of the board; the Fiduciary enters the picture by refining this budget into investment terms and then spelling out the strategic benchmark and its specific parts in order to be able to monitor the greater number of asset managers that may be employed.

Another objection reported in the survey is that the Fiduciary Management concept in essence is really nothing new. But as has been shown, this is not correct.

Meanwhile, there is evidence for the perception expressed by a number of respondents that foreign fiduciaries are taking over the management of Dutch pension capital. But here reality is more complex than it initially appears. Foreign companies may have won more Fiduciary Management contracts than Dutch suppliers, but that development does not directly imply that there is a flow of assets under management going abroad. A substantial volume of pension fund assets were already being managed by foreign asset managers. Indeed, the experience so far is that the market share of foreign asset managers has increased with the introduction of Fiduciary schemes, but the trend is not as dramatic as suggested by merely looking at the foreign market in Fiduciary Management. What this outflow represents is an indication that the high quality in asset management available abroad has become discernable. It is true that until 2007 most Fiduciary contracts were being won by foreign firms, but this picture has been changing. Dutch investment houses have been slow to react to this new development, but as 2007 was unfolding, there were signs that they were gaining market share.

Costs are an issue in pension fund management, especially in the Netherlands, where many pension funds succeed in getting assets managed at very low fees. In fact, Holland is quite notorious for this in the asset management world. While it is difficult to feel comfortable handing over pensioner's money to highly-paid managers who generate losses in adverse markets, it would be penny-wise and pound-foolish to hire managers only on the basis of low fees. It is the net excess return that is important. And having a performance-related fee structure can align the interests of managers and the fund, and can lead to a stronger pension fund.

In short, there is still a long way to go in convincing many pension funds of the merits of Fiduciary Management. Some 45 percent of the funds familiar with the term and its meaning indicated that it is not the answer to their needs. However, an equal number say Fiduciary Management addresses issues that concern them, while 10 percent say they do not know, or leave the question unanswered.

In analyzing these survey results, KPMG concludes that Fiduciary Management is more than a buzzword, and the firm points out that this type of management only produces meaningful results if and when its building blocks are precisely tailored to the characteristics and risk profile of a specific fund. In evaluating the role of the fiduciary, KPMG adds that the pension fund enters into a relation in which the Fiduciary Manager oversees, integrates, and coordinates all aspects of the pension fund's operations. While KPMG divided a pension fund's activities into tactical and operational aspects, this may not be fully accurate. The strategic aspects should be overseen, integrated, and coordinated as well.

That is not to say that the Fiduciary should have to define the entire strategy—the fund's management should do that. But the pension fund's management should evaluate strategic proposals from a range of choices shaped for it by the Fiduciary. These proposals are based on the neutral risk budget that the fund has to choose as the most appropriate one.

KPMG correctly points out that the Fiduciary Manager differs from the old-time balanced manager in that the Fiduciary is focused on the total approach of the pension fund and does not have to focus only on the interests of the asset management side of the organization. A good Fiduciary Manager determines the needs of his or her customers from an independent point of view.

KPMG concludes that because of the Fiduciary Management's integrating approach to pension issues, it is a good choice for a fund in seeking optimization of the investment management. A fund cannot and should not delegate all of its responsibilities. A Fiduciary can make operational decisions, but the board remains responsible for the strategic decisions that a pension fund must make regarding general goals as well as specific asset allocations, benchmarks, and liability matching. This is in line with Dutch regulations and with the European IORP directive in that respect.

Finally, KPMG notes that in considering Fiduciary Management, a pension fund cannot follow the principle of one size fits all. If traditional models represent one end of a spectrum and the Fiduciary Management model represents the other, KPMG discerns all kinds of mixes that can fit the characteristics of specific funds. The most important are the risk profile and the accompanying investment strategy. A fund that chooses a deliberate defensive, low-risk strategy will have less need for the expertise of a Fiduciary than a fund that is pursuing more complexity in investing. The nature and structure of a pension fund organization plays a role as well. According to KPMG, the construction of the Fiduciary mandate should seamlessly fit the existing organization and its competences and infrastructure. It should be added that this indeed should be the case, but only if all of these attributes are already sound. It is very well conceivable that the issues leading to the consideration of a fiduciary structure could and should lead to a change in the existing organization. In fact, it is frequently the case that the division of labor between board and Fiduciary changes the responsibilities of parts of the organization so much, that the organization itself is changed.

The latest development in the Fiduciary Management field is a trend that has been called Fiduciary in-sourcing. At the end of 2006, a large Dutch pension fund recognized the need for more specialist managers, but it also realized that its in-house capabilities for monitoring a whole new team of managers would be insufficient. After seeking external advice regarding which managers to hire, the fund hired an outside specialist company to monitor them. The plan sponsor said the main reason not to choose a full-fledged Fiduciary mandate was the feeling that the fund would then have too little contact with the investment world, and in due course it would lose the expertise in this field that it felt it should have. As in other debates over outsourcing, the plan sponsor was fearful that there would be a hollowing out process if it gave up too much of its involvement in the investment process; once this involvement was diminished, the fear was that the remaining core of knowledge and expertise would wither, leaving the fund unable to properly assess what was going on in the investment world and incapable of resuming the activities it had outsourced if it ever wanted to do so.

It is important to note that these considerations were made by a fund with enough assets under management to be able to maintain an investment team strong enough to execute certain complex strategies, such as an active overlay policy. This fund felt it needed to have a team working together with the outside monitoring agency in order to check whether the managers deliver what they promise and to be able to replace managers if needed. The crucial element in this structure, however, is risk budgeting. Fiduciary in-sourcing this way is a flexible application of the fiduciary concept, but does it go far enough? Having a good fleet of external managers may produce good results within the strategic policy with its active accents, but when the risk budget is not calculated correctly, the gains will be far lower than the foregone returns of the application of a better risk budget.

The basic question therefore is, whether or not the risk budget is determined optimally. The answer is in the in-house expertise, which should be such that a good translation of the asset-liability study into a risk budget can be made and all the managers receive the correct amount of risk. In this field a good fiduciary has strong credentials, and the jury is out as to whether a midsized pension fund can do the same thing as well.

BEYOND THE NETHERLANDS

There is no reason to think that only the Dutch environment would be positive for the development of the Fiduciary Manager concept. In all of the major developed countries, financial regulations are growing increasingly strict and complex, and the new International Financial Reporting Standards pose challenges to all publicly traded international companies. To diminish the impact of pension funds on their balance sheets, many companies are likely to seek greater separation from these pension funds. This tendency requires a stronger governance structure, and Fiduciary Management is delivering just that. Moreover, when there are less-favorable market conditions, this situation influences investment possibilities and future returns in all countries, and it heightens the appeal of finding better ways to organize and oversee the investment management function.

So there is every reason to believe that the Dutch example of this new concept will take hold in other financial centers. In fact, some indications of that are already visible. Pension services, performed by traditional asset managers in the United States are slowly being broadened, and in Germany, Austria, Switzerland, UK, Japan, and the Middle East there is also greater attention being paid to the fiduciary management concept. In some of these countries fiduciary agreements have been signed.

FIDUCIARY MANAGEMENT PLUS

As has been shown, Fiduciary Management provides a way to help pension funds respond to pressure from regulators for better governance and to new accounting rules. But a number of pension funds (and some smaller insurance companies) are opting for a more dramatic version of Fiduciary Management. They not only want the Fiduciary to perform the tasks described in previous chapters (advice, portfolio construction, manager selection, monitoring, and reporting), they also want the Fiduciary involved in areas normally confined to the board, such as benefit oversight and governance. Depending on the existing legal specifications and possibilities, the Fiduciary Manager would assume responsibility for relationships with plan participants and policyholders.

Contracts have been signed in which a Fiduciary acquires the asset management responsibilities of the fund. In other contracts, the Fiduciary's role in overseeing the asset management function is enlarged to include some of the legal obligations toward policyholders or participants. In this case, for example, the buyer assumes or renegotiates the rights of the beneficiaries, sometimes incorporates existing staff within its own organization, and then it essentially runs the pension fund.

The question of who determines premium levels and the nature of the liabilities can be the attributes that determine the distinction between a new asset management agreement and actual acquisition of a pension fund. When premiums and liabilities are taken over by the buyer, within the existing legal entity or within a newly negotiated one, it is essentially an acquisition. When premiums and benefits—and the way they are periodically renegotiated—stay intact, such an agreement comes down to a broadly defined asset management agreement.

In general, an acquisition can be viewed as an extension of the Fiduciary mandate, with all the benefits associated with Fiduciary Management. However, one pitfall associated with such a takeover may be found in the asset management agreement that goes along with it. The acquirer is generally interested in undertaking this transaction because of the future revenues to be generated from the asset management activities. This kind of acquisition can also be a way for a Fiduciary Manager to buy market share in a growing market, thus demonstrating that it is a significant participant in the market.

The acquisition price in these circumstances can be high, since many bidders may want the contract. Once the deal is struck, the asset management agreement can contain elements, relating to this high price. In this way, it is possible for the new asset managers to manage as many assets in-house as possible in order to earn fees and recoup the money invested in the deal. The management fee levied in this setting is not likely to be as competitive as it would be in an open bidding process within a strict Fiduciary Manager contract.

When these two elements come together—choosing an in-house party instead of a best-in-class manager and paying relatively high management fees—the arrangement misses two important benefits of a Fiduciary contract. In the worst-case scenario, in fact, this arrangement turns into an expensive balanced mandate that provides what is nearly the complete opposite of the benefits of a fiduciary contract.

If the financial components of a pension fund, that is premiums and benefits, are taken over, it is fair to say that the fund barely continues to exist. The most important variables of the pension system are handed over to the buyer. This resembles the situation when an insurance contract is purchased, and the pension fund is reduced to a wrapper for an insurance product. Since the buyer of a pension fund may be an insurance company, the line between asset management and insurance becomes a very thin line indeed.

CHAPTER 10

Summing Up Fiduciary Management: What It Is and Is Not

As we have seen, a good Fiduciary Manager plays a very important role in supporting the management of a fund, yet the Fiduciary is not a replacement for the actual managers of a pension fund. Fiduciary Managers oversee an important set of tasks: They advise the management in terms of assets and liability matching; they construct an efficient investment portfolio; they select the managers to run that portfolio; they monitor these managers; and, finally, they provide regular reports to the fund management on each of these tasks. This array of duties makes the Fiduciary a full-fledged partner in the process of managing the pension fund, a process in which clear lines of responsibility have been drawn.

GOALS, POLICY, AND RESPONSIBILITIES

Most of the academic literature on management argues that the quality of an organization's decision-making process is an important determinant of the degree of success that the organization will have in meeting its objectives. This idea is important in understanding pension funds because many pension fund departments or organizations have generally not been created with the objective of being an efficient producer of pension-related services. Indeed, many pension fund organizations were created by the personnel or human resources departments of the plan sponsor without much thought given to their capacity to make good decisions.

O'Barr and Conley[1] go as far as to argue that the organizational structures of many pension funds seem to be historical accidents. That may well be the main reason why they concluded that the common themes at many pension plans seem to be responsibility-shifting and blame-deflection. Instead of managing pensions, these organizations try to manage blame. Another of their findings is also relevant: strong personal relationships with consultants and investment managers seem to be a top priority at many pension funds.

In line with these results, in a 1996 study in which 50 senior pension fund executives were interviewed, Ambachtsheer, Boice, Ezra, and McLaughlin[2] found the following reasons were most frequently cited reasons for failing to achieve excellent results: poor decision-making processes (98%); inadequate resources (48%); and lack of focus or clear mission (42%). The consequences of these findings are clear: improvements in the nature and content of the decision-making process are essential in order to achieve a better pension product and a better way to deliver that product to the clients.

Times have changed since the late 1990s. Benign equity markets proved only temporary, and high investment returns are not easily attainable. Well-funded pension plans and contribution holidays are far less common. A combination of market developments and new regulations has put institutional investors in an environment in which their activities are compared to best practice and often found wanting. Blame-management has to be replaced by effective pension management.

Fiduciary Management, by its nature, can play a major role in achieving this. The findings of Ambachtsheer, Capelle, and Scheibelhut[3] indicate where it fits in. According to their research, the principal drivers of a pension fund's performance are

- Clarity about the pension proposition and risk-bearing
- Clarity about board and executive responsibility
- Clarity about board composition and skill set
- Willingness of the board members to evaluate their own effectiveness as well as that of the fund's management
- High levels of trust.

The Fiduciary Manager identifies and clarifies risks and spells out precisely which risks can be managed effectively. These risks are related to the nature of the investment assets and their interaction with market developments. The Fiduciary will not take ultimate responsibility for the asset-liability study and its uncertainties, nor for the choice of the asset mix and accompanying chances of underfunding. These are issues for the board of directors to resolve, as are issues having to do with contributions and the level and structure of benefits provided. Shifting responsibilities with respect to oversight of asset management to the Fiduciary Manager relieves the board from being obliged to assemble detailed asset management skills. Instead, they can concentrate their active decision making on other areas, and limit their role in overseeing investment matters to ensuring that the required skills are being brought to bear on this task.

The party who accepts significant responsibility for the management of plan assets must be willing to be evaluated according to the highest standards for that mission. The board, in turn, is implicitly evaluated for its decision to hire this party. Effectiveness is measured by using transparent and objective data. By nature, the oversight tasks assumed by the board result in a deeper understanding of important issues as well as closer ties between the board and the Fiduciary. A high level of trust is essential in handing over the management of a substantial amount of money. It is earned by the way the Fiduciary fulfils his or her duties.

O'Barr and Conley note that strong personal relationships with consultants and investment managers are seen as important for pension funds. This finding can, of course, complicate an objective assessment of their performance. The involvement of the Fiduciary Manager also implies strong personal relationships, but these relationships are between the board and the Fiduciary and not necessarily the various service providers. In the Fiduciary Manager system, the distance between the board and the asset managers becomes greater and this is positive, as it helps ensure an objective attitude in judging the managers, as shown below. Meanwhile, the board's ties with the Fiduciary are based on a professional division of labor.

Ezra defines best practices in pension management in a way that makes them identical with Fiduciary Management. In his words,

The acceleration of multi-manager structures is evidence of Fiduciary Management taking hold. Recent evidence is there, that the question "Why" has been changed into the questions "What," "How," and "Who." Fiduciary Management has become accepted as a necessary part of good governance.[4]

In his view, the players and contents of a decision-making process are essentially the same whether this process is designed for a corporation or for a pension fund or other institutional investor. He summarizes the governance matrix for a company or other organization as shown in Table 10.1.

The governance matrix of an institutional investor is the same, except that some players have different names. See Table 10.2.

Decisions have to be taken by one layer, and by the same token, the task of overseeing decisions, has to be limited to one layer. In the case of an institutional investor, Ezra defines three areas of decision making, in declining order of importance, shown in Table 10.3.

A focus on managing blame can only be prevented from occurring when "decides" and "oversees" are not found in more than one row.

From Table 10.3 it is clear that the Fiduciary is not simply some new variation on the traditional balanced manager. There can and should be

TABLE 10.1 General Governance Matrix

Group/Role	General Description
Board	Decision on direction and goals
Executive	Decisions on the means and establishing the organization structure
Workers	Production of the product or service
External consultants	Research and advice

TABLE 10.2 Institutional Investor's Governance Matrix

Group/Role	General Description
Board	Decision on direction and goals
Fiduciary Manager	Decisions on the means and establishing the organization structure
Investment managers	Production of the product or service
External consultants	Research and advice

TABLE 10.3 Pension Fund's Investment Governance Matrix

Fiduciary/Decision Area	Asset Liability Policy or General Risk Management	Manager Structure and Selection	Security Selection
Board	Decides and oversees	Oversees	
Fiduciary Manager	Inputs	Decides	Oversees
Asset managers			Decides
External consultants	Inputs		

a reliance on specialization in devising a structure in which a group of investment managers each manage a portion of the portfolio.

Table 10.3 also indicates the difference between "ultimate responsibility," which always resides with the board, and "immediate responsibility," which can and should be delegated to the Fiduciary. This delegation is associated with the second layer of decisions and has to be delegated to asset managers in case of investing.

It should be noted that effective governance does not exclude the possibility that the Fiduciary Manager is actually a part of the fund staff. When an institutional investor has sufficient resources and assets to manage the entire investment process, the Fiduciary Manager role can be delegated to an internal officer or division. However, in this case, it is critical that one condition be met—conflicts of interest have to be avoided—and this means that a Fiduciary Manager who is an employee of the pension fund should not have any goals or obligations other than serving as an effective Fiduciary Manager.

The same is true if the external Fiduciary also manages assets. A pension fund should not rule out the possibility that an external organization could fulfill this dual role of Fiduciary and asset manager. The chosen Fiduciary could very well be an experienced asset manager since he or she needs to be intimately familiar with all aspects of asset management. Excluding the Fiduciary as a possible asset manager would imply that one condition of a good Fiduciary contract has not been met: employing the best asset managers that are available. However, the asset manager's activities in the role of Fiduciary Manager should always be directed toward achieving the best fiduciary result. The Fiduciary Management agreement should regulate this dual assignment and should detect possible conflicts of interest and indicate the ways how to handle them.

The key message from Ezra is that decisions have to be taken by one layer in the organization and that the subjects of the decisions are strongly tied to the responsibilities of each layer. In the case of institutional investors, it is clear that the board is responsible for the most important aspects of balancing risks and returns, and this responsibility cannot and should not be delegated. The critical concerns in this area are

- *Determining the basic investment policy*, including the appropriate risk budget, the strategic asset mix which fits that budget, and the accompanying benchmarks for measuring results. The Fiduciary's posture in this area will be more reactive than proactive. The risk budget and the asset mix are the responsibility of the fund and cannot be delegated. That mix is the most important determinant of returns over time. Of course, the Fiduciary can and should assemble information for decisions about the risk budget and asset mix, and he or she should also advise on the best benchmarks to be used after the strategic mix has been decided upon.
- *Determining critical aspects regarding the ways in which the investment policy should be implemented:* for instance, how much active management; in what form (overlay or not); whether or not to hedge currency positions and bridge the duration gap. These elements should not be underestimated; the complexity grows in most cases compared to other execution models.

- *Exercising final decision-making responsibility* on the overall policy of the fund.
- *Communicating policies and processes* to all of the fund's constituencies, including regulators, stakeholders, the press, and the public.

While major decisions must always be the board's responsibility, it is obvious that the Fiduciary is a major contributor to the quality of the management provided by the institutional investor. In Ezra's view, a basic characteristic of a Fiduciary is taking the attitude that he is a partner in the undertaking and not simply someone hired to perform a list of tasks. This attitude is reflected several ways.[5] To begin with, a Fiduciary needs to have a reputation for long partnering relationships. That is why a number of the organizations offering fiduciary services started life as pension funds or have a consulting background. They are known to have longer-term commitments to their customers and to emphasize advisory services. Along the same lines, the Fiduciary Manager needs to have a reputation for collaboration, not for deal making. Of course, investing is about transactions and making deals, but these should grow out of the tasks delegated by the board and should not take on a life of their own.

A true Fiduciary Manager treats clients as long-term partners, not as a source of quick profits. This by no means implies that a fiduciary contract should not be profitable for the Fiduciary. In the financial world, relationships cannot exist for the long term without mutual financial benefits. But profits should originate from the efficiency of the processes devised to serve the interests of the fund and from the benefits that the client has received from the services that have been purchased.

In achieving an effective Fiduciary relationship, it is critical to ensure that interests are aligned, not conflicting. In institutional investing the amounts of money involved are generally so huge that there will inevitably be potential for conflicts of interest as well as opportunities to cheat.

Ambachtsheer, Capelle and Lum[6] posed the following two important questions regarding attributes of a pension fund's system of governance:

- Have CEO perceptions of strengths and weaknesses in their governance and management practices changed?
- Can we discover additional insights into the drivers of investment performance?

In order to find an answer, they compared two surveys of the pension fund industry (undertaken in 1997 and 2005). These surveys involved plan sponsors in the United States, Canada, Western Europe, and Australia/New

Zealand. One of their findings was that the three statements that consistently received the lowest scores with respect to the subject of governance were:

- Our fund has an effective process for selecting, developing, and terminating its governing fiduciaries.
- My governing fiduciaries examine and improve their own effectiveness on a regular basis.
- My governing fiduciaries do *not* spend time assessing individual portfolio manager effectiveness or individual investments.

The tasks of selecting, organizing, and terminating asset managers for reasons of underperformance or inefficient use of the risk budget are among the principal duties of a Fiduciary Manager. The Fiduciary's effectiveness in performing this work is supposed to be measured constantly and objectively, and the plan sponsor does not have to evaluate individual portfolio managers and individual investments, because the Fiduciary performs these tasks.

FIDUCIARY MANAGEMENT CAN ENHANCE PRODUCTIVITY

The Fiduciary "merely" supports and carries out decisions that are actually made by a fund's board. Nonetheless, the decisions made by the board frequently differ in character when a Fiduciary is engaged. Investment policy almost certainly will change with Fiduciary support for two reasons. One is that the way decisions are made is altered because of the additional expertise the Fiduciary provides to the board in such areas as portfolio management, risk management, and manager research.

The capabilities of the board are very limited at small and midsize institutions, but this situation changes markedly with Fiduciary support because of the knowledge and expertise the Fiduciary brings to the decision-making process. Secondly, the range of actions that a board can choose to pursue is much broader when it has a Fiduciary Manager who can implement its decisions.

The division of labor that is possible when a fund board has a Fiduciary Manager enables the fund to be more fully engaged in other tasks, such as communicating with the regulatory agencies when new legislation is under consideration. Even in these instances when substantial attention has to be focused on this new legislation, the Fiduciary may enable the board to undertake the tasks in the investment area with greater expertise and sophistication. Because of the small size of many pension fund organizations, the range of the staff's skills and knowledge is often surprisingly limited.

The Fiduciary not only makes it possible for a wider range of asset classes to be investigated, he or she also helps ensure that the available risk budget is used optimally.

This is, by far, the most important contribution of Fiduciary Management. And because more asset classes and investment approaches are considered, more are likely to be utilized, and this brings improvements in potential returns and in risk management. Meanwhile, internal conflicts of interest, such as plan sponsor versus members or retirees, can be dealt with in a more objective and professional way because of the existence of a Fiduciary, who is knowledgeable about the plan yet an independent third party. The Fiduciary can also bring the expertise needed to meet new demands from regulators.

WHAT FIDUCIARY MANAGEMENT IS NOT: A SIMPLIFICATION

While it should be clear that there are a number of advantages to be gained by having a Fiduciary Manager, one thing will not be achieved: the decision-making process will not become simpler or easier. While the Fiduciary provides advice and expertise, he also opens the door to greater complexity and sophistication in the choices that a board must confront. More investment alternatives are brought into consideration, and the specification of investment policy often requires more study than before. Exercising oversight and control is more complex when a fund utilizes more asset classes, more sophisticated investment strategies, and perhaps even more external managers. Balancing of risk and return plays a more prominent role in more sophisticated approaches to pension management, and risk management is not an easy task.

Fiduciary Management can, however, support these processes and improve the quality of the decisions taken. As indicated earlier, the character and content of the decision-making process are at stake, and in this context a study by Risseeuw, ter Wengel, and Rutte highlight another important characteristic of certain pension funds.[7] While large organizations generally have large ambitions as well as greater resources, and small organizations pair small ambitions with small resources, midsize funds often face a mismatch between their aspirations and possibilities. They find themselves having limited resources but ambitious goals. As has been noted in earlier chapters, Fiduciary Management can bridge this disparity. Ambitious goals can be reached when small or midsize funds delegate appropriate decisions to a Fiduciary.

COMPARISONS WITH OTHER INVESTMENT MANAGEMENT MODELS

Fiduciary Management distinguishes itself favorably from other models of investment management and operation in several respects: Compared to balanced mandates, for example, Fiduciary Management provides better overall risk management and avoids the fallacy that one investment manager can be the best in a number of different asset classes. The old idea that it is possible to diversify risks by using more than one balanced manager clearly does not solve this problem because most balanced managers are likely to be fashioning the same response to the same market circumstances. Proper systematic risk management becomes almost impossible when several balanced managers are employed. Fiduciary Management greatly improves the prospects of achieving an approach to investing that brings appropriate diversification and risk management while maximizing opportunities to achieve attractive returns.

Fiduciary Management is not necessarily better than careful and coherent in-house management. But it is fair to say that only the largest funds have the resources required to do everything by themselves. And even then, these large funds have good reason to delegate certain tasks, particularly specialized investment management. Even the largest institutional investors cannot assemble the expertise that specialized investment houses have. Nor are they likely to be willing and able to provide the same level of compensation to specialized investment experts as what is likely to be offered by investment management firms.

Moreover, these institutions cannot replicate the culture that is useful in supporting those with specialized expertise. Being the only private equity expert at a pension fund is not the same as being part of a team of people at a private equity firm, for example. Thus, in-house management of all the assets is not a very workable structure for most institutions, while a Fiduciary Management concept is one of the best structures to integrate external management into the overall management of a portfolio.

There are some who advocate a middle-of-the road solution in which institutions of a certain size would manage part of their investments themselves. Some suggest that when assets surpass $10 billion, some 30 percent of those assets could and should be managed internally, and this percentage should increase with the size of the fund. This seems reasonable if one condition has been met. Calculation and apportioning the risk budget should be defined across the entire portfolio, and it should be warranted that allocation of risk over the internally managed portion is correct. No risk should be left unused and, of course, apportioning should not imply surpassing the overall risk budget. What may be even more important is safeguarding the beneficial effects of integrating management and risks to achieve more efficient risk/return characteristics. This kind of middle of the road approach requires sophisticated integration of the various parts of the portfolio in determining the strategic and tactical investment policy.

Institutions that are smaller than the very largest, but large enough to be able to formulate and conduct a proprietary investment policy, can hire external managers to do the actual investing. But this requires substantial in-house expertise about all the present and future alternatives, and a continuous monitoring of the field of external management in order to be sure the fund is working with the best managers. These tasks are also demanding for all but the very largest funds.

Meanwhile, simply insuring liabilities is a very costly approach, as well as being an approach that essentially decimates the pension fund as an organization. There is no more room to formulate and execute a proprietary policy with respect to premiums and investments. Fiduciary Management can, in fact, be regarded as the opposite of this model.

There is now a body of working experience about Fiduciary Management to join with the theoretical principles underpinning the concept in providing convincing evidence that this approach offers significant benefits as a way of organizing the management of pension funds and other large pools of institutional capital.

The organizational clarity and effectiveness that can be achieved using a Fiduciary Manager are shown graphically in Figure 10.1.

Over the course of the last century, pension fund management has moved from complete centralization—all decision making was in the hands of a pension officer at a plan sponsor and his or her bank or insurance company—to sweeping decentralization, in which a pension fund is guided by consultants as well as substantial numbers of external investment managers, none of whom have any obligation or opportunity to think about the broad issues facing the plan. Fiduciary Management provides a middle way, harnessing the expertise that specialists can provide in investment management and other areas with the broad perspective and sense of responsibility that can only be obtained when concern for high-level issues is concentrated in a single office with broad powers as well as responsibilities.

THE CONCEPT'S CLAIMS

After defining the broad pallet of tasks and contributions of the Fiduciary Manager, and comparing this to the results achieved under other forms of governance, the case may seem persuasive–or pretentious.

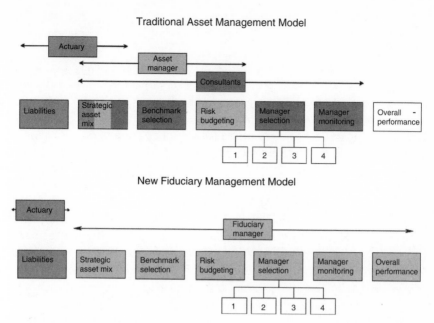

FIGURE 10.1   A Simple Comparison of Traditional and Fiduciary Management

In discussing all the different elements of Fiduciary Management, perhaps it seem as if an ideal world is being described, one which is being compared to real world models that always fall short of the ideal. We have contrasted Fiduciary Management with models in which risk budgets are cut in bits without integration at portfolio level, too few asset categories are considered, managers are engaged whose mandates are not integrated with others, and so on. The Fiduciary Management approach seems to offer improvements in all of these areas.

Whether or not these improvements will be realized however, ultimately depends on the quality of the Fiduciary Management services. A well designed search process must be able to deliver a knowledgeable and able Fiduciary. He has to have shown expertise in all the elements of the advice and construction phase and be able to intertwine this expertise with a well-developed process for the selection of excellent investment managers.

Of course, the ideal of maximizing the use of the calculated risk budget and gaining the highest possible return will never be fully achieved. Uncertainty will always interfere with even the best theoretical constructs. So risk budgets will inevitably be exceeded with a certain regularity or they will be idle in part during certain periods, and returns will disappoint in certain markets. Nonetheless, an investment fund should aspire to approach the ideal as closely as possible by defining a tolerable risk budget, translating it into an investment model and having it executed by the best managers available.

To be sure, these tasks are difficult. Recognition of this complexity has sometimes led to Fiduciary contracts being doled out to two Fiduciary Managers instead of one. The reasoning behind this procedure of employing two Fiduciaries is, in essence, a simple one. When the concept of balanced managers is no good, because one player cannot be the best in all fields, the same should hold for the Fiduciary Manager.

However, if the concept of balanced management is not persuasive because one manager cannot be the best in all areas, the same is true for a Fiduciary Manager. One can argue that a division of labor is almost always possible in the case of fiduciary management, but the allocation of tasks must be done carefully. Portfolio construction, including risk management, and manager selection are two areas of expertise so closely interrelated that a division of labor is hazardous. The division of labor might better be applied to areas such as reporting and performance measurement, where custodians have traditionally been active.

Specialization as such does not harm the Fiduciary concept, but total responsibility for the various services is no longer clear cut when Fiduciaries are combined. When a disappointing investment result is a consequence of investment managers underperforming, for example, the party responsible for manager selection can be held to account. But that may not be feasible when underperformance is a consequence of the relevant risk budget having not been used completely. Questions arise as to who is responsible for this underutilization, who will decide whether or not to do something about it, and when, and who will actually intervene. And how will intervention take place? Will the manager selection process be adapted? Or is the spare risk budget allocated to other assets? Who is taking responsibility for this change? These are the kind of questions which will inevitable occur in the course of managing blame and in most cases these questions cannot be answered unambiguously.

Costs of Fiduciary Management are also important. There is an extra layer of fees imposed compared to the traditional management model, and one must ask if this kind of expensive expertise, talent and experience is affordable, especially for the smaller institutions. Experience shows it is. As has been noted, the portfolio construction process is improved because without Fiduciary Management most pension funds cannot marshal equivalent manpower and models. The same is true in assessing potential asset classes and investment managers.

McKinsey* argues that Fiduciary Management is a solid replacement for internal asset management. For a €100 million pension fund, organizing this Fiduciary setting, according to McKinsey, costs some 50 basis points in terms of assets under management, versus some 10 basis points for funds larger than €5 billion. Then, it is merely a rhetorical question as to whether a small fund can realize relative outperformance of 40 basis points. The fiduciary can gain economies of scale in reducing costs and, can probably realize outperformance in returns. If the sole criterion is cost, McKinsey is positive in assessing the Fiduciary concept as well. McKinsey's starting point is a basic cost level of 10 basis points, which is partly compensated for by internal cost reductions of 5 basis points. Avoiding possible underperformance adds x basis points, but this can never be an argument in favor of Fiduciary Management because an institution can index its investments. Supposing an outperformance of y basis points, a fiduciary contract thus delivers $x + y - 5$ basis points, possibly to be deducted with a performance-related Fiduciary fee, but in that case there is outperformance, which improves the picture. Experience has already shown that this formula implies a positive result.

Last but not least, Fiduciary Management provides advantages in the field of governance. Compared to partial outsourcing, Fiduciary Management delegates tasks more appropriately even as it brings a more simple structure in which there is one party to address risk, return, and quality of reporting. The ultimate responsibility for the entire portfolio is presented to the board in a structured way. In governance, as in other aspects of pension fund management, Fiduciary Management is not the be all and end all, but it offers a better governance model than that which exists at most small and medium-sized institutional investors.

---

*See footnote 2, Chapter 9.

Appendix

Suppliers of Fiduciary Services

This appendix is devoted to an overview of a number of organizations offering Fiduciary Management services. Investment management companies, banks, and institutional investors who are seeking to offer Fiduciary Management services have been asked to provide a short description of what they think are the main ingredients of the product they are offering. It is important to note that *these descriptions are in their own words*. That seemed to be the most equitable way to have their services described. And we are not judging or comparing the various offerings that are described.

While every effort has been made to identify and contact companies offering Fiduciary Management services, the number of companies that supply these services is no doubt greater than the number that is represented here.

The contributors are not categorized, and they are listed in the order in which their reports have been received. This listing is followed by a brief evaluation of some of the different attributes that are mentioned by the various providers.

1. SEI Investments, Amsterdam, Wassenaar, The Netherlands.
2. Kempen Capital Management, Amsterdam, The Netherlands.
3. ING Investment Management, The Hague, The Netherlands.
4. AXA Investment Managers, Schiphol Airport, The Netherlands.
5. Goldman Sachs Asset Management, New York, USA.
6. Merrill Lynch Investment Managers, Amsterdam, The Netherlands.
7. Aegon Nederland N.V., The Hague, The Netherlands.
8. Altis Investment Management AG, Zug, Switzerland.
9. Mn Services, Rijswijk, The Netherlands.
10. Schroder Investment Management Ltd., London, England.
11. Interpolis Pensioenen Vermogensbeheer, De Meern, The Netherlands.
12. Blue Sky Group, Amstelveen, The Netherlands.
13. AZL Group, Heerlen, The Netherlands.
14. Lombard Odier Darier Hentsch & Cie, Amsterdam, The Netherlands.
15. ABN Amro Asset Management, Amsterdam, The Netherlands.

16. State Street Global Advisors, Boston, USA.
17. Cordares, Amsterdam, The Netherlands.
18. Fidelity, Amsterdam, The Netherlands.
19. SPF, Utrecht, The Netherlands.
20. Fortis Investments, Utrecht, The Netherlands.
21. Credit Suisse. London, England.

Fiduciary Management at SEI

The first point to be made about the term "Fiduciary Management" in the Dutch market is to say that the fiduciary concept is primarily an Anglo-Saxon one that does not explicitly exist in the Netherlands as there is no trust law as such. Therefore the term is not strictly applicable to the Dutch market, although of course the notion of entrusting the administration and management of your assets to a third party is easy enough to understand.

SEI presents itself is as a provider of outsourcing business solutions for investment processing and asset management. Another way of looking at it is that it allows you to hand over day-to-day management, while retaining ultimate control. It's perhaps better to think of it in terms of allowing pension fund executives to focus on the key elements of their jobs by allowing some of the technical aspects to be outsourced in a relationship of trust and confidence.

SEI's approach is to offer responsibility for asset allocation, risk management and budgeting, portfolio construction, manager selection, and monitoring and reporting. Other features could include strategic advice with respect to Asset and Liability Modeling, the effects on the sponsor's finances of asset allocation decisions in the pension fund, and the adherence to the new FTK rules.

As in any outsourcing relationship, there are a number of potential pitfalls that any client must take into consideration. These include the structure of the Fiduciary Manager and the degree to which its owners are truly committed to the business. Clients need to consider the independence and objectivity of their outsourcing partner. They need also to take into account the credibility of the manager-of-managers process. Along with confirming viability of a stated track record, questions here should include: What are the firm's committed resources? What is the quality of both the research and portfolio construction processes? Think about what skills and experience the manager really brings to the table—for example, how many managers do they review? What is their goal in combining multiple managers—that is, alpha generation or risk control?

Maybe what is most important to consider, as an outsourcing partner, is whether this is a core business. Finding a partner that will continue to be around and who will reinvest to maintain and improve his services can make all the difference in the long term. Another point to ponder is strategic advice. This is important because outsourcing risks loss of in-house expertise. It is unwise to outsource strategic decisions, unless your outsourcing partner will give the client access to the latest thinking and can transfer expertise to the client. Finally the client needs to consider the extra layer of costs that the asset manager will bring. It should be noted, however, that with a large enough outsourcing partner, the economies of scale can claw back some of these extra costs through cheaper arrangements with underlying managers and additional services being included.

All this takes on extra relevance at the current time due to the forthcoming implementation of the FTK (Financieel Toetsings Kader, the Dutch regulatory framework), a seismic shock to the market. This is a trigger event that will make life a lot harder for pension funds. Alongside this are new corporate governance issues and new international financial reporting standards. The FTK will introduce a new way of measuring liabilities and a more onerous stress test—as well as minimum funding requirements.

Amid all this, pension executives will want to focus on strategic human resources issues and indexation matters—especially at relatively smaller schemes that don't necessarily have the firepower of the giant Dutch plans. Such people may well find it absolutely prudent to delegate what for them are the more operational and less relevant tasks.

So, in summary, there's a lot to think about. But there's a lot to be gained if you take your time and choose correctly.

Bart Heenk
SEI Investments (Europe) Ltd
Amsterdam, The Netherlands.

Fiduciary Management at Kempen Capital Management*

The fiduciary approach of KCM is based on the following fiduciary beliefs:

- Fiduciary Management is a state of mind and not an investment product. At KCM each client is assigned a dedicated team of Fiduciary Managers

---

*Kempen Capital Management (KCM) is a Dutch Fiduciary Manager based in Amsterdam. It is certain that Fiduciary Management is the most effective way for institutions to obtain their financial goals and to ensure appropriate governance.

acting as the client's personal investment staff. The team speaks the language of the client and has experience in all aspects of investment management.

- Clients are always in the driver's seat. The Fiduciary Manager supports the client in a broad range of activities, but will not and cannot take over the fiduciary responsibility of the client.

- Clients, external advisors (like actuaries and investment consultants), and the Fiduciary Manager can only be successful if they work in close cooperation.

- The interests of the Fiduciary Manager have to be completely in line with the client. This is expressed financially in the management fee arrangements.

- An ever-changing and more complex world makes a dynamic approach to asset allocation absolutely necessary. Static strategic asset allocation is inefficient.

- The ultimate target is to create (absolute) returns versus the liabilities of the institution. Relative investing in comparison with a market benchmark is only relevant if this benchmark meets the primary goals of the client.

- Selecting best of breed managers adds value for the client. When selecting active managers, KCM focuses on return-driven managers that have an outspoken investment style and are aligned with the investor. The approach will be less benchmark-driven and will not be aiming at asset gathering.

- Investment policies and risks have to be structured and evaluated in an integral way. Optimization of portfolios within an asset category or on a regional basis is often sub-optimal and leads to overdiversification and high, unnecessary risks and costs.

The core business of Fiduciary Management is being an effective, strategic partner for the institutional investor in all aspects of investment management. From the broad range of fiduciary services that KCM offers, the allocation process, illustrated by Figure A.1, will be discussed in further detail. The starting point is the analysis of the financial objectives of the institution. These can be translated into a model portfolio (minimum risk portfolio) that matches the pattern of the nominal liabilities plus the extra return goal of the fund (e.g., for indexation). This will serve as the benchmark for the Fiduciary Manager. Given the overall risk constraints of the client, the investment portfolio is split into two main building blocks: the matching portfolio and the return portfolio.

The matching portfolio aims to reduce the interest rate and/or inflation mismatch risk to acceptable levels. The return portfolio consists of low

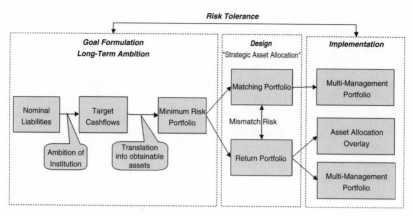

FIGURE A.1 Allocation Process

correlated assets delivering an attractive extra return. In order to realize this, a multimanager structure is implemented to cover various investment categories and investment styles. The construction will be integrally optimized in accordance with the institution's objectives and within the risk tolerance (risk budget). It may contain both non-benchmark driven and benchmark-driven/passive managers.

The ever-changing economic environment implies that the long-term asset allocation policy will not always be optimal and that opportunities for extra return will arise. To benefit from investment opportunities and to use the investment risk budget efficiently at all times, medium- and short-term asset allocation strategies are implemented as well. Medium-term allocation is valuable, but often neglected. It is driven by valuation and momentum and enables the institution to dynamically allocate around the strategic allocation in the medium term. By choosing an overlay implementation one avoids expensive trading of (physical) securities.

To summarize, KCM distinguishes itself from other Fiduciary Managers by (i) dedication—not a product but a culture, in line with the client, (ii) experience—multidisciplinary team of fiduciary pioneers in the Netherlands, (iii) dynamic strategic allocation—dealing with the non-stationary world, (iv) integral approach—liability driven, avoiding sub-optimisation, and (v) management—return driven multimanagement approach.

Jan Bertus Molenkamp, Hans Rademaker
Kempen Capital Management
Amsterdam, The Netherlands.

Fiduciary Management at ING Investment Management

Although a household name in asset management, ING Investment Management is not immediately identified with fiduciary asset management. Yet, we have long offered this service to several of our largest Dutch clients, both pension funds and insurance companies. Our combined asset management and insurance background and many years of expertise in liability-driven asset management, account for a balanced focus on both risk and return. It is this experience and liability-driven approach that distinguishes us from many other managers.

BEYOND FIDUCIARY MANAGEMENT

The strategic services provided by ING Investment Management go beyond traditional asset management or multimanagement. We focus on efficient management of the client's total balance sheet, taking the pension fund's liabilities as the starting point. We offer pension funds a "modular" package of solutions to the difficulties they face, on the basis of their specific needs and situations. We ensure that the investment portfolio always has the optimum structure, taking into account the risks that the client is willing and able to run with respect to his liabilities and the applicable laws and legislation.

FOCUS ON CLIENTS' SPECIFIC SITUATION

The ultimate goal of our strategic service is an investment portfolio that is tailor-made to the client's specific situation and liability structure. Using the analysis of the pension fund's assets and liabilities, the optimum portfolio is constructed in a series of steps. We apply regular checks to ensure that this portfolio continues to match the client's specific situation. If this is not the case, the optimum portfolio is reconstructed and implemented accordingly.

Our *modus operandi* focuses on enabling clients to take informed decisions on their investment portfolio. This requires close consultation, whereby we ensure that clients possess the required expertise and information in order to make sound decisions.

FIGURE A.2 Areas of Expertise

COMPLETE STRATEGIC SERVICE LEADS TO TAILOR MADE SOLUTION

Our strategic service comprises four different areas of expertise (shown in Figure A.2):

1. Strategic Investment Policy Advice
2. Total Asset Management
3. Organizational Support
4. Client Servicing

STRATEGIC INVESTMENT POLICY ADVICE

The basic principle for our strategic investment policy advice is a detailed Asset Liability Management (ALM) analysis or continuity analysis. This analysis forms part of our proprietary Strategic Asset Allocation (SAA) process. Together with the client, we follow the various steps of the process, which results in a complete investment portfolio with optimum portfolio allocation for the client.

When conducting ALM studies, we work closely with experienced actuarial firms. We supervise the execution of the whole study and provide important input, such as views on different macroeconomic indicators. This analysis results in advice on the optimum portfolio allocation across the investment categories: bonds, equity, real estate, and absolute return products. See Figure A.3.

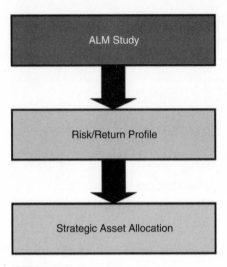

FIGURE A.3   From ALM to Strategy

ALM Scan Enables Interim Alterations

An extensive ALM study is usually conducted every three or five years. In practice, however, interim alterations are often needed. We provide a solution for this: *the ALM scan*. This is a shorter version of an ALM study and can be conducted more frequently. The long-term ALM study is thus periodically complemented by an update. The ALM scan includes all the latest developments on the part of the pension fund and takes into account changes to the capital markets' risk/return characteristics.

ALM Study Results in Portfolio Composition

The ALM study or scan, the distinguishing factor, results in an allocation across the different investment categories. By further diversification within these categories, we can reduce the portfolio risk even more. Using our SAA model we advise on the opportunities for further optimizing the investment portfolio. In doing so, we take into account specific wishes with respect to, for example, transparency or liquidity.

TOTAL ASSET MANAGEMENT

Once the correct positioning has been established, we advise on the composition of the investment portfolio. This means that we select those investment products that best match the optimum positioning determined earlier.

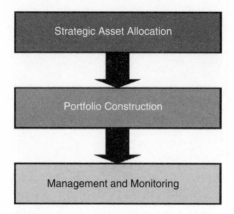

FIGURE A.4 Total Asset Management

We make this selection from our own extensive ING product range, a mix between ING and other managers, or build a multimanager portfolio from investment products offered by other asset managers. The final portfolio will therefore contain a combination of various investment products. Skilled portfolio management and monitoring ensure that the portfolio contains the correct combination of investment products at all times and that this combination is managed actively and efficiently. See Figure A.4.

ORGANIZATIONAL SUPPORT

With regard to organizational issues, we offer clients support in a number of different areas, such as dealing with operational issues or providing support at pension board meetings. The major benefit for clients is that they can focus more clearly on their strategic objectives and their responsibilities as director or manager of a pension fund.

CLIENT SERVICING

In the case of client servicing, the mainstay of our policy is that a client of ING Investment Management has one central point of contact: the relation management team. For the client, this team is the portal to our organization. Specific tasks of the relation management team include visiting clients to discuss the portfolio and reporting on the development of the portfolio.

ING COMMITTED TO FIDUCIARY MANAGEMENT

Our commitment to Fiduciary Management is illustrated by the fact that we have formed a completely new department that will focus especially on strategic fiduciary services. This department consists of several teams and has an independent position within our organization. See Figure A.5.

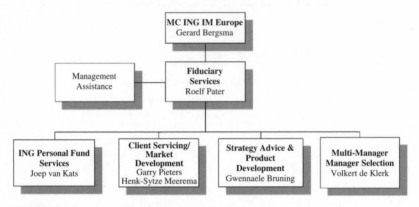

FIGURE A.5 Department of Fiduciary Management

Our strategic service provides a made-to-measure investment solution. From asset liability management to portfolio construction to manager selection; we carefully construct the optimum investment portfolio in several clear and logical steps. We do this together with the client and take into account the client's total balance sheet. We have, through the nature of our business as a bank, insurer, and asset manager, the necessary expertise on all the different areas at our disposal.

Garry Pieters
ING Investment Management
The Hague, The Netherlands.

Fiduciary Management at AXA Investment Managers

Fiduciary Management can mean a lot of different things to a lot of different people. As a consequence, what is probably the most important thing when entering into a fiduciary relationship is a full and deep understanding of the services that will be provided and where the responsibility begins and ends for all the parties involved. Communication is absolutely key from the beginning of a fiduciary relationship.

For us, as a Fiduciary Manager, the challenge is to integrate all the different (internal and external) expertises and services into one solution that exactly fits the needs of our fiduciary partner. In order to build an efficient solution we have organized ourselves in a simple and efficient way, with one team within being responsible for the overall solution, our Pensions group, part of our Investment Solutions Division. It's like a plug and play exercise where the Pensions group draws on the different expertises within and outside AXA IM to maximize the outcome for our partner. The most commonly used and simplified structure looks like the one shown in Figure A.6.

The organization described above has the following features:

- There is a clear communication line with the partner on the overall solution and a single point of entry for the partner: the Pensions group/Investment Solutions.
- There is a dedicated structure for manager selection: AXA Multimanager.
- Financial Engineering provides advice on the strategic asset allocation based on the liabilities profile of the partner.
- The LDS team manages the liability risks on the overall portfolio (e.g., interest and or inflation risks).

With our insurance background we understand the challenges of institutions trying to meet and outperform their long-term liabilities while having to take into account the regulatory and accounting constraints that often are in conflict with those long-term goals. Our solutions are built around

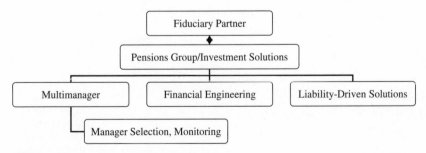

FIGURE A.6 Simplified fiduciary structure

those same principles, protecting solvency, reducing volatility and maximizing returns in the long run. Our people speak the same language as our partner's actuaries and advisors. Here is a quick introduction to our different teams.

AXA MULTIMANAGER

AXA Multimanager is a dedicated entity within AXA Investment Managers. The team has been working since 2000 in setting up a focused and dedicated multimanager approach for our clients. It can deliver a full range of multimanager solutions either solely external or in combination with AXA IM Investment Expertises. (See Figure A.7.)

AXA Multimanager has a rigorous process in selecting, monitoring (managers and risk budgets), and controlling on an overall level our partners' externalized portfolio. This includes GTAA & Currency overlays if applicable.

FINANCIAL ENGINEERING

With our insurance background we have developed our own internal financial engineering system called S.M.A.R.T. This tool helps us and our partners to create a well diversified and risk optimized portfolio for the long term, taking into account the client's specifics but also, for instance, costs of diversification or relevance of the diversification. (See Figure A.8.)

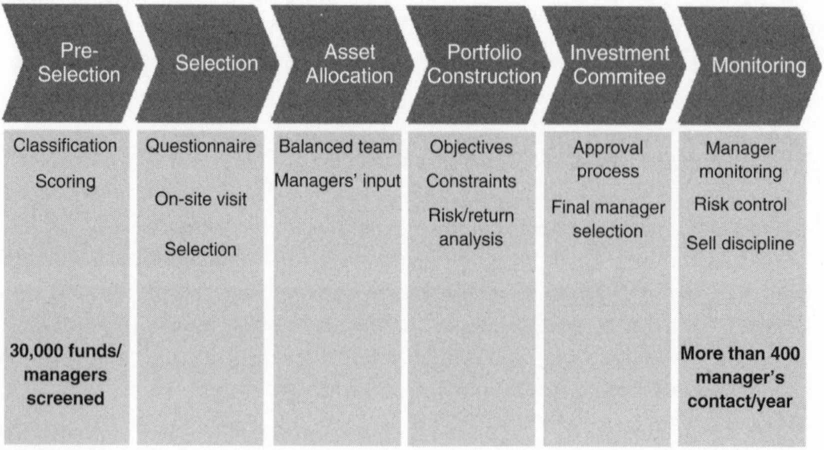

Pre-Selection	Selection	Asset Allocation	Portfolio Construction	Investment Commitee	Monitoring
Classification	Questionnaire	Balanced team	Objectives	Approval process	Manager monitoring
Scoring	On-site visit	Managers' input	Constraints	Final manager selection	Risk control
	Selection		Risk/return analysis		Sell discipline
30,000 funds/ managers screened					More than 400 manager's contact/year

FIGURE A.7 Multimanager process

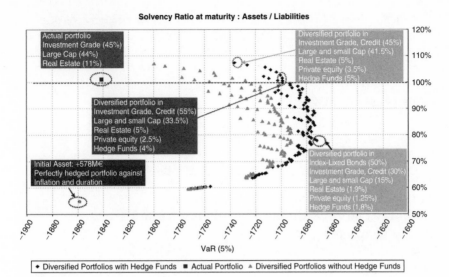

FIGURE A.8   Optimizing portfolios

LIABILITY DRIVEN SOLUTIONS

Within this team we manage the overall interest rate risk of the assets versus the liabilities. Currently this team manages around €23 billion in assets. With our independence from investment banks we can offer our clients a full service, multicounterparty solution and full transparency of costs. The team takes care of ISDA, CSA negotiations, monitors the efficiency of the overlay, and adjusts if needed. Our middle office takes care of collateral management. Clients can opt for a bespoke overlay or an efficient investment in our Pooled LDI Vehicle: AXA IM Horizon Funds.

PENSION GROUP/INVESTMENT SOLUTIONS

These teams are responsible for the overall solution, attributing risk to the other teams (tracking error versus the liabilities), integrating the input from the different teams and managing the relationship with the fiduciary partner. The team can implement its own TAA capabilities or do so through AXA Multimanager. It is a highly experienced team that can draw on all other internal resources within AXA IM that are relevant for the mandate.

Fiduciary Management is one of the most exciting and challenging developments in recent years. It benefits us as a company as we grow with our clients to build better solutions and a more in-depth relationship and on the other hand benefits our partners who can leverage our in-house knowledge and weight. For the relatively smaller institutions it is an efficient way to stay independent and on the other hand have all the necessary tools of a big house in hand to maximize the risk-return trade off. This is how we are organized ourselves.

Stefan Baecke
AXA Investment Managers
Amsterdam

Fiduciary Management at Goldman Sachs Asset Management

Fiduciary Management involves outsourcing the design, implementation, and oversight of a pension fund's investment program to one provider, the Fiduciary Manager. The relationship between the sponsor company and the Fiduciary Manager functions as a partnership: both parties work side by side to address the needs of the pension fund.

The role of the Fiduciary Manager is based on five central components:

- Strategic investment advice
- Portfolio construction
- Selection of external portfolio managers
- Investment performance monitoring
- Customized and consolidated reporting

There are a number of complex issues in running a pension fund. Each client has a unique liability profile, with varying funding and cash flow needs. The flexibility inherent to the fiduciary-managed approach allows for a more integrated program, which in turn can better help target the unique needs of each client. Specifically, there are efficiencies to be gained from (1) an *improved risk and return profile* achieved from planning the most efficient use of assets at the total fund level; (2) *time savings* on the part of the pension fund, since there is only one point of contact and one set of consolidated reports; and (3) *flexibility* to change the structure of the fund in step with changes to liabilities or market conditions.

Consequently, the partnership with a Fiduciary Manager allows pension funds to focus on the high-level strategic objectives, leaving the Fiduciary Manager in charge of the actual implementation of the investment strategy.

FIDUCIARY MANAGEMENT PROCESS

First, the Fiduciary Manager's responsibilities begin with providing strategic investment advice to the pension board, usually incorporating data from the Pension Board's actuary and consultant. For the most part, this investment advice focuses on reviewing the strategic asset allocation and asset liability modeling to ensure that it is consistent with the overall plan.

Second, a key responsibility of the Fiduciary Manager is to design an Active Risk Budget that will determine how the active management returns are expected to be generated to meet the long-term investment objectives of the pension fund. The risk budget is designed within the context of the pension fund's liability profile, asset allocation, and risk tolerance. The aim is to take the most risk in the asset classes and sub-asset classes where you are the most rewarded for taking that risk—in other words, where you can find the most skilled managers with the best quality information ratios.

Third, the practical part of portfolio construction is the selection of external managers. The Fiduciary Manager must conduct extensive manager research and due diligence to identify suitable/appropriate investment managers for the underlying portfolios. The Fiduciary Manager constructs portfolios of managers, negotiates fee agreements and legal contracts, and executes these on behalf of the pension fund.

The fourth part of the process is the investment performance and risk monitoring. Risk and performance are monitored at the underlying portfolio level and also at the total fund level. State of the art Fiduciary Managers use several different real-time attribution systems in order to maintain the integrity of the risk management process, which ranges from viewing the manager's most recent buys and sells in the portfolio to monitoring the manager's adherence to investment guidelines.

Lastly, the Fiduciary Manager collects all reports from underlying investments and consolidates these to meet the agreed-upon specifications. The goal is to provide accurate, timely, and relevant high-level reporting and presentations to the board of the pension fund.

ACCRUING BENEFITS OF FIDUCIARY MANAGEMENT

One significant advantage of appointing a Fiduciary Manager is measurable accountability: one party is involved in the complete range of investments; one party is unambiguously assigned responsibility; and there is one point of contact for all aspects in managing the investments of the pension fund. The right Fiduciary Manager will have the capability to recognize what the client requires and has the solutions for the complex issues facing modern investment management.

The key to hiring a credible Fiduciary Manager is to select an organization with the expertise and in-depth, practitioner's knowledge of all aspects of investment management—from strategic asset allocation, risk budgeting, and active alpha generation, to successful external manager selection and sophisticated risk-monitoring capabilities.

Ruud Hendriks
Goldman Sachs & Co
London, England/New York, USA

Fiduciary Management at Merrill Lynch Investment Managers

PHILOSOPHY

Definitions of Fiduciary Management differ widely within the marketplace. At Merrill Lynch Investment Managers (MLIM), Fiduciary Management means a flexible partnership whereby it takes

1. Full responsibility for the day-to-day management
2. Acts as trusted adviser for strategic decisions
3. Takes responsibility for overall performance of the scheme, including selection and monitoring of external managers

We focus on improving performance by eliminating managers' distraction by allowing trustees and sponsors to delegate all nonessential tasks. At the same time, MLIM explicitly recognises the higher cost associated with Fiduciary Management and its implications for performance. It counteracts the potential drag on performance by using external managers in a cost-effective manner and applying the cost discipline of a single transparent annual management fee. MLIM's pragmatic philosophy also entails that the usefulness of a fiduciary approach is judged on a case-by-case basis against the following key criteria:

- Time and cost efficiency gains
- Improved performance
- More focused and professional asset allocation
- Better risk controls
- Greater transparency and accountability
- More educated and knowledgeable trustees

An initial cost-benefits analysis should ensure that these benefits outweigh the additional costs. If not, MLIM would suggest alternative and less comprehensive forms of portfolio management.

PRACTICE

Trustees are able to delegate virtually all tasks and responsibilities to MLIM. This includes dealing with administrative, compliance, legal and custody issues, and so forth. Under MLIM's fiduciary model, they remain, however, solely responsible for deciding strategic asset allocation and observing their statutory trust management duties.

Once the investment objective is set, MLIM takes responsibility for the overall portfolio performance. This facilitates selection of the most appropriate manager and a more efficient use of dynamic tactical asset allocation.

Reducing management and trustees' distraction improves performance. However, to avoid the resulting performance gain being undermined by the higher costs associated with Fiduciary Management MLIM applies various cost-reduction measures:

- *Single Fee*. This imposes a strong cost discipline on its fiduciary process.
- *Judicious Manager Selection*. MLIM seeks best-of-breed performance, but will only source externally via its dedicated multimanager research platform if the additional cost can be offset by higher performance.

Equally for subsequent manager changes, MLIM takes into account the considerable costs in terms of transition management fees and managers' distraction.

- *Cost-Efficient Portfolio Construction*. Sources of alpha and beta are separated so that only expertise in alpha generation is bought, with sources of beta being managed passively or via an overlay construction.
- *Economies of Scale*. MLIM can deliver considerable economies of scale via its global platforms and the use of fiduciary building blocks.
- *Other Cost-minimizing Measures*. These include the use of currency and other overlay techniques, securities lending, and cash management.

While it remains the responsibility of trustees to take the strategic asset allocation decisions, MLIM's independent Strategic Advice and Strategic Investment Groups can help trustees gain a better understanding of their requirements (including their liability profile and risk appetite) in terms of overall investment strategy and risk budget.

In MLIM's view, comprehensive and continuous risk management is an important component of Fiduciary Management. MLIM can rely on its independent Risk and Quantitative Analysis Team for the monitoring of both internal and external investment managers.

Ensuring good and swift communication with trustees and scheme sponsors via dedicated local staff is another key ingredient of MLIM's fiduciary partnership. This includes providing a single and customized reporting feed. In addition, MLIM believes that using a single clean fee enhances transparency and accountability as it puts the onus on MLIM to provide the best costs-benefits solution.

For MLIM, educating and advising trustees is another essential fiduciary task. As well as organizing seminars and writing educational material, MLIM considers its ability to act as trusted adviser particularly relevant in the regulatory area where MLIM can assist clients with new developments.

In summary, key reasons why clients choose MLIM as Fiduciary Manager are

- Ability to offer a comprehensive Fiduciary Management partnership and a wide range of LDI and non-LDI products for a single annual management fee
- Focus on cost-effectiveness—through efficient use of open architecture, economies of scale, and judicious portfolio construction that ensures only expertise in generating alpha is being bought
- Strategic commitment to the local market (including sizeable local resources and expertise)
- Track record in multimanagement both domestically and internationally

■ Global resources including strong in-house strategic advice and tactical asset allocation capabilities

Leen Meijaard
Merrill Lynch Investment Managers
Amsterdam, The Netherlands.

Fiduciary Management at Aegon

How does AEGON communicate the concept of Fiduciary Management as a new trend? Simply by doing what the company has been doing for many years: by offering institutional investors a comprehensive concept for all value-adding components relating to asset management. AEGON offers this service via its 100 percent subsidiary TKP Investments, an organization that has its roots in the Dutch pension world and that has provided full-service support for well over 15 years. Currently TKP Investments manages more than €9 billion for a number of Dutch pension funds. Needless to say, this requires a strong relationship based on trust.

STRATEGIC ADVICE

Fiduciary Management starts with a comprehensive asset-liability management study to map the pension fund's risk environment. In doing so, the fund's strategic starting points, the development of its commitments, scenarios for macroeconomic trends, and the resulting choices made within the investment classes are taken into account.

Asset Management According to the Multimanagement Principle

TKP Investments distinguishes itself on two points from most of the other providers of Fiduciary Management. First, we have opted for asset management via investment funds in which clients can place their fixed-interest, equity and alternative investments. The management of the resources placed with these funds is subsequently outsourced to several specialist asset managers according to the multimanagement principle. Combining the respective qualities of these excellent managers, who each have their own style, will result in a greater chance of consistent outperformance in each phase of the investment cycle. The combination of asset management via investment funds and multimanagement makes for an efficient and optimal form of Fiduciary Management.

Selection and Monitoring of External Managers

The selection process developed by TKP Investments is very intensive and aimed at selecting the very best managers per (sub) asset class. Important criteria are the investment philosophy used (Is it comprehensible?), the investment process (How do investment decisions come about?), staff and organizational structure (Is the organization sufficiently robust, and how are people kept motivated?), performance (Is the performance achieved consistently?) and diversification (To what extent does the manager we select add value to the portfolio, and is the risk of the total portfolio reduced?). The performance of the managers we select is monitored intensively and on an ongoing basis through portfolio information, market information, company information, attribution analyses, and risk and return criteria.

Value for Money

The management fees on the investment funds are relatively low because, due to the volume of the mandates to be placed, TKP Investments has a favorable negotiating position and we pass on the pricing benefits we achieves to our clients. Also, a performance-related fee has been agreed with all the external managers, guaranteeing the external manager's maximum efforts. The investment funds, incidentally, also apply a performance-related fee, as a result of which all parties involved have parallel interests.

RISK MANAGEMENT

Risk management is of crucial importance to Fiduciary Management. If irregularities are not noticed, or noticed too late, the relationship based on trust between the pension fund and the executor can be seriously impaired. For TKP Investments this may have adverse effects on the client level, the level of investment funds, and the manager level. Per external manager *ex ante* tracking errors are recorded, which are very frequently tested against the *ex post* figures realized. Agreed-upon restrictions are analysed on a daily basis by the external administrator, the custodian, and TKP Investments' investment administration.

REPORTING

Written reports of the results achieved are made on a monthly, quarterly, and yearly basis. These reports present the performance figures in a uniform way that allows comparison in accordance with the GIPS standard. In addition, a performance audit ensures that the performance figures presented are correct. The Fiduciary Manager's tasks also comprise the periodic reports to the regulator. The account manager ensures that the relationship based on trust between the pension fund and the executor is maintained via proper communication and a sound provision of information.

THE BENEFITS OF FIDUCIARY MANAGEMENT

Fiduciary Management comprises the outsourcing of all asset management activities of a pension fund. This requires extensive knowledge and expertise in many areas. Only in this way can the vital relationship of trust be built up with the client. TKP Investments has its roots in the pension fund world, has extensive experience in all relevant areas, and meets the quality standards of many independent organizations that have thoroughly tested the processes, systems, and procedures. With the proposition of TKP Investments, AEGON offers an efficient form of Fiduciary Management in particular to middle-sized pension funds. They can benefit from the skills of an experienced executor with extensive knowledge of the Dutch pension funds issues, and from the qualities of the best asset managers in the world, at low cost.

Frans van der Horst
Aegon Nederland N.V.
The Hague, The Netherlands

Fiduciary Management at Altis

Fiduciary Management defined as "CIO Support."

COMPANY BACKGROUND

With the emergence of more and more specialist investment expertise, the fiduciary multiasset, multimanager concept has become increasingly popular. However, its actual implementation is not that simple. At Morgan Stanley, the Altis team was a pioneer of the concept, with one of the longest track records in the European industry. Between 1996 and 2004, the team developed an investment process that focuses particularly on the quality of implementation—in other words, on risk management and manager research. The necessity for a fiduciary to be independent in its manager selection subsequently led to the start of Altis Investment Management in

2004. The company is based in Zug, Switzerland, with offices in Amsterdam and London.

A crucial step in the company's evolution was the realisation that its added value—making multiasset portfolios perform more consistently—does not come from any hard-to-define intuition or gut feeling. Rather, it stems from disciplining asset allocation and manager selection, enabled by solid systems and in-depth analysis.

INSOURCING OR OUTSOURCING?

The definition of Fiduciary Management has become very broad indeed. In contrast, Altis defines a very narrow role for itself. It acts as a specialist that is *insourced* to support the investment process of its clients—rather than as an asset manager to whom the entire investment process is *outsourced*. As opposed to gut feeling, systems and analysis lend themselves well to the insourcing option.

TWO CHALLENGES IN MULTIASSET, LIABILITY-DRIVEN PORTFOLIOS

Increasingly complex investment markets mean allocating to a far wider range of assets than before, integrating external managers and specialised products. Liability-driven strategies typically add another layer of complexity through the use of derivatives and complex instruments. As a consequence of all this, institutional investors need to add resources and expertise in two areas:

- Manager research
- Multiasset portfolio construction and risk management

The fiduciary concept is a logical answer to both of these points. There is a need for arm's length impartiality in manager selection, and it requires significant resources to build the expertise. Doing so in-house may not be the right answer, nor is a conventional asset manager the logical partner.

FIDUCIARY MANAGEMENT AS CIO SUPPORT

The question for institutional investors still remains: Does all this necessarily mean outsourcing of the complete portfolio to a Fiduciary Manager, or is there a more cooperative alternative? Insourcing specialist fiduciary *services* while keeping performance responsibility in-house may be an attractive option, depending on the institutional investor's own situation and ambition. Altis aims to fulfil that role.

Manager selection and portfolio construction are the core problems in any fiduciary portfolio. There is clear evidence that if a multiasset strategy is not carefully constructed, it can actually add more to volatility than to performance—which has proven to be a very real problem in practice. The reason is that in a multiasset portfolio, selection bias can impact the asset allocation severely. There is always the risk to invest more in past performance than in sustainable alpha skills. Selecting managers with good track records tends to create an asset allocation bias to whatever market factors have had strong momentum in recent years. This makes multiasset/multimanager portfolios very vulnerable to changes in market climate. Good examples were the stubbornly maintained growth exposure of many multimanager portfolios in 2000–2001, and more recently in 2006, the often dramatic overweight of small caps, a by-product of selecting managers with good track records after years in which small caps had performed well (see Figure A.9).

Altis believes that the solution to the combined problem of manager selection and portfolio construction should be found in process, data, and

FIGURE A.9 Weight of Technology Stocks in Portfolio

analytics—not in subjective judgment alone. The interesting thing is that these more technical aspects lend themselves well to insourcing into a client's existing investment process.

TECHNICAL SKILLS: THE ABILITY TO ANALYZE

Performance attribution on historical holdings is the obvious tool to separate past performance luck from sustainable alpha skills. Across the industry, this holdings-based research is a poorly developed manager selection instrument. Altis has built a data center that holds the full holdings history of a universe of hundreds of competing managers in which its clients may be invested or interested.

Building such a data center is not something that belongs to the core business of an institutional investor—yet it is an essential element in his manager selection process. This is the first component that clients can insource into their investment process using Altis: manager selection based on long-term performance attribution, separating sustainable skills from other factors in a manager's past performance.

The second component is portfolio construction—controling the aggregated exposures of multiasset portfolios. It is hard to see the aggregated exposures of a portfolio that is a mix of passive vehicles, active separate accounts, funds, and derivatives. Again, the answer is essentially a technical one. Altis maintains a monthly risk management system at the client's office, enabling a *see through* across all investments into the underlying, aggregated asset allocation exposures and risk factors. Crucially, it allows what-if studies to see how the addition of a manager, a swaption, or any other investment vehicle, impacts the portfolio's information ratio, its VaR and its surplus-at-risk.

The top of Figure A.10 shows holdings-based research that reveals how a manager made his track record. The bottom of the figure shows the aggregated risk management is a basic requirement for managing complex portfolios. Sharing such systems with clients is a basic part of Altis' services.

EXPERTISE: THE ABILITY TO DRAW CONCLUSIONS FROM ANALYSIS

A cooperative involvement with a client's portfolio carries one significant disadvantage compared to discretionary fiduciary solutions. Manager selection and portfolio construction recommendations tend to lose their relevance if the advisor is too far removed from the portfolio.

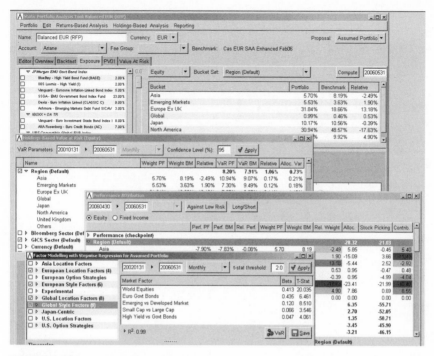

FIGURE A.10   Holdings-Based Research for Manager Tracking

Over the past ten years, the team at Altis has developed a work process that combines the level of involvement that a discretionary manager has, with the cooperative approach of CIO support. The monthly updated risk management system ensures a good macro view of what is happening in the underlying asset allocation of the portfolio. This tool allows a practical, hands-on asset allocation and manager selection discussion on the topics that arise from the portfolio analysis. And that is how effective integration of a fiduciary support specialist into an existing investment process is made possible.

SUMMARY

Altis believes that a cooperative approach to Fiduciary Management can be a very attractive option for institutional investors. It keeps performance responsibility under control of the CIO and reinforces the investment process where it is needed. A sophisticated analytical infrastructure, and a hands-on work process are the essential ingredients in this form of fiduciary service.

Oscar Vermeulen
Altis Investment Management AG
Zug, Switzerland.

Fiduciary Management at Mn Services

Forgoing an attempt to place the phenomenon of the Fiduciary Management product in its proper historical perspective, one cannot really fully avoid reflecting on its coming to be for a moment. Within an environment of high interest rates and an actuarial rate of return of 4 percent virtually anyone could run a pension fund. Circumstances have changed, and sustaining a 100 percent coverage ratio in the light of future solvency requirements has become a lot more complicated. Not so long ago, pension funds were the financiers of the state. ABP, the largest pension fund in the Netherlands, would gobble up about 40 percent of the total of the government bond issues in any given year.

This picture looks completely different now. Until the early 1990s, the Dutch state pension funds could only invest a very limited percentage of their holdings outside of their own borders and were almost completely obliged to resort to the domestic financial markets. In this context, the pension fund for Metalworking and Mechanical Engineering (predecessor of Mn Services), which was not bound by these limitations, was one of the first large pension funds to make its move towards diversification, using a flexible multimanager approach. This philosophy, which the pension fund used for its own investments, has been maintained unimpaired after the formal split off of its servicing organization in 2001. Mn Services was created with the pension fund for Metalworking and Mechanical Engineering as its sole shareholder. Building on the concept that had already been developed within the pension fund, Mn Services started offering its wide area of products and services, to third parties including pension funds outside the metal industry sector.

In Mn Services' view, Fiduciary Management is a Total Concept. It does not suffice anymore to do a proper analysis of the asset side of the balance. The liabilities side has become equally important if one wants to make a proper judgment on how a strategic asset mix should be composed. After the analytical phase, the most appropriate strategic asset mix will be established, based on the specific situation of the pension fund in question.

It should be clear that during this phase thoughts about the desired risk profile will be taken into account. Normally after the formal acceptance of the proposed asset mix by the investment committee and the board of the pension fund, the investment teams will then start executing the proper construction of the portfolios. Transitions are always executed in a multidisciplinary task force environment to make sure that market exposure is maintained, while keeping costs under control.

The Fiduciary Manager has to be a flexible multimanager in many respects, not just multiasset but also within an asset class multimanager and even multistyle. The Fiduciary Manager also has a choice, to either offer a service based on full internal management, full external management, or a combination of both. Advantages of internal management, be it full or in part, are as follows: a better feeling with markets and the ability to execute the selection process from a deeply rooted experience and knowledge of the market itself. Examples of some of the advantages of external management are independence and flexibility. The often-mentioned argument of a deemed conflict of interest when executing asset classes in-house is not in all cases a valid one. By submitting the internal asset managers to the same stringent demands that count for external managers, most of this criticism can be silenced. By scrutinising asset managers on criteria-like performance, long-term track record, style drift, and so forth, virtually the same independence can be achieved. In case of lagging returns that last for several reporting periods, the organization will have to demonstrate that claims of treating all managers according to the same criteria are being substantiated by replacing underperforming asset managers. In the past this situation has occurred at Mn Services, and appropriate steps have been taken.

The last steps in the process are administration, reporting (legal, client), monitoring (risk control) and, crucial, the constant interaction with the pension fund itself. Key words in this part of the process are *transparency, best-of-class execution, quality of servicing*, and *separation of duties*.

This concept of Fiduciary Management is supported by the structure of the investment management organization of Mn Services, which is based on the following structure:

- relationship management and strategy
- asset management
- administration and reporting

Essential is the role of the relationship manager, not only the normal point of contact of the pension fund, but also the internal responsible person representing the clients' interests within Mn Services itself. The structure also supports the integrated concept of servicing of the whole process lifecycle of Fiduciary Management, in which all departments fill in their part of the process.

One of the drivers of the success of Fiduciary Management has been that in the last couple of years the pensions fund industry has been confronted with a whole string of legislative and regulatory measures, and pressure to stay in control is coming from all sides. For some funds the pressure may become too high, and solutions for outsourcing in full or in part are sought after.

The board of a pension fund who accept that the various (sub) tasks, including investment strategy, reporting, risk management, and strategic choices, are handled in a fragmented way, work like an orchestra without a conductor.

Fiduciary Management goes a number of steps beyond the traditional balanced mandate solutions because the role of the conductor is clearly included this way. It is not really a single product solution but rather a flexible philosophy logically resulting in an integrated way of working. The service provider and customer have to form a partnership in order to achieve an optimal strategy. Crucial for the success of this partnership is to jointly look at those components of the product that best fit the demands and needs of the customer. The customer clearly maintains the final responsibility but the service provider can absorb many tasks and thus make the life of the managers and board of the pension fund or institutional investor a lot easier. This will allow them to focus on their core responsibilities of properly running their "business," which include establishing a policy on indexation and premium as well as participant communication.

In addition to the service components already mentioned before, similar to advice in the field of investment policy, other tasks such as risk management and control as well as transition management should, in the opinion of Mn Services, be included in the Fiduciary Management concept. It goes without saying that the more mundane tasks of reporting to the customer and regulatory bodies should also be included in the standard service offering.

It is this integrated and thorough approach that has put Mn Services on the map as one of the leading providers of Fiduciary Management in the Netherlands. The concept however is exportable and is of interest for other countries in Europe. The increased role of the European Union in developing legal standards with respect to both investment management and pension funds makes Fiduciary Management likely to become an interesting proposal, which will have an impact in other European countries as well. We conclude that Mn Services is considered to be one of the founding fathers of the concept and also one of the most successful ones and that Europe will be one of the next steps Mn Services will have to take to continue on this successful route.

Erik Hulshof
Mn Services
Rijswijk, The Netherlands

Fiduciary Management at Schroder Investment Management

Schroders—Fiduciary Management Process
Dedicated advisory service

Schroders has been managing assets on behalf of pension schemes and insurance companies for over 200 years. Schroders believes in building long-standing relationships with our clients, and inherent in that concept is the provision of sound long-term fiduciary advice. Schroders Fiduciary Management focuses on understanding individual client situations and maintaining an ongoing dialogue with the client as markets and circumstances change. This consultative style is implemented by a 25-strong multiasset team that is responsible for Fiduciary Management and meeting clients' objectives, based on the following philosophy and beliefs:

- Each investor has different return objectives, risk attitudes, and constraints.
- Portfolios should be constructed to reflect this individuality.
- Investors' preferences can change through time.
- Portfolios should include liability management (nonrisk assets) and diversified growth components (risk assets).
- Investors should consider the entire spectrum of investment opportunities and techniques.
- Understanding and managing risk is a critical part of the process.

SMART: OPTIMIZING, MONITORING AND REPORTING

Schroders has developed a proprietary risk tool, SMART (Schroder MultiAsset Risk Technology, see Figure A.11) to model the optimal allocation to assets and active strategies, with an explicit focus on the volatility of the overall return relative to cash or liabilities. It is an open architecture and flexible system, in which external managers' assets, Schroders' portfolios, and derivative-based passive products can be analysed. Market risk (beta) and active risk (alpha) are modeled separately, to provide an understanding of the optimal amount of active risk and passive risk in the portfolio and how the risk and fee budgets should be constructed. SMART also takes into account that some asset classes, particularly alternatives, do not display a normal distribution of returns—and models this risk (called "fat tail" risk).

The in-depth understanding of the interrelationship between assets and their overall volatility provided by SMART allows Schroders' fund managers to manage the overall risk of the portfolios (see Figure A.12).

Schroders   Schroders Multi-Asset Risk Technology   **SMART**

Portfolio Report   Portfolio Distribution   Portfolio Paths   Portfolio Contribution

muehlns

Options

Print

Excel

PDF

Optimisation : DGF UK Strategic   Portfolio : New

SMART Portfolio Report	Weight	Benchmark	Active	Return	Contribution to Return	Contribution to Risk	Contribution to Excess Return	Contribution to Active Risk
Inst Specialist UK Equity Fund	10.0%	0.0%	10.0%	1.6%	0.2%	0.1%	0.2%	0.1%
Schroder UK Alpha Plus	5.0%	0.0%	5.0%	4.0%	0.2%	0.1%	0.2%	0.1%
UK Smaller Companies Fund	3.0%	0.0%	3.0%	2.8%	0.1%	0.0%	0.1%	0.0%
Passive FTSE W North America	0.0%	0.0%	0.0%	0.0%	0.0%	0.0%	0.0%	0.0%
US SMID	5.0%	0.0%	5.0%	2.5%	0.1%	0.1%	0.1%	0.1%
Specialist Europe ex UK	6.0%	0.0%	6.0%	2.3%	0.1%	0.1%	0.1%	0.1%
Passive FTSE W Europe ex UK	0.0%	0.0%	0.0%	0.0%	0.0%	0.0%	0.0%	0.0%
Passive TSE 1st Section	0.0%	0.0%	0.0%	0.0%	0.0%	0.0%	0.0%	0.0%
Japan Smaller Comp Fund	2.0%	0.0%	2.0%	2.5%	0.0%	0.0%	0.0%	0.0%
Inst Pacific Fund	3.0%	0.0%	3.0%	1.6%	0.0%	0.0%	0.0%	0.0%
SIDMF	3.0%	0.0%	3.0%	1.6%	0.0%	0.0%	0.0%	0.0%
Property Composite	3.0%	0.0%	3.0%	1.0%	0.0%	0.0%	0.0%	0.0%
Inst Global Equity Fund QEP	5.0%	0.0%	5.0%	1.3%	0.1%	0.0%	0.1%	0.0%
Global High Yield Debt	8.0%	0.0%	8.0%	1.5%	0.1%	0.1%	0.1%	0.1%
Bluebay EMD	8.0%	0.0%	8.0%	2.0%	0.2%	0.1%	0.2%	0.1%
Global Property Securities Fund	10.0%	0.0%	10.0%	1.5%	0.2%	0.1%	0.2%	0.1%
Passive DJ AIG Commodity	0.0%	0.0%	0.0%	0.0%	0.0%	0.0%	0.0%	0.0%
Global Active Value	8.0%	0.0%	8.0%	8.5%	0.7%	9.2%	0.7%	9.1%
Private Equity Beta	3.0%	0.0%	3.0%	13.7%	0.4%	6.5%	0.4%	6.5%
GSAM FX Fund	5.0%	0.0%	5.0%	7.0%	0.4%	1.6%	0.4%	1.6%
Hedge Fund Composite	3.0%	0.0%	3.0%	9.0%	0.3%	1.0%	0.3%	1.0%
Cash (GBP)	10.0%	0.0%	10.0%	4.5%	0.5%	0.0%	0.5%	0.0%
Inflation (GBP)	0.0%	100.0%	-100.0%	2.6%	0.0%	0.0%	-2.6%	0.3%
FTSE All Share	22.0%	0.0%	22.0%	7.7%	1.7%	24.1%	1.7%	24.1%
FTSE Small Cap ex. IT	3.0%	0.0%	3.0%	9.1%	0.3%	4.0%	0.3%	4.0%

FIGURE A.11   SMART, the Risk Tool

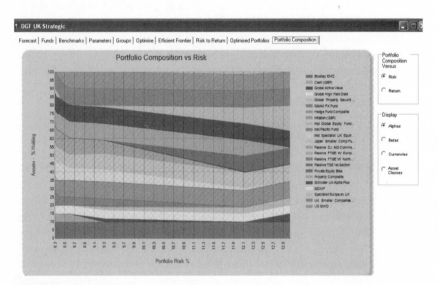

FIGURE A.12   Portfolio Composition versus Risk

MANAGER RESEARCH AND SELECTION PROCESS

Manager research is a key element in an open architecture structure like Fiduciary Management. In the initial stage of our manager selection process Schroders works closely with Standard & Poor's Fund Research. The initial quantitative stage involves screening their database of over 100,000 funds and searching for consistently strong risk-adjusted performance within each asset category. In the qualitative stage of the process, Standard & Poor's Fund Research analysts visit the managers identified to conduct in-depth interviews and to score managers objectively on five key parameters: strength and depth of investment team; workload; experience; investment processes; and risk processes and procedures.

Schroders' MultiManager Team uses this in-depth research as a starting point. The team ensures the recommended funds complement the other investment funds or managers in the portfolio—ensuring an appropriate diversification across different investment styles (see Figure A.13).

The team also re-examines performance track records, looking at risk-adjusted historic return to evaluate how each manager has performed in different cycles of up and down markets.

The second stage of the process is to examine each (equity) fund's characteristics and risk exposures by running security level holdings data through a proprietary system called PRISM (Portfolio Risk Investment Strategy Manager) and a return-based style analysis in order to assess the fund's performance in varying market environments—useful for distinguishing luck from skill. Finally, several meetings with the asset manager will contribute to a deeper understanding of the strengths and weaknesses of products, investment management processes, and the key personnel involved.

The PRISM model provides a detailed insight into the level of risk being taken in multimanager portfolios as well as identifying individual positions that contribute to the risk of the portfolio. PRISM identifies active risk, size, beta, nonindex positions and sources of risk by decomposing portfolios into stock-specific, sector, country, and characteristic exposures. It is important to be able to measure and manage a portfolio's exposure to style characteristics as styles behave differently according to market and economic conditions. Schroders' managers use PRISM to ensure that they do not take unintended risk, to make sure that stronger risk contribution corresponds to stronger views, and—not least—to make sure that the aggregate risk is still sufficient to deliver alpha.

Portfolio Risk Investment Strategy Manager *Page 1 of 8*

Name:	GlbValLux - QEP Live Data		20 April 2007
Benchmark:	MSCI World		Currency USD
Region:	Total Portfolio	No. Stocks(ex/inc Funds) 912	912
		Number of Funds/Futures/Index Options: 0	

Predicted Risk

Tracking Error	5.4%
Tracking Error (APT)	2.2%
Beta	0.98
Benchmark Volatility	13.0%
Absolute Fund Volatility	13.9%

(Figures from Barra unless otherwise stated)

Active Risk Decomposition (Barra)

Stock specific factor	5.3%
Industrial sectors	6.3%
Countries	17.3%
Risk indices	71.0%
Market risk	0.1%

Supplemental Statistics

Concentration of risk to 30% of Specific Risk[2]	27
Concentration of risk to 50% of Specific Risk[2]	73

[2] *Number of stocks which make up X% of the predicted Specific Risk*

Active money(top 10 positive)	4.3%
Active money(top 10 negative)	-8.7%

Number of stocks in benchmark	1880	
Benchmark coverage(common money)[3]	17.7%	
Absolute Active Positions	164.60%	

[3]*% of benchmark accounted for by fund positions*

	Mean	Median
Positive active position	0.09%	0.06%
Negative active position	-0.05%	-0.02%
No. of positive active positions	875	
No. of negative active positions	1635	

Portfolio Concentration	Fund	B'mark
Top 5 Stocks	2.4%	5.6%
Top 10 Stocks	4.7%	9.5%
Top 20 Stocks	9.1%	15.5%
Top 50 Stocks	21.4%	27.4%

Non-Index Stocks Held	% of Fund	Specific Contrib.
Ryder Sys Inc	0.43%	0.03%
Bmw Sta	0.42%	0.02%
Conocophillips	0.42%	0.02%
Alliance & Leicest	0.41%	0.01%
Integrys Energy Group Inc	0.41%	0.01%
Total weight of non-index stocks	42.06%	1.37%

Value At Risk[4]	Confidence Interval	
	95%	99%
Relative VaR	2.5%	3.6%
Fund Absolute VaR	6.5%	9.2%
Benchmark Absolute VaR	6.1%	8.6%

[4]*VaR horizon is one month, returns assumed to be normally distributed with mean zero.*

Change in net weight[5]	Change
Zurich Financial Ser	0.41
Bnp Paribas Eur2	0.40
Basf Ag	0.40
Qantas Airways	-0.18
Sanmina-sci Corp	-0.33
Electrolux Ab	-0.36

[5]*Change in fund weight less change in benchmark weight (only indicative of purchases and sales)*

High Contribution to Beta[6]	Beta	Active	Contrib.
Procter & Gamble Co	0.08	-0.71%	0.65
Johnson & Johnson	0.24	-0.66%	0.50
Nestle R	0.35	-0.56%	0.37
Glaxosmithkline	0.40	-0.60%	0.36
Exxon Mobil Corp	0.80	-1.64%	0.33

Low Contribution to Beta[6]	Beta	Active	Contrib.
Intel Corp	2.25	-0.45%	-0.56
Nokia Oyj	2.22	-0.36%	-0.44
Cisco Sys Inc	1.73	-0.58%	-0.42
Ericsson Tel. Ab-b	2.95	-0.20%	-0.39
At&t Inc	1.44	-0.88%	-0.39

[6]*Contribution to active portfolio beta. Calculated as active weight * (beta -1), multiplied by 100.*

Active Weights By Market Cap Range

Currency (USD)

Barra analysis on this page excludes 0.27 % of the portfolio.
Barra analysis on this page excludes 0.09 % of the benchmark.
APT analysis on this page excludes 0.26 % of the portfolio.
APT analysis on this page excludes 0.10 % of the benchmark.
NB. This report is based on unaudited data. Any Funds or Futures will be decomposed into their constituent stocks and integrated with direct holdings.

FIGURE A.13   Portfolio Risk Investment Strategy Manager

DYNAMIC MANAGEMENT OF PORTFOLIOS

Schroders' view is that the allocation to the nonrisk and risk assets should not be static over time, which requires us to think in a much more holistic way. For example, opportunity (risk premiums) and wealth (funding ratios) generally move in opposite directions. Pension funding ratios tend to improve when equities outperform bonds, but when equities materially outperform bonds, future opportunities tend to decline.

Schroders' approach moves the focus away from benchmarks to risk budgets and opportunity. When wealth measures, such as the funding level, are the main driver, the key metric has become the fund's liabilities, and it is against the fund's liabilities that the risk budget is measured.

NONRISK ASSETS

Schroders takes a pragmatic view of (the degree of) liability matching, allowing for the uncertain nature of future cash flows and future mortality. Liability-driven investment comes in many guises, from monitoring and managing the interest rate and inflation sensitivity to a complete cash matching solution. Various forms are applicable depending on maturity, funding level, and attitudes towards risk by trustees or sponsors.

RISK ASSETS

The objective of the risk assets is to deliver returns over long-term liability growth in order to improve the funding level of the fund, and in a less volatile manner than has been the case historically. Pension funds should maintain equity exposure but, in addition to this, should enhance portfolio diversification structurally and tactically by diversifying across a variety of growth assets in what Schroders is calling a Diversified Growth portfolio. Where appropriate, Schroders believes in the benefit of isolating the manager's skill and outperformance (alpha) by removing unwanted market risk (beta) that creates volatility. This is called portable alpha—a technique that would be part of Schroders' approach in Fiduciary Management. The technique of combining matching assets and growth assets is also implemented in Schroders' own pension fund in the UK.

For pension funds that do not have the scale, expertise, staff, and monitoring capabilities to achieve this level of diversification, Schroders has developed a pooled portfolio, Schroder Global Diversified Growth Fund. According to the new Financial Assessment Framework (FTK) in the

Netherlands, the Diversified Growth portfolio leads to a lower solvency requirement than a traditional equity portfolio. Pension funds or plan sponsors can either profit from the lower solvency requirement, or can increase the allocation to risk assets at the same level of risk to improve the expected return of the pension fund significantly.

MONITORING AND REPORTING

Risk monitoring takes place throughout the entire process. Reporting and responsibility for Fiduciary Management clients is in the hands of a 25-strong multiasset team, headed by Curt Custard, directly under Alan Brown, head of Investment and executive member of the board.

Allan Brown, Curt Custard, Willem van Gijzen
Schroder Investment Management, London, England.

Fiduciary Management at Interpolis

Interpolis Financial Pension Management

At Interpolis Pensioenen Vermogensbeheer ("Interpolis"), fiduciary asset management is part of the Financial Pension Management service that Interpolis offers its clients. Financial Pension Management anticipates legal requirements and social developments that are relevant to a pension fund, such as FTK, IFRS, and Pension Fund Governance.

RISK MANAGEMENT AND OPTIMIZATION OF THE RISK/RETURN PROFILE

Financial Pension Management makes it possible for the trustees of a pension fund to shape and implement its financial and risk policy in an integrated fashion, using all the management tools at their disposal. It enables the trustees to shape risk management and to optimize the expected return, given the fund's required risk profile.

WHAT DOES THE FINANCIAL PENSION MANAGEMENT PROCESS LOOK LIKE?

In implementing Financial Pension Management, Interpolis goes through the following steps with its clients:

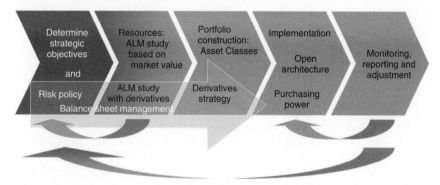

FIGURE A.14 Implementation of Financial Pension Management

1. Determination of the strategic objectives
2. ALM studies on the basis of market value and derivatives strategies
3. Portfolio construction
4. Implementation
5. Monitoring, reporting, and adjustment

This process is illustrated in Figure A.14.

STEP 1. DETERMINATION OF THE STRATEGIC OBJECTIVES

In this step of the process, based in part on the ALM studies mentioned below, Interpolis will periodically analyse the premium, indexation, and investment policy and advise the trustees. The strategic investment policy is adjusted to the indexation and premium policy of the fund, taking into account the interest rate sensitivity of the liabilities and the net assets of the fund (balance sheet management).

STEP 2. ALM STUDIES ON THE BASIS OF MARKET VALUE AND DERIVATIVES STRATEGIES

In preparing the above advice Interpolis uses ALM studies with different policy alternatives, including the use of derivatives strategies. It has been shown in practice that for a pension fund these studies often lead to a more specific formulation of objectives, as expressed in the desired risk/return profile. The results of these studies ultimately lead to strategic choices on such matters as investment policy, often combined with the use of derivatives. Besides interest rate risk, this step also examines the equity risk, inflation risk, and currency risk.

STEP 3. PORTFOLIO CONSTRUCTION

Based on the determined strategic investment policy, Interpolis designs an investment portfolio, including the financial instruments to be used in order to reduce risks (interest, inflation, equity, and currency hedges) and the asset classes. The decisive factor is further optimization of the risk/return profile.

STEP 4. IMPLEMENTATION

Implementation breaks down into several components. Interpolis increasingly uses derivatives for risk management on behalf of its clients. Strategies to reduce the interest rate risk, in particular, are given great emphasis. This can be through the use of swaps or swaptions, but also a combination of these (dynamic hedge strategy). Interpolis then elaborates the aforementioned asset classes in detail. In the interest of the pension fund, a so-called open architecture is used (fiduciary asset management), herewith the fund is able to benefit from Interpolis's purchasing power.

STEP 5. MONITORING, REPORTING AND ADJUSTMENT

Besides reporting on investments, derivatives reporting is also carried out. For the purposes of risk management to be performed, Interpolis will, on a daily basis, value the hedge positions, make any payments as required, and carry out collateral management. At the same time as reporting on the pension funds, mostly on a quarterly basis, reports will be made on the market development and effectiveness of the hedge. This allows the funds to follow the development of assets and liabilities as well as the compensation offered by the hedges. If required, action can be taken to adjust the hedge position in response to changes in the balance sheet composition, policy changes, or market movements.

Interpolis will also continuously measure the results of the operational asset managers and monitor whether they stay within the limits of the granted mandate and achieve their targets. Where necessary, Interpolis will replace operational asset managers. Interpolis consolidates the results of the operational asset managers and reports these to the funds.

Besides reporting on asset management, Interpolis also reports on the strategic risk profile, since this can change as a result of market movements, among other things. Based on the findings and new information, Interpolis advises its clients on a continuous basis and adjusts the process. As such, the entire Financial Pension Management process is a cycle that continually repeats itself.

Tom Boltje
Interpolis Pensioenen Vermogensbeheer
De Meern, The Netherlands.

Fiduciary Management at Blue Sky Group

At Blue Sky Group we feel that much of the new concept called Fiduciary Management is not as new as is often claimed.

The focus of a dedicated manager of pension funds like Blue Sky Group is to execute and advise about policies that are solely to the financial benefit of the pension funds that we serve. The level of alignment of interest between our company and our pension funds clients has always been very high. Since Blue Sky Group originated from a large corporate pension funds office, serving the pension funds' best interest has become common practice. This is not necessarily true for all of the suppliers of Fiduciary Management services today.

The case for offering Fiduciary Management stems largely from the increased attention to balance sheet management by pension funds after the implosion of equity prices in the early 2000s. It became clear that most of the asset management products were often just partial solutions in that respect.

The approach that Blue Sky Group takes at Fiduciary Management comprises four integrated services:

1. Continuous balance sheet management through the use of integrated ALM and risk management modeling techniques.
2. Diversification management within the portfolio to optimize the risk and return characteristics of each portfolio.
3. Multimanagement of specialized external asset managers within an efficient pooling structure in which portfolio segments can be managed either passive, enhanced, or active, dependent on the likelihood of generating alpha at acceptable levels of management fees.
4. Performance and risk control, both at the balance sheet level (liability risk) and at the investment portfolio level (active management risk).

These four services combined describe the integrated Fiduciary Management process that Blue Sky Group offers to clients. We recognize, however, that other institutions may apply Fiduciary Management to parts of this process. Of course, elements of the process can be excluded as desired.

MANAGING LIABILITY RISK

It will not be a surprise that Blue Sky Group finds the liability risk the dominant risk within a pension fund portfolio. Instrumental to Blue Sky Group's approach is the use of the ORTEC model for asset liability management. Since 2000 it has been fully integrated within the company. Actuaries and investment researchers work closely together in managing balance sheets.

We were early to realize that if one wants to look into the "genetic code" of a pension plan, one should be able to perform an ALM study within the organization. To make this work, close cooperation was established between the Investment Strategy Research department and the Actuarial Department. Combining both capabilities enhances the understanding of the pension plans enormously. This is clearly a benefit of a dedicated pension fund servicing organization. Our combined efforts go far beyond traditional ALM modeling.

It is often assumed that an ALM study is sufficient to set an appropriate strategic asset allocation for a pension plan. However, our experience tells us that there is much more to strategic asset allocation than an ALM study alone. Much can be done to improve the management of the balance sheet of a pension plan. Research and advice aimed at that is what we see as an important part of Fiduciary Management.

An example may clarify our stance. When, by the end of 2000, the Board of Trustees of the Pilots Pension Plan of KLM asked for a way to reduce the downside risk of equities using derivatives, Blue Sky Group established a connection with a risk management consultancy firm in the Netherlands that was able to model the effects of derivatives within our ALM tool. It resulted in a solution that has effectively reduced the downside risk of the solvency rate at acceptable cost. This derivatives solution proved to be a leap forward in terms of our balance sheet management capabilities.

The desire to apply equity options to strategically hedge the downside risk of equities enforced proper management of both derivatives and collateral. It also enhanced the capabilities of the back office function at Blue Sky Group.

ALTERNATIVE INVESTMENTS

Proper balance sheet optimization is able to determine the sensitivities of asset mix changes to variables like the probability of underfunding, the ability to protect against inflation, the level and volatility of the premium and of more of such target variables that are crucial to the board of trustees to reach their goals.

There are limits to the extent to which assets can be modeled within an ALM model. In a long-term–oriented model it is largely useless to refine the asset mix to the level of asset class segments that are likely to improve the overall portfolio diversification. For that reason most of the diversification optimization within asset classes is performed within an asset-only context. Blue Sky Group uses the outcome, an enhanced time series of optimized returns per asset class, in the ALM studies that it performs for its clients. We test the effectiveness of including alternative investments within our balance sheet optimization procedures. Applying both empirical and/or market research and, if necessary, desmoothing techniques allows us to reveal the degree to which alternative investments can help to improve balance sheet management. Contrary to what is often proclaimed by the supply (or sell) side of the financial markets, the outcomes are not often in favor of new instruments.

STATE-DEPENDENT DURATION MANAGEMENT

To give another example of the importance of balance sheet management optimization, we find that there are no easy solutions for pension funds that want to phase out the interest rate risk in their balance sheet through the use of swaps or swaptions. We regard many of the product offerings to pension funds as quick fixes rather than fine-tuned instruments that tackle the problem adequately. It is insufficient just to mimic the liability cash flows by adding some sort of duration completion overlay.

Our balance sheet optimization research shows that a proper duration management solution makes use of nominal and inflation-linked swaps or swaptions in dynamic combinations that are solvency-rate dependent. The ambition level to index pension rights with future inflation appears dependent on the current and future state of the solvency of a pension plan. At low solvency rates, the indexation ambition is implicitly nominal. Nominal swaps appear a sound solution in that case. But at high solvency rates the picture changes, and inflation-linked swaps become the optimal solution. In between, combinations of nominal and inflation swaps serve best. This can only be shown in rigorous ALM models that are able to capture the particularities of nominal and inflation-linked swaps. We see, however, few solutions being offered today that appreciate such state-dependent characteristics. True Fiduciary Management should offer such refined solutions. That is what we aim for at Blue Sky Group.

Such careful determination of pension management solutions apply to all four levels that we described earlier. As early as in 1999 Blue Sky Group switched from internal to external management. A core-satellite approach was adopted to discern between actively and passively managed segments of the financial markets. A pooling structure was created in order to be able to efficiently channel our multimanager portfolios to a larger client base. Finally, Blue Sky Group adopted a risk budgeting system to exploit active management opportunities within the portfolio. That timely business process redesign helped us to meet today's demand of pension plans.

REALISTIC ALPHA MANAGEMENT

As a second part of the Fiduciary Management offering, our efforts in the multimanagement business are geared towards hiring highly specialized asset managers. We are willing to pay high fees to asset managers who are able to deliver sufficient and persistent alphas at a reasonable level of additional risk. But empirical research has shown that alpha delivery is not feasible within every segment of the financial markets. Therefore, we do not want to pay active fees in segments in which the likelihood of positive and persistent alpha is negligible. In such segments we choose passive management and, in some instances, enhanced management. Decisions are made with full recognition of the all-in cost structures in each segment. This leads us to make realistic alpha promises to our clients, that minimize regret from paying too much for illusive or, at least, disappointing excess returns. We consider this as another important task for any Fiduciary Manager.

As yet another observation, we find that much of the alpha that is offered by active managers stems from investing beyond a specified benchmark. The problem with that is, of course, that pension funds pay high active fees for partial exposure to structural risk premiums that could be captured at lower cost by expanding the benchmark to other segments of asset classes. In other words, what is called alpha often is not more than enhanced diversification across asset segments that offer different (levels of) risk premiums. We would argue that such diversification should be enacted by the pension fund itself and should not be left to a manager who exploits it to claim alpha capabilities at a high fee. Delivery of alpha should not rest on benchmark misuse.

FIDUCIARY RESPONSIBLE FEES

Within a Fiduciary Management environment, the fee structure deserves special attention. Ultimately the Fiduciary Manager should be rewarded for achieving an investment return that meets or surpasses the threshold return demanded by the liabilities. To the extent that asset components are perfect matches to liability components, the return threshold is straightforward. The matching portfolio, as this part is often called, is easily manageable and a fixed fee for the Fiduciary Managers seems appropriate.

This is different for the management of the assets that do not perfectly fit the liabilities, or the return portfolio. By definition there will be a mismatch of returns between the liabilities and the assets within that part of the overall portfolio. It is not straightforward how the Fiduciary Manager gets rewarded for managing this part of the balance sheet. It should be recognized that the excess returns of the return portfolio are volatile. Although the Fiduciary Manager will do its utmost to minimize them, negative excess returns cannot be ruled out. Given the inherent volatility of the excess returns, a performance-related fee for managing the return portfolio makes sense. To warrant for negative excess returns, for which the Fiduciary Manager should feel the pinch, a so-called high watermark may be applied.

WIN-WIN SITUATION

A Fiduciary Manager should do everything that is in the best interest of the pension fund. Therefore it would be wise for such a manager to refrain from internal management of assets completely. It is sometimes claimed that internally managing straightforward asset segments, like government bonds or domestic equities, can be cost-saving compared to more expensive external management. We question the viability of this argument, since it introduces self-interest of the Fiduciary Manager with the earnings stream that he generates through the fee that is charged for the internally managed assets. It is unlikely that a Fiduciary Manager will "fire" himself in case of underperformance of his benchmark. Clearly this is not in the interest of a pension fund, and pension funds should be keen on avoiding such conflicts of interest between the Fiduciary Manager and the fund. When set up properly, Fiduciary Management can surely result in a win-win situation for both.

Fons Lute
Blue Sky Group
Amstelveen, The Netherlands.

Fiduciary Management at AZL Group

"AZL NV" Integral outsourcing.

INTRODUCTION

The very concept of fiduciary asset management, which originates from private banking, is subject to inflation. More and more, asset managers and consultants to traditional pension funds management organizations offer products that seem to be fiduciary. The question is which definition of *fiduciary* these parties use. The introduction of concepts such as semi-fiduciary, fiduciary +, indicates that the pension world is also still at odds with this concept. Another question is whether *fiduciary* is indeed a distinguishing term, or whether it only serves for the provider to position himself in the market.

AZL NV (AZL) relates the term *fiduciary* primarily to the pension fund's need, and only secondly to the content the service provider claims to give to the concept. Fiduciary can best be translated according to the Dutch concept of *goed rentmeesterschap*; in which context the fiduciary, as if he were the pension manager himself, takes all actions the pension fund requires, whether this concerns parts of the trustees' responsibilities or the integral service. The concept of fiduciary in this context goes beyond a standard service level agreement and involves an alignment of interests between the client and the executor.

Considering the Dutch pension market, we can establish that many management organizations that are linked to one or more pension funds effectively fall under this concept and have been using the concept of fiduciary for many years.

This paper discusses the concept of fiduciary as specified by AZL. A concept that is the product of AZL's ambition and which in brief boils down to AZL NV's intending to perform the pension fund function as optimally as possible in all its facets.

THE CONCEPT OF INTEGRAL INSOURCING

AZL's target group consists of Dutch pension funds. Specifically for the integral concept AZL focuses its services on small to medium-sized pension funds, measured in number of participants or assets under management.

In particular for this type of pension fund it is difficult to constantly respond to the continuous changes in the environment, legislation, and increasingly tight regulatory requirements. Often, directing the pension fund is only one of the tasks of the pension fund trustee, who consequently finds it hard to carry the total (integral) responsibility.

The concept of integral insourcing offers the pension fund trustees a service that enables it to take control and fill in the integral responsibility. This is done by appointing a Fiduciary Manager who, as if it were the management bureau of the pension fund itself, is responsible for the complete execution by the pension fund.

AZL offers the pension fund trustee a model whereby the complete management of the pension execution can be outsourced by the pension fund. Within this model the trustees are supported by one client team that can cover the entire range of pension products and on behalf of the pension fund trustees supervises and selects the executors of the policy formulated by the trustees.

AZL's services focus on the pension-wide problems and defines its objectives accordingly. In this framework, it has found itself unable to restrict itself to the implementation of the investment part of the process. Therefore it is difficult to compare the concept of AZL NV with the fiduciary form in the narrow sense. AZL does more than simply select and direct asset managers.

The integral approach is necessarily based on the assumption that an outsourcing approach aimed at sub-responsibilities, from the point of view of the trustee, will only lead to elevating the problem to a higher level of abstraction. The trustees themselves continue to supervise the various service providers and will find it hard to remain in control. Figure A.15 shows AZL's integral model.

FIDUCIARY RISK MANAGEMENT

In the foregoing, we elaborated on the AZL concept for the present pension issues for small(er) to medium-sized pension funds. AZL finds the solution in an integral outsourcing to the Fiduciary Manager.

The discussion about the determination of the ambition levels of the pension funds and the steering of the financial risks of the funds therefore takes place from the integral perspective. In this discussion, AZL has in particular a steering task towards the trustees.

Discussing this with the various stakeholders and translating this into a practical policy framework is an essential part of what AZL has designed as fiduciary risk management. Fiduciary risk management encompasses the

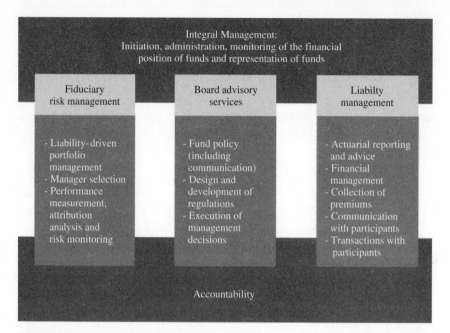

FIGURE A.15   AZL's Integral Model

management's entire decision-making and implementation process, starting with formulating the ambitions up to the actual implementation of the investment portfolios. The focus of AZL's advice is aimed in particular at providing support to the management in formulating its policy frameworks. Not before this is done, can AZL provide the instruments aimed at building up the actual investment portfolios.

With respect to the implementation and the policy choices, AZL's added value for the client consists of determining and detailing the optimal solution for the client. AZL's task (fiduciary risk management) is a coordinating role, creating access to various solutions. Offering various in-house solutions for asset management is not a necessity, but AZL must have the expertise to assess the quality of the products to be purchased.

This said, alignment with the interests of an (individual) pension fund for an insourcer like AZL, with various smaller and mutually different pension funds as clients, means constantly choosing between generating economies of scale and creating flexibility. When purchasing specific services for the client, AZL's implementation model is therefore aimed at creating economies of scale, and on the other hand at retaining sufficient flexibility to offer tailormade solutions independent of the standard (and efficient) products. Within AZL, offering tailormade solutions has led to building up

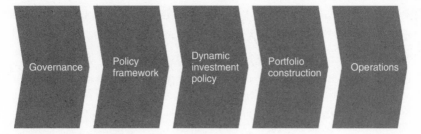

FIGURE A.16   Expertise in the Investment Process

expertise in certain specific areas of the investment process, as shown in Figure A.16.

TO CONCLUDE

The concept of Fiduciary Management is relatively new in the Dutch pension world. This is also apparent from the different content given to the concept by the various providers. An integral approach of fiduciary pension management is, however, a concept that is as old as the Dutch pension system itself. Within this concept the emphasis is constantly changing, and new insights are emerging. Like its fellow integral service providers, AZL is convinced that integral outsourcing is the only tenable solution for smaller funds and is therefore constantly engaged in optimising its services on behalf of the pension funds.

A next step in the services provided by AZL is to fill in the concept of fiduciary, the alignment of the interests between the outsourcer and insourcer in a more concrete way. In this context AZL is investigating the possibility of joining the managing committee of the pension fund.

Walther Schapendonk
AZL Group
Heerlen, The Netherlands

Fiduciary Management at Lombard Odier Darier Hentsch & Cie

Fiduciary Management or open architecture/multimanager solutions are gaining popularity within the investment community. Whether these investment solutions are the Holy Grail for the future remains to be seen: the jury is still out. A partnership approach towards delivering services to trustees is key within the whole investment process. Whether this will have to take place via a fiduciary arrangement is the question to be resolved for the coming years.

Within this section we will focus on one important element of Fiduciary Management/open architecture: portfolio construction. Since a major part of institutional portfolios are invested in fixed income, we have focused on the hidden alphas, and thus opportunities, within a fixed income environment.

ON THE ADDED VALUE OF FIXED INCOME TACTICAL ASSET ALLOCATION

Why would one pursue an active allocation investment policy within a fixed income portfolio? The overall risk of the fixed income portfolio is low compared to the other traditional asset classes. Even the most risky fixed income asset classes, like emerging markets and high yield, have a volatility that is only half of that of equities. From an equity perspective, volatilities of all fixed income asset classes are more or less equal. And given that all fixed income classes, regardless of their specific characteristics, are exposed to general interest rate movements it is not strange that perceived correlations are high. So why bother? Looking at correlations of bonds within a specific fixed income asset class, this conclusion could be valid. Fixed income markets have developed rapidly especially in Europe since the introduction of the euro. Derivatives and information technology have greatly increased the efficiency of the EMU government bond and euro credit market. At the same time new markets like euro high yield, inflation-linked, and converging Europe have emerged as new investment opportunities. Analyzing the return patterns of all the sub-asset classes suggests however that euro fixed income markets are not that similar at all. Various fixed income markets do react differently to changes in the economic environment. Return distributions are not stable over time, and thus correlations are not. These time-varying correlations pose investment opportunities by tactically allocating assets to those asset classes that promise the highest risk-adjusted returns. But then again, are the return differentials large enough to create alpha in the portfolio?

We have chosen for a simulation approach to answer that question. Not that a performance attribution cannot provide a convincing analysis, but results can depend heavily on the chosen model and the classifications that are used. Furthermore it can be hard to pinpoint the nature of a trade. The addition of a specific corporate bond to the portfolio implicitly has a duration impact, it is an allocation to credits, and it is a selection of this specific issuer. To overcome this, we have chosen for a model- and classification-independent analysis.

We have collected monthly excess returns versus EMU government bonds of indices of the following fixed income asset classes: euro inflation-linked, euro credits, converging Europe (in local currency), emerging markets and global high yield, the latter two hedged to euro. Excess returns versus EMU government bonds are used, as this is the natural opposite for an asset allocation decision for a euro-benchmarked investor. We assume that the portfolio has a strategic holding in each asset class. The period covers the start of EMU at January 1, 1999, till December 31, 2005. The following allocation strategy is applied: if over the next month an asset class outperforms EMU government bonds, an overweight position is implemented. This implies however, that the investment manager always chooses the "correct" (e.g., overweight when an asset class outperforms and underweight when underperforming) allocation.

To reflect the imperfectness of the investment manager, the "correct" allocation is modified in such a way that its frequency equals the information coefficient or skill of the manager. We have chosen 0.55 as the information coefficient of the investment manager. The strategy is repeated month after month throughout the whole observation period and rerun for 1,000 cycles to achieve statistically stable results. The allowed allocations are typical for the size of the overweight or underweight positions in those markets in a normal euro aggregate portfolio context. It does not necessarily mean that each allocation decision consumes *ex post* an equal part of the risk budget. Because we use index returns, all results with respect to returns and risk are due to the allocation strategy and do not include any selection effects, nor duration effects or costs.

Table A.1 shows the allocation, the achieved annual excess return, *ex post* tracking error, and information ratio when the strategy is applied to an asset class in isolation and for all asset classes together.

We conclude that an active allocation policy only applied to the less risky asset classes inflation linked and credits, adds about 10 basis points annually. Allowing for investments in more risky asset classes increases the excess return with an additional 26 basis points to about 36 basis points annually. Moreover it greatly enhances the efficiency of the portfolio. To illustrate this, we have plotted (see Figure A.17) the distribution of excess returns, when allocating in isolation to an asset class and when all asset classes are part of the investment universe.

As can be seen, the distributions of excess returns, when allocating only to the individual asset classes, are concentrated, except for converging Europe. The excess return distribution in the broad portfolio is centered much more to the right. Although its variance is somewhat larger, the

TABLE A.1 Added Value of Fixed Income Tactical Asset Allocation

Asset Class	Allocation	Annual Excess Return (in Basis Points) (Standard Deviation)	Tracking Error (Basis Points)	Information Ratio
Inflation-Linked	+/− 7,5%	6(8)	23	0.25
Credits	+/− 10%	3(4)	12	0.24
Converging Europe	+/− 6%	14(20)	54	0.26
Emerging Markets	+/− 3%	7(9)	26	0.28
Global High Yield	+/− 3%	6(10)	26	0.23
All		36(25)	66	0.54

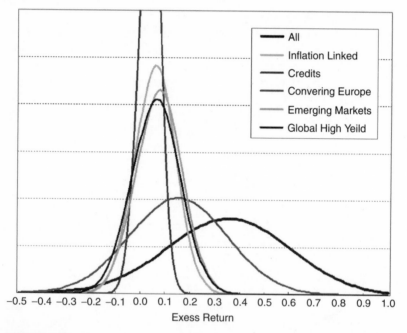

FIGURE A.17 Distribution of Excess Returns

probability of generating an excess return below zero is only 8 percent.[1] The probability of having negative excess returns when allocating to just one asset class is +/−25 percent, regardless of the asset class. These diversification benefits cause the information ratio to increase from roughly 0.25 for each asset class separately to 0.54 when all asset classes are allowed.

In the above simulation we have assumed that investment decisions are made every month and positioning is adjusted accordingly. Although this may seem very active for an asset allocation policy, Figure A.18 indicates that it pays off to actively manage the portfolio to that extent. Again, the information coefficient is set at 0.55 and allocations to all asset classes are allowed.

If the investment decisions are made less frequently, the excess return declines rapidly. When the forecast period is one month, the excess return is 36 basis points. Increasing this period to about once a quarter, the excess return declines to only 20 basis points. As the tracking error is stable (as allocations do not change) the information ratio declines with the excess return. If decisions are being made only once a year, the information ratio is just one third of the information ratio of the monthly investment cycle. This phenomenon has a statistical basis. As the number of investment decisions decreases, the variance around the expected information coefficient increases; for instance, the number of poor investment decisions increases (with an information coefficient less than 0.5) and thus the final excess return decreases.

So far we have assumed that the investment manager is right in 55 out of 100 decisions. Improving your skill dramatically improves the investment results. Table A.2 shows the information ratio in relation with the information coefficient and the forecast period.

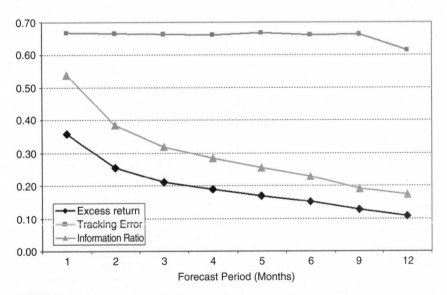

FIGURE A.18 Effects of Monthly Rebalancing

TABLE A.2 Information Ratio versus Information Coefficient and Forecast Period

		Forecast Period (Months)							
		1	2	3	4	5	6	9	12
	0.50	0.00	0.00	0.00	0.00	0.00	0.00	0.00	0.00
	0.55	0.54	0.38	0.32	0.29	0.26	0.23	0.19	0.17
Information Coefficient	0.60	1.04	0.78	0.59	0.49	0.44	0.40	0.31	0.35
	0.65	1.55	1.12	0.89	0.77	0.66	0.57	0.50	0.49
	0.70	2.07	1.51	1.21	1.00	0.90	0.77	0.65	0.69
	0.75	2.59	1.90	1.49	1.26	1.10	0.97	0.80	0.88

If the investment cycle is one month, an increase of only 5 percent of the information coefficient from 0.55 to 0.60, results in an increase in the information ratio from 0.54 to 1.04! Furthermore a manager with roughly a quarterly investment cycle has to have 5 percent more skill to be as efficient as a manager with skill 0.55 who makes monthly decisions. An even less active manager, with a six-to-nine-month cycle, needs another 5 percent additional skill to be equally efficient. Reversing the argument: if an investment manager does not have any skill (information coefficient < 0.5) he'd better be very passive.

We realize that a simulation study cannot replace actual investment results. By recognizing that an investment manager has limited, but positive skills, combined with realistic portfolio positioning we have shown that fixed income tactical asset allocation does add value, both in terms of excess returns and in enhancing the portfolio efficiency.

In doing so we have illustrated the value of the fundamental laws of active management:

- Expanding the investment universe results in higher (although not unlimited), but most importantly in more stable excess returns.
- If an investment manager has skill, it pays off to be active.

Lombard Odier Darier Hentsch (LODH) has a long-standing experience in fixed income asset management and open architecture services. Fixed income tactical asset allocation is an integrated part of the investment tools used in our discretionary, tailormade mandates.

LODH embraced the open architecture/multimanager concept in 1991, which reflects the entrepreneurial philosophy of LODH. The success is shown by a steady growth of assets under management with close to 12 billion euros now (June 2006) in this concept.

Generating lasting added value in a volatile environment requires a flexible investment approach. An active investment style that invests in collective third-party instruments enables the manager to take account of changes in market behaviour. LODH are and have to be able to respond to new market conditions by using different investment styles (Growth, Value, Large/Mid/Small Caps, etc.) offered by the best specialists for each investment category. In a proactive way we provide our opinion on institutional trends.

Niels de Visser,
Lombard Odier Darier Hentsch & Cie (Nederland) N.V.,
Amsterdam, The Netherlands.

Fiduciary Management at ABN Amro Asset Management

FIDUCIARY MANAGEMENT AND LIABILITY DRIVEN INVESTMENT

Both these concepts are hot in the investment management industry in the Netherlands in 2006 and most likely will be in the years to come. Although Fiduciary Management and LDI are two different concepts, ABN AMRO Asset Management believes that LDI is the solid base for a fiduciary mandate. A true Fiduciary Manager should make optimal use of a pension fund's risk budget while managing the assets against liabilities. This ensures that the Fiduciary Manager is close to the core of the pension fund and can act as a true partner.

CURRENT ENVIRONMENT

Liabilities are key. The introduction of FTK and Fair Value accounting rules, such as IAS 19, requires pension costs calculated against market rate ("fair value"). Within fair value, the value of the liabilities moves up and down with changes in interest rates. Many pension funds have assets (existing portfolios) with short durations (five years) and liabilities with long durations. Hence, huge interest rate risks have become visible.

We believe that this current environment calls for a fundamental reassessment of the way pension funds approach investing. The traditional approach of trying to outperform a benchmark is no longer adequate.

Instead, investors need to explicitly link assets to liabilities. All in all, fair value has created demand for liability-driven investments (LDI).

LIABILITY-DRIVEN INVESTMENTS

LDI is about making optimal use of the pension fund's risk budget in managing the assets of a fund vis-à-vis the liabilities. In an LDI context, part of a fund's assets can be used to closely match the liabilities in order to minimize associated risks. In addition, the "remainder" of a pension fund's portfolio can serve to generate upside potential consistent with the fund's overall risk strategy.

At ABN AMRO Asset Management, we consider the different elements of LDI to comprise

- Analysis of assets and liabilities
- Consideration of a full range of asset classes to utilize multiple sources of return
- Risk budgeting versus liabilities with ongoing monitoring
- Explicit capture of both Alpha and Beta returns
- Dynamic Management to react to realized returns and the resulting changes to the funded ratio

The Fiduciary Manager has an active role in translating the fund's goals into a meaningful and understandable LDI-design.

Key Element 1: Analysis of Asset and Liabilities

The first step is to help the pension fund to come to a fuller understanding of its liabilities and how to better align assets with liabilities. Our approach begins with the use of our proprietary advisory model to identify the strategic asset mix satisfying the fund's risk/return criteria. It thoroughly models possible future financial market and interest rate risk scenarios. We believe that most clients can improve the ratio of expected return versus risk of large losses by further diversifying risky investments.

Key Element 2: Consideration of a Full Range of Asset Classes to Utilize Multiple Sources of Return

The next step is to provide appropriate vehicles for implementation. We offer integrated solutions in which a part of our client's portfolio is used for hedging purposes, while the rest is used to generate excess return in relation to your liabilities.

The so-called hedge portfolio will be designed to match the pension fund's required duration and interest-rate sensitivity. Typical techniques include duration and cash-flow matching, by using bonds, interest rate swaps or swaptions. Meanwhile, the yield-enhancing portfolio element will be broadly diversified across multiple products/asset classes to generate excess return on top of the liabilities. These include not only traditional assets such as equities but also more specialized ones, such as emerging markets, and alternatives, such as TAA and leveraged products.

Key Element 3: Risk Budgeting versus Liabilities with Ongoing Monitoring

Risk budgeting determines the overall risk constraints, the aggregate target outperformance, how much of this will come from market exposure (beta), and how much from active management (alpha). We also monitor the implementation and adapt it where necessary due to changes in market conditions and in the funded ratio.

Key Element 4: Explicit Capture of Both Alpha and Beta Returns

In addition to traditional equity and fixed income, sources of alpha and beta may include those shown in Table A.3.

In a fiduciary mandate, the universe of alpha and beta opportunities is endless. We will advise clients on the added value of adding new asset categories to their portfolio.

TABLE A.3 Sources of Alpha and Beta

Beta	Add new asset classes — Real Estate — Commodities — Etc.	Diversify within existing asset classes — High yield — Credits — Etc.
Alpha	Add exposure to skill — TAA — Hedge funds — Other portable alpha — Etc.	Remove constraints — Long only → long + short — Use of derivatives — Etc.

Key Element 5: Dynamic Management

LDI provides the opportunity to manage portfolios in a dynamic way, allowing us to take into account realized returns and the resulting changes to the funded ratio and make changes on a regular basis. For instance, we might increase investments in risky assets when the funded level has increased. Dynamic management also offers some defense of the funded ratio in the face of adverse movements. It is vital in a fiduciary mandate to monitor and measure the exposures of the external managers, particularly in a dynamic management context.

WHY ABN AMRO ASSET MANAGEMENT?

We see Fiduciary Management and LDI as a partnership. We will help the client to understand his liabilities comprehensively and how to better align assets with liabilities. We will provide a customized solution, a fiduciary portfolio with a broad range of asset classes and managers, based on his risk profile and preferences. Establishing such a liability-driven investment solution requires setting up an interactive process between client and fiduciary. It is a close relationship. The pension fund will keep some control of how the risk budget is spent, and it will be able to take strategic and tactical decisions.

ABN AMRO Asset Management has a well-resourced and experienced LDI team with more than 35 investment professionals and financial engineers. The LDI team is responsible for managing quantitative and liability-driven investment strategies, as well as interest-rate hedging solutions, with total AUM of over 6 billion euros.

We believe that ABN AMRO Asset Management is unique in offering an integrated LDI package. We understand the changes affecting pension trustees. We have developed a solutions-based approach to liability-driven investments. We provide the specialist services necessary to design and implement a liability-driven investment approach tailored to clients' goals and targeted return as a foundation for a fiduciary portfolio.

Karin Roeloffs
ABN Amro Asset Management
Amsterdam, The Netherlands

Fiduciary Management at State Street Global Advisors

State Street Global Advisor's
Office of the Fiduciary Advisor

The concept of Fiduciary Management has gained hold in recent years. Plan sponsors around the world have been slowly moving away from the traditional approach of internal plan management to partnering with firms willing to work as a Fiduciary Manager. Pension plans and plan sponsors find the need for pension management skill and analysis of an ever-increasing level of complexity of asset management strategies. The staff may not have the expertise in-house; thus many have decided to seek experienced professionals outside their organization to assist. Those services usually include familiarization and analysis of the plan's liabilities and assets, its asset allocation design, and the processes for investment manager selection, ongoing manager oversight, and reporting to the plan sponsor. Many plan sponsors find that having a Fiduciary Manager has proven beneficial in focusing the company on their core competencies while meeting its fiduciary obligations to participants.

State Street Global Advisor's Office of the Fiduciary Advisor (OFA) has played the role of Fiduciary Manager for its clients since 1995. OFA has worked with clients whose needs span a wide range. Those clients fall under two specific groups. The first type falls under the category of the small to midsize plans with a relatively small staff responsible for many aspects of the company's operations. These clients typically do not have the required time or expertise to spend on all of the functions necessary to fulfill their fiduciary responsibility. The solution that has been most successful for them has been an approach that utilizes a structured "manager of managers/fund of funds" solution that provides plan sponsors with access to multiple managers within each asset class. By structuring the investments in this fund of fund structure, it provides a lower-cost option for achieving diversification within each asset class and provides access to "best of class" managers selected by OFA that would be difficult to invest with small asset sizes. While strong performance, better management, and improving funded status are implicit objectives of managing any plan, the additional benefits to midsized plans working with a Fiduciary Manager include gaining scale and skill in a cost-effective manner.

The second type of client is the larger client with more custom requirements. These companies typically have a larger staff handling the plan assets but are in need of a prudent expert in coordinating and managing the entire process. As with the smaller companies, internal resources are trying to balance both the goals of the company and the responsibilities to the participants in the plan. A Fiduciary Manager such as OFA can step in and take on most of the day-to-day management of the plan so that the company can continue to focus on its core business. With the larger plans, a more customized solution can be used as the assets are large enough to achieve economies of scale within individual managers rather than a fund of funds approach. Along with strong performance, better management, and improving funded status, the key benefits for larger plans include greater efficiencies across research and execution, and improved service levels that come with centralizing services with an experienced Fiduciary Manager.

No matter what type of category a plan falls under, the same key elements of the process are followed from start to finish. The process begins with the planning and implementation process. At this stage, it is important for the Fiduciary Manager to work very closely with the plan sponsor to understand the goals and objectives of the company and understand the risk tolerances that the company is willing to take. From here, the Fiduciary Manager can begin the process of building the plan structure. OFA, as a Fiduciary Manager, will typically handle the following:

- *Comprehensive Asset/Liability Review.* Using the most recent actuarial data available, both assets and liabilities are analyzed to show the impact on the plan under various scenarios.
- *Asset Allocation Design.* Using the output from the asset liability study, the asset allocation is chosen from one of the recommended mixes that fall on the efficient frontier.
- *Investment Policy.* Create or update the plan's investment policy to incorporate the new strategic asset allocation and investment guidelines that need to be followed.
- *Fund/Manager Structure.* Select and implement the investment managers for each asset class and establish the proper fund structures at the trustee/custodian for the monthly accounting.
- *Ongoing Oversight.* Provide monthly and quarterly reporting back to the plan sponsor on the status of the plan, including manager performance and due diligence updates, plan performance, asset allocation, market reviews and forecasts, funded status of the plan, and educational topics.

As a fiduciary, a plan sponsor needs to make sure that the Fiduciary Manager hired to provide the outsourcing services will perform its tasks with the same or better standard of care than the plan sponsor would perform himself. As plan sponsors and pension managers articulate their needs, their main goal is finding a solid partner with a long, successful heritage as a fiduciary and a proven process to implement and manage the plan assets.

Kathleen Mann/Robert Rijlaarsdam
State Street Global Advisors
Boston/Amsterdam

Fiduciary Management at Cordares

PENSION RISK MANAGEMENT FOR INDIVIDUALS

Pensions are important. For many workers pensions are something in the far-distant future. They prefer to leave the management of pensions to the pension fund. The pension fund takes away worries of employees. The Netherlands has a strong tradition in collective pensions, where pension liabilities are predominantly financed by capital accumulation, and participants can look forward to a pension income linked to a reasonable replacement rate compared to their previous salary. Volatility of financial markets, lower interest rates, and more stringent pension regulation, however, have made employers much more aware of the real costs of pensions. Also, new accounting rules (IFRS) that emphasize mark-to-market valuation, have revealed the P&L and balance sheet sensitivity for pension liabilities. All these factors have increased the pressure on the trustees of pension funds in recent years. The growing complexity of risk and asset management has contributed to the growth of solutions that focus on fiduciary solutions for asset management. Now, a trend is emerging towards application of these insights for innovative individual pension accounts.

In addition to the development of pension plan design in collective pension plans, interest in defined contribution (DC) solutions is growing. In DC, the employer pays a yearly pension premium, but the participant bears most of the risks. The employer and the pension fund have transferred the risks with regard to such matters as interest rates, investment returns, mortality, and longevity to the employee. Of course, this offers an upside to the participant (better returns), but at the same time the participant has a real possibility of income shortfall. Defined contribution is gaining ground: in the UK, a strong shift from DB to DC has taken place. In Sweden, individual accounts have been introduced amounting to 2.5 percent of salary within the collective pillar I pension scheme. Outside Europe, such as in the

United States and Australia, but also in Chile, DC has experienced strong growth. However, the experiences with DC differ per country. This is due to the fact that many of these DC plans lack important features that are available in collective schemes. At the same time, there is a strong need for tailormade solutions. Trends towards individualization require adapting to personal circumstances and ambitions of participants. In this way, Fiduciary Management also extends to an individual financial planning dimension.

An individual pension solution in which the participant has to decide on his or her own pension investments requires investment and financial planning expertise of the participant. The average participant is lacking this knowledge. Therefore, in a common DC plan participant will realize too late that he or she has accumulated not enough capital in order to reach a desired pension income. Many DC plan participants in the United States have found out that the DC account contained too little capital, but also in Sweden participants that invested their DC contribution in equities have gone through this experience.

Research of DNB (Dutch Central Bank), the consumer organization Consumentenbond and pension web site Pensioenkijker.nl show that the level of knowledge and interest in pensions is limited with the average worker. This is worrisome in this time and age when pension plan designs are adjusted. DB pension rights have been hollowed out because of added conditionalities with regard to adjustments for cost-of-living increases. Furthermore, many pension schemes have switched from final pay to indexed average pay as a benchmark for the replacement rate. The latter has led to the transfer of price indexation risks from plan sponsor to participant. A number of plan sponsors have limited their total pension expenses, thereby transferring the risks of underfunding to the participants of the plan. Examples of this strategy include the chemical company AkzoNobel, the retail company VendexKBB (now Maxeda), and the bank assurance company SNS Reaal Group. Also, the number of participants in individual DC plans has increased (sometimes these DC plans apply to employees with regard of their income above some ceiling, such as 50,000 euros per year). The restructuring of the pension sector thus leads to a redistribution of risks between employers and employees and a pension premium that mirrors true pension costs. Given the information asymmetry with regard of the pricing of pension risks between employers and employees, more attention is needed for the end-user (participant) perspective.

Employees should benefit from intelligibility of their future income provision. Without doubt, DB's promise of a pension income linked to the current salary, adds to its popularity. In 2005, a survey under Dutch adolescents showed that they prefer a pension income with a replacement of 70 percent of final salary. But appearances may be deceptive: fewer years of participation in the plan, personal circumstances (such as a divorce), changing employers, but also inflation may spoil this target. Traditional DC does not offer a solution to this: it is difficult for individuals to plan finances properly over such a long horizon. Behavioral Finance theory shows the limitations of human behavior with regard to investment planning. Therefore, it is necessary to develop pension solutions that fit well to personal circumstances and aspirations of consumers and mimic the benefits of collective pension schemes, but on an individual level.

In order to align the interests of employers and employees it is important to realize that

- Employers benefit from a transparent cost for pensions and no open-ended liabilities.
- Employers benefit from competitive conditions of employment; in this respect, pension benefits can be seen as postponed salary.
- Employees benefit from transparency with regard to expected future pension income, preferably including proper adjustments for inflation.
- Employees benefit from freedom of choice with regard to personal circumstances, like income level, family type and size, and so forth.
- Employees benefit from diversification of certain risks, such as mortality, longevity, disability.
- Expertise in the areas of risk management, asset management and a cost efficient administration serves the interests of both employers and employees.

There is a need for a pension solution that brings insight and choice with regard to risk taking and future pension income to the individual. Figure A.19 illustrates the capital accumulation and payout for an individual: this exhibit presents individual pension risk management in a nutshell.

At a glance, the participant can examine his or her pension condition. Based on a certain saving rate, the participant can work towards a predetermined target capital that is necessary to provide for the expected future pension benefit. First, a basic layer of guarantees can be established for this target capital. In principle, the participant can buy pieces of zero coupon bonds: these bonds offer a one-time future pay out and mitigate interim interest rate risks. By yearly buying pieces of secure target capital, a participant can accumulate a target capital needed for future pension income. At retirement, part of the target capital can be used for buying annuities. Uncertainty with regards to the conversion of target capital into target income can be mitigated by adding flexibility to the duration of the bonds that are being bought. Also, as maturities of these zero bonds increase over time, it will become possible to buy future pension income right away.

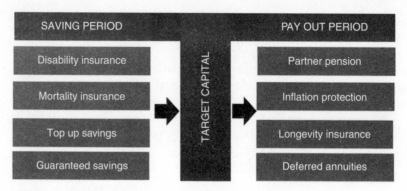

FIGURE A.19   Overview of the Individual Pension Account

It is also possible for the participant to invest partly in risky capital in order to enjoy a return on a risk premium.

The amount to invest in risky assets will be dependent on the ability and will of the participant to take risks. This is also dependent on other sources of future income and other assets the participant might possess (such as a house). Taking risks in a balanced way will lead to a higher expected target capital, which can be used for additional future income. A participant may also decide to make an additional allocation to invest in certain alpha and beta investment products, but the idea is to offer an investment solution that takes the burden of investment timing and selection away from the uninformed investor. Next to the decision on the target capital or income needed, the participant can decide on whether or not to insure disability, mortality risk, and/or income for family members. It is also possible to let the participant decide on the type of annuities (fixed or variable term, inflation correction). For all these participant choices, proper defaults will also be included.

This approach to providing a secure indexed pension income, including the insurance of certain risks, provides an outcome similar to what a DB plan can offer, but this time it is structured in an individual framework. It also aligns the interests of employers and employees. The cost of this future pension income is calculated based on market pricing. Risks that can be shared by participants are mitigated through insurance; transfers that are not transparent will be excluded: it is WYSIWYG (What You See Is What You Get). For the building blocks, suppliers can be selected that offer the best value for money, in terms of risk/return and other costs.

In individual pension plans, it is possible to decide on which risks to take and which risks to hedge out. Figure A.20 gives an example of which risk can be hedged. The risks of inflation, returns, mortality, and disability

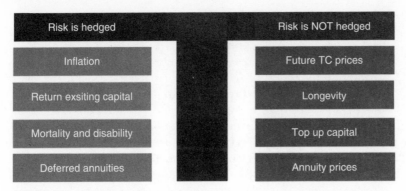

FIGURE A.20 Examples of Hedged Risks in an Individual Pension Account

can be hedged. Also, for deferred annuities with limited duration pricing is available. However, other risks are difficult to hedge. Future prices of zero bonds (target capital) will be dependent on future interest rate developments. Risks with regard to longevity are difficult to trade. The returns on top up capital that is invested in alpha and beta risks is volatile over time, and also future annuity prices will be dependent on interest rate and other market developments.

A participant can choose for security by locking in returns and insuring against all risks. However, there is optionality. Some participants might allow for risk taking in the saving period by investing in top up capital because their situation allows for some volatility in target capital. Participants might also decide on taking on some longevity risk, because they have the option to work longer (either because they are entrepreneurs or they have specific skills). Also, if a participant has other means (assets), he or she can prefer more risky investments or other moments of transition to annuity income.

The individual pension account is no longer theory in the Netherlands. A recent example is a new pension product for self-employed that want a flexible pension solution. Most self-employed are not taking part in a collective pension scheme. Their only options are to buy insurance or to invest personally in an investment account. These choices are costly, require financial planning skills, and offer limited income security. A new interest group "Alternatief voor Vakbond (AVV)" now offers a pension solution that is developed by Cordares and is based on previously discussed methodology. Since early 2007 a first release of this product is available.

In the coming years, the individual pension account will develop in flexibility and importance, next to current collective schemes. It will especially cater to those that are not able to take part in collective schemes and to those that want to supplement income from a collective scheme. It also provides a solution for collective schemes that have transferred many risks to employees. Financial markets already prepare for the increasing appetite for guaranteed and (deferred) annuity products. The growing interest of individuals in taking care of their future pension income, increasing wealth in the private sector world wide, but also adjustments in the asset allocation of institutional investors support this development. In the search for yield, new specific alpha and (advanced) beta investment products will become available for individuals. This will also allow for more specific risk-return choices for individuals.

The growth in long-duration and inflation-indexed bond instruments and the development of derivative markets offer additional building blocks for the individual pension accounts. Specific risks with regard to mortality and longevity will become better tradable in the near future. Consolidation and specialization in the financial sector will lead to commoditization of investment products and will drive down cost of administration. Technology will allow for customization of individual accounts to serve particular needs.

Individual pension accounts also offer a solution to employers that want to derisk their balance sheets with regard to pension risk. Individual pension accounts offer a solution that can be win-win for sponsor and employees. Actuarial advisors can translate current pension rights in terms of target capital and/or income, which form the basis of the splitting up of the assets to individual participants (including current buffers). Future pension contributions should also be set in a way compatible to at least the current plan. A switch to individual pension accounts of this type also allows for scalability and application in countries with another institutional and fiscal setting.

Individual pension accounts bring Fiduciary Management to the individual level, applying a similar type of risk management used for collective schemes. Innovations in pension plan design and risk management pave the way for further developments of these accounts. Individual pension accounts and personal pension risk management provide individuals the building blocks to secure their future pension income needs in a transparent and WYSIWYG way.

Alwin G. Oerlemans & Jeroen M. Tielman
Cordares
Amsterdam

Fiduciary Management at Fidelity

Fidelity Corp. (FMR) founded in 1946, Fidelity International (FIL London) established in 1969

- One of the world's leading active asset managers
- Investment management our core business
- Stable organization through: private ownership structure
- Organic growth of assets under management
- FMR Corp and FIL manage over 872 billion of equity assets and €437 billion of fixed income assets.
- Network of offices—local presence, globally integrated

Fiduciary Management

- Fidelity seeks to partner with pension funds and their consultants in order to develop a 100 percent tailormade solution.
- Our approach to Fiduciary Management stands for "best in class" fund management, objectivity, and total transparency, a commitment to delivering alpha and true independence as there is no affiliation with an investment bank.
- By seamlessly combining our institutional multimanagement skills with our LDI solutions we are able to construct the long-term solution fitted to the fund characteristics of your organization:
  - Active overlay strategies
  - Return portfolio solutions:
    - Over 20 years of Institutional multimanagement expertise with over €20 billion under management
    - Fully dedicated and very experienced team focusing on dynamic institutional multiasset and multimanager management
    - Success of the Fidelity "best in class" approach in combining the best uncorrelated sources of alpha
    - Tactical Asset Allocation (TAA) capabilities, based on our proprietary research, with a proven track record
  - Integrated Matching Portfolio solutions:
    - All types of liability matching products on a tailormade basis
    - Innovative approach to managing fixed income assets and derivatives resulting in strong alpha-generating products for your customized defined risk profile
  - Collateral management
  - Monitoring & Risk management

Not only do we apply our own proprietary risk management systems to the management of your assets, we guarantee an objective and transparent approach by hiring an independent third party to monitor our decisions (see Figure A.21).

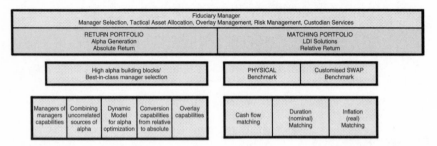

FIGURE A.21   Fiduciary Services

Gillian Schonauer
Fidelity
Amsterdam

Fiduciary Management at SPF

INTRODUCTION

SPF Beheer was founded more than ten years ago. Since then we have acted as a Fiduciary Manager on behalf of Stichting Spoorweg Pensioenfonds and Stichting Pensioenfonds Openbaar Vervoer. The number of participants involved amount to 100,000 with total assets reaching almost €14 billion. The assets are diversified over equities, fixed income, real estate, private equity, infrastructure, and opportunistic investments.

SPF Beheer is uniquely positioned to exploit its capabilities in the area of Fiduciary Management. The reasons are threefold. First, over the past ten years we have had a straightforward discussion and open approach with our clients so we are aware of their needs. Second, we see the relationship with our clients as a long-term partnership whereby we act on behalf of our clients and our clients only. Third we are excellently equipped to advise on strategic and operational issues. In total more than fifty people are engaged in asset management.

FIDUCIARY MANAGEMENT

We define Fiduciary Management as an integral and objective solution for clients with different needs. We regard Fiduciary Management as a long-term partnership in which solutions are provided for strategic, tactical, and operational issues accompanied by tailor made reporting.

Figure A.22 provides insight in how we see a Fiduciary Manager acting on behalf of his clients.

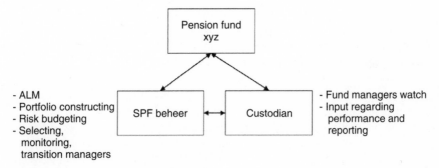

FIGURE A.22 Fiduciary Management

The role of a Fiduciary Manager starts with cementing a long-term relationship and giving advice on a broad spectrum of strategic issues, assisting pension funds with implementing the requirements set by the regulatory bodies. To be able to perform an excellent job and provide tailormade solutions, we limit the number of clients involved. On the development of liabilities and assets we go to great lengths to obtain the necessary information. Also—on the aspects of risk and perception of risk, a lot attention is given. State-of-the art asset liability management studies provide us with data to advise our clients on the asset mix. Depending on the needs regarding matching assets and liabilities, we define a matching portfolio and a return portfolio. The goal of the first portfolio is to synchronize duration of liabilities and assets, while the second is to create room for maximizing excess return.

The best managers are selected, under the constraints of the defined risk budget. We make use of an extensive database. We give high importance to select the best, simply because their returns make the difference. To make sure that an optimal portfolio of managers is selected we have a model in place. To ensure that the external managers do what they promised, we monitor them closely. Every day the risk profile per manager is calculated and the portfolio of external managers is monitored. Deviations from the risk budget agreed upon are corrected promptly.

We want every manager to add value in a portfolio of managers. To make sure that no value between managers is destroyed we tend to set up a portfolio consisting of a small number—5 to 12—of managers. Besides that, we are keen to limit management fees as much as possible where we make use of our purchasing power.

In case of a manager not performing or not complying to his mandate we will act swiftly to dismiss him. The accompanying transition process is carried out with great care. Ample evidence is present pointing out that a great deal of value can be destroyed during a transition process. Therefore we have selected a few transition managers with access to ample liquidity while maintaining market exposure. By the way, over the past ten years we have fired only two managers.

Managers selected are a combination of external managers and in-house managers. In house we focus on specialties like private equity, direct real estate, credits, and strategic equity portfolios. We believe that the combination of internal and external management gives us an edge to stay on top of developments in asset management and to adequately judge performance.

We consider reporting as the tool of communication comprehending information from in-house managers, external managers, custodian, and financial markets. Top-level insight is given on return and risk levels, both per asset class and per manager and, of course, portfolio wide. It is obvious that the custodian plays a major role as fund watcher and an independent source of information for our clients.

SUMMARY

SPF Beheer expects the demand for Fiduciary Management to explode in the years ahead. The causes for that have to do with increased regulation, the need to find extra return and, most important, the need for an institutional investor to have a reliable partner.

The long-term relationships SPF Beheer has built with our current clients on strategic and operational issues provided for ample experience in Fiduciary Management. Open communication and proactive decision making in the interest of the client make the difference on a strategic level. On an operational level we are well suited to select the best—a few—managers and monitor them closely. Reporting on the results in a client-based format is necessary to be able to explain the developments in the investment portfolio.

Given our long-lasting experience SPF Beheer is in perfect shape to tap on future possibilities regarding fiduciary tasks on behalf of current and potential clients.

Wim van Iersel
SPF
Utrecht

Fiduciary Management at Fortis Investments

FIDUCIARY MANAGEMENT: TAKING THE CONCEPT FURTHER

The world is becoming increasingly challenging for institutional investors. Tighter restrictions, more complex financial markets, and product proliferation mean that defining investment policies is becoming harder and harder.

At Fortis Investments, our primary goal is creating and providing solutions for our clients. We seek not only to understand the issues that our clients face, but to tackle them in ways that fit as closely as possible with their specific needs. Our innovative investment philosophies and organizational structure are integral parts of our approach to servicing our clients. Crucially, we do not just consider our clients' liabilities, but we consider how their assets should be invested in relation to these liabilities.

A FOCUS ON SOLVING OUR CLIENTS' PROBLEMS

Fortis Investments' organizational structure makes it ready to provide a comprehensive Fiduciary Management service. With 20 autonomous investment centers, each responsible for the management of a single asset class, we have the front-office skills to deliver the right investment solutions. Our multimanagement team has long experience in bringing together other managers' products into our fiduciary clients' portfolios. In addition our LDI team is highly experienced in matching the duration and interest exposure of our clients' liabilities. Besides this, we have the right back office support in place to satisfy our clients' risk management and reporting requirements.

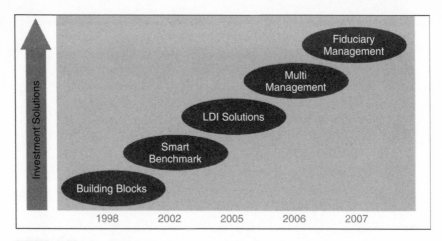

FIGURE A.23   How Our Investment Solutions Have Developed Over Time

Figure A.23 illustrates how our range of investment solutions has evolved over time. From a position of managing simple equity and bond funds, our offering has grown in complexity to incorporate absolute return vehicles, hedge funds, structured products, funds of funds, and liability-driven investment solutions. These can be combined to form tailormade solutions for our Fiduciary clients.

As we discuss later, Smart Benchmarking and multimanagement form the heart of our approach to Fiduciary Management, while performance measurement, risk control, and reporting are essential supports for this concept. Our dedicated Fiduciary Investment Officer, who acts as the liaison between the client and Fortis Investments, oversees and controls the whole portfolio management service.

A MODULAR APPROACH

We employ a modular approach to Fiduciary Management—an important distinguishing feature of our service. This enables us to offer each client a tailormade solution appropriate to their individual needs (see Figure A.24).

STRATEGIC INVESTMENT ADVICE

Studies have shown a portfolio's strategic allocation is by far the largest determinant of its risk and return characteristics, so getting this right is

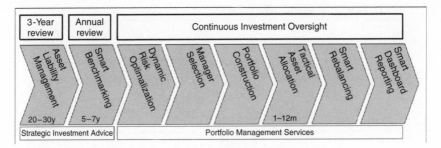

FIGURE A.24   Fiduciary Management Service Involves a Number of Steps

a crucial part of our service. Our recommendations are made up of two key components: an Asset-Liability Management study, and our Smart Benchmark concept.

ASSET-LIABILITY MANAGEMENT STUDY

This forms the basis of our strategic asset allocation recommendation. It involves close collaboration with consultants, who have in-depth knowledge of this area. Our dedicated Fiduciary Investment Officer coordinates the process, while the consultant retains responsibility for the study, which results in a recommended allocation—the Standard Strategic Portfolio (SSP).

SMART BENCHMARKING AND STRATEGIC RISK MANAGEMENT

Fortis Investments goes on to improve upon the initial SSP, producing a Strategic Portfolio (SP) using its Smart Benchmark approach. This innovative concept is based on the observation that a portfolio's expected risk can be considerably reduced by increasing the number of asset classes within it. In practice this means that given a particular risk budget, we create a portfolio with a higher expected return than that of the initial SSP by incorporating additional asset classes.

In determining each client's SP we consider their assets, cash flows, and liabilities, together with the expected returns, risk levels, and correlations of the various asset classes under consideration. These variables are determined by a proprietary tool, which is based on the widely-used Ibbotson model.

PORTFOLIO MANAGEMENT SERVICES

Our Portfolio Management Services consist of Continuous Investment Oversight, Dynamic Risk Optimization, Manager Selection, Portfolio Construction, Tactical Asset Allocation, and Smart Rebalancing.

CONTINUOUS INVESTMENT "OVERSIGHT"

Once the strategic portfolio (SP) has been defined, Fortis Investments assumes entire responsibility for the Fiduciary client's portfolio. Specialists from a number of our teams are involved in this service: in particular our Asset Allocation and multimanagement investment centers, our LDI team, Risk Management, and Reporting. The whole investment process is controlled by our Fiduciary Investment Officer who is a permanent representative of Fortis Investments in the investment committee and board meetings of the fiduciary client.

DYNAMIC RISK OPTIMIZATION

This is closely related to the Smart Benchmarking concept and involves continual monitoring of the funding ratio. Central to the process is attempting to minimize the likelihood of lower-than-expected portfolio returns while maintaining upside potential.

MANAGER AND FUND SELECTION, IMPLEMENTATION AND MONITORING

Our manager selection process involves finding the funds that bring the most diversification to our clients' overall portfolios. We pay close attention to each manager's investment style and philosophy, investment processes, and the capabilities of their staff as well as their corporate governance procedures.

Our multimanagement investment center has access to a very broad universe of funds managed by specialist external managers with which we construct our clients' portfolios. These can be made up of a unique combination of traditional asset classes alongside more exotic products such as hedge funds, GTAA, private equity, and specialized absolute return vehicles. We closely monitor developments at each manager and their performance on an ongoing basis.

We are aware of the potential conflict of interest involved in selecting our own funds, so we ask each client to set a maximum quota for investment in Fortis Investments' products. This guarantees the independence of our Fiduciary Management team, while enabling our clients to benefit from those of our products that are most suitable for them.

SMART REBALANCING

Smart Benchmarking is the process of allocating investments across different asset classes in an attempt to achieve the best possible risk/reward ratio. However, it is inevitable that over time different asset classes will produce different returns, causing the portfolio to move away from its initial composition. Our Smart Rebalancing process doesn't just involve automatically bringing the portfolio back in line with the SP at the end of each month—it avoids the effect of routinely selling assets that are performing strongly and buying assets that are not doing so well. Rather than following a typical, automated, rules-based approach to rebalancing, our process is more active, based upon our views of the prospects of each asset class.

SMART DASHBOARD REPORTING

Institutional investors require regular updates on how their assets stand relative to their liabilities, so we have developed specialized monthly reporting for our fiduciary clients, called Smart Dashboard reports. These one-page documents contain key data on assets and liabilities.

CONCLUSION

Fortis Investments' Fiduciary Management service was the logical next development in our range of tailormade investment solutions for institutional clients. Coordinated by our dedicated Fiduciary Investment Officer, our approach is transparent and flexible, and its modular nature means that tailormade solutions can be discussed and implemented seamlessly. Our one-stop service means that our clients' management teams have more time to concentrate on other concerns.

Christiaan Tromp
Fortis Investments
Utrecht

Fiduciary Management at Credit Suisse

Pension fund trustees have rightly moved from the traditional "managed balanced" investment strategies in favour of capturing the best opportunities from the proliferation of assets now available. One downside, however, is the tendency for diversification to lead to dispersal, with the strength of the parts lacking coordination at the center. Credit Suisse's fiduciary proposition is designed to remove this weakness.

The Credit Suisse fiduciary model aims to ensure that a diversified portfolio is properly managed in terms of both investment ideas and practical operational support. Credit Suisse becomes, in effect, the pension fund trustees' Chief Investment Officer, overseeing the investment proposition at every level: strategic, tactical, and operational.

It is a one-stop solution, taking overall responsibility for fund management, including the appointment of specialist managers. We adopt a multifund approach, with Credit Suisse's advice covering the full range of investment opportunities and risk control issues, including multimanager, core/satellite, liability-driven investment frameworks, multiasset class solutions, and the use of derivatives and alternative assets as appropriate.

The Credit Suisse approach has four modular parts which can be taken up individually or together to provide a comprehensive solution:

STRATEGIC ADVICE ON INVESTMENT POLICY

The first component in a fiduciary proposition is to analyse the fund's asset and liability profiles to determine the best way forward, which could include the use of a liability-driven investment (LDI) framework. Analysis and proposals for an investment strategy center around:

- Return objectives (minimum threshold return, a policy on excess return, and return periods)
- Risk budgeting (maximum volatility, probability of shortfall, appropriate tracking error, downside risks including value at risk and loss prevention monitoring)
- Assets (appropriate asset classes—including synthetics and alternatives—as well as weightings and bandwidths, optimal diversifications and currency hedges or overlays)
- Indices and benchmarks (selection of comparative indices and other relevant benchmarks and peer groups)

ASSET MANAGEMENT SOLUTIONS

Assets are grouped under broad headings such as fixed income, equity, private equity, currency, property, commodities, hedge funds, and insurance-linked products. Sample portfolios are tested for the impact of diversification and risk, including long-term, risk-return analysis of selected asset classes. Forward simulation models are created using historic risk premiums typical of a number of different economic environments. These are matched to economic phases likely to predominate over the next 5–10 years to help establish a forward risk profile.

With asset allocation decisions generating the most significant long-term investment returns, an active approach helps capture value from markets at every phase. Credit Suisse has a highly developed, disciplined, and market-proven process to ensure optimal long-term value from tactical asset allocation on a global scale across all traded asset classes. Asset allocation flows into portfolio construction so that ideas, debate, risk control, implementation, and constant review and refinement are embedded characteristics of our overall process.

Portfolios are managed within quantified guidelines developed to create a tailored solution. Acceptable guidelines can include almost any combination of investment techniques, including currency hedging and overlays; active, fixed weight and no-trading strategies; maximum and minimum asset restrictions; absolute or relative performance targets; risk adjustment; and liability-driven approaches.

ORGANIZATIONAL AND OPERATIONAL SUPPORT

In our fiduciary role, Credit Suisse can support the board of the fund's corporate sponsor as well as the trustees to ensure that the pension fund is managed in a way that is appropriate to the interests of all stakeholders. We report to both the board and the trustees on legal and regulatory risks as well as on the likely impact of developments within the financial markets. Operational, legal, and reputational risks are included in our integrated approach to risk management.

Credit Suisse has detailed procedures for monitoring portfolios and external managers. These include computation of Value at Risk according to internationally accepted standards (Basle II, as supported by the Bank of International Settlements), monitoring factors such as style drift, extended or excessive positions, analysis of draw-downs, and position concentrations.

CLIENT SERVICES

Ensuring strong, ongoing client support is key to the Credit Suisse fiduciary offering. Essential elements include detailed performance reports, client visits, and conference calls. A dedicated client relationship manager is assigned to liaise between the client and their consultant and the portfolio manager. Credit Suisse also ensures portfolio structures are optimized for tax purposes.

Paul Bourdon
Credit Suisse Asset Management Ltd
London

An Overview of Fiduciary Management Providers

The first important observation to be made on the basis of this chapter is the sizable number of providers of Fiduciary Manager services. When the first worldwide Fiduciary Management mandate was brought to the market in mid-2001, only eight organizations put themselves forward as being able to do the job, while two companies indicated they could fulfill part of the requirements and were working on extensions of their capabilities. A half dozen years later, the number of providers that we are able to list has increased to more than 20, and there are surely others that we missed. Moreover, there is good reason to believe the number of providers will continue to grow in response to increasing interest in the Fiduciary Management approach.

The Fiduciary concept lends itself to execution in two ways. The Fiduciary may enable a pension fund to outsource a number of tasks and restrict itself to basic strategic issues. Or the Fiduciary may act like a front office for the pension fund. In that way, an institution insources all of the tasks it wants to have done yet excluded from its responsibility.

While the two approaches may seem very different at first glance, the practical execution of the Fiduciary duties is not all that different. Depending on the level of expertise at a pension fund, the insourcing variant can be used to communicate more directly within the context of the fund and therefore create more room to exercise greater influence on the Fiduciary. This last point hints at a complication in which the responsibilities between fund and Fiduciary Manager should not be intertwined. In the insourcing model, the pension fund may feel it has the steering wheel in its hands, but, in fact, the same goes for the outsourcing variant, even though actual operations can be executed at more of a distance.

One striking difference among the suppliers of Fiduciary Management services listed above appears to be in the area of asset management services. Some firms offer an in-house asset management product, or even several products from their own stable, while other Fiduciaries outsource asset management completely. Those who don't offer these services often argue that this separation is a necessity if the Fiduciary Manager is to be completely objective and dispassionate in providing advice on the selection and retention of managers. Those who do offer asset management services say they only use their own services when appropriate, and they argue that there are benefits to the client from having a Fiduciary who has firsthand experience in managing assets.

This is a decidedly tricky debate. When a firm has an in-house investment product and advocates it to its Fiduciary Management clients, it should qualify as best in class, and the supplier should be able to demonstrate this characteristic to the client beyond reasonable doubt. While quality is important, however, there is also the issue of cost. Fiduciary Managers typically offer in-house investment management services at a relatively low cost. This can be very attractive when a low-added-value product is concerned because costs can devour a large part of the returns on these products. Conversely, in the case of a very expensive product, such as alpha overlay, for example, a low-cost in-house product can also be attractive.

But there is a more fundamental consideration: a fund must judge whether this supplier is putting forward its product because it genuinely believes it is the best alternative for the client or because it simply sees an easy way to put more assets under management and generate additional fees.

Choosing the right partner is not an easy job in the first place, and the potential intermingling of what may be conflicting interests makes the job harder. To make things even more complicated, several suppliers play a middleman role: They offer a manager-of-managers product, in which they pool assets run by several managers and offer these pools to the client. Most providers say these in-house pools or products are a cost-effective way to gain plain vanilla market exposure or reach a specific goal, such as increasing duration in fixed income. But others emphasize that they go to great lengths to avoid possible conflicts of interest, and, consequently, they never offer in-house products.

While virtually all providers stress that statutory trust management duties stay with the board and cannot be delegated to the Fiduciary Manager, some providers assume responsibility for the strategic asset allocation while others emphasize that they follow directives from the board and restrict themselves to advising the board about alternatives in this area. Some Fiduciaries offer advice in determining the strategic objectives of the fund.

While a number of institutions would consider this overstepping, others might welcome some help in this field as well. The latter are most likely to be smaller institutions, which may find themselves grappling with a broader range of investment possibilities in the fiduciary framework than they faced before. The broadening of investment policies and products can open a fund to more ambitious goals than they could have defined and pursued before they had a Fiduciary Manager.

Fiduciaries also take several approaches to thinking about asset management strategies. While some offer an overall policy for the total portfolio, others make a distinction between liability management and developing a return portfolio. In theory, it can be instructive to separate the actual portfolio into a restricted (liability-driven) component and an unrestricted (return-driven) component, thus making the client aware of the goals and risks of the fund. But an optimal use of investment possibilities would seem to require considering the portfolio as an entity. Making artificial divisions of the portfolio can give clients inaccurate ideas about the actual investment policies and the use of the risk budget.

A few managers suggest that the concept of Fiduciary Management is not new. In advocating this point of view, they refer to themselves as a provider of several services that are part of a Fiduciary framework. To some extent, they are right: Fiduciary Management is nothing more, or less, then the optimal execution of the strategic and tactical investment policies that are the direct consequences of the strategic decisions taken by a fund. A large pension fund with all the required know-how and staff translates this strategic policy into investment strategies and asset management policies on its own. The Fiduciary Manager seeks to do precisely the same thing in those cases in which the fund lacks the know-how and the staff to carry out these tasks.

Every well-organized and well-staffed pension fund can boast of being its own Fiduciary Manager. However, the overwhelming majority of pension funds lack the know-how and the staff to carry out these tasks on their own. That is why there is a pressing need for Fiduciary Managers. Many pension funds and many other institutional investors need a Fiduciary to deliver the right tools to compensate for shortcomings in their own expertise and to integrate the vast range of investment management needs and aspirations into an efficient execution model.

All suppliers are client-driven, as is the norm in the financial world. However, within this framework, significant differences are discernable. While some Fiduciaries strongly emphasize governance and decision making, others stress the investment policies they think are conducive to achieving the best outcome from that decision process. To a certain extent, Fiducia-ries can be labeled as advisors—with a role as an investor or as investors who perform an advisory role as well. Frequently, this label reveals the pedigree of the supplier. This interpretation of the fiduciary role contains an implicit statement about the relative importance these suppliers attach to advice versus asset management. The client then has the opportunity to choose the provider offering the most appropriate services. Experience shows that most pension funds considering the introduction of a Fiduciary Management tend to feel their organization can sustain tests of governance, and they stress their lack of capacity in evaluating risks and financial markets as the principal reason they are seeking a Fiduciary Manager.

Some providers of fiduciary services believe it would be wise for the plan sponsor to have the Fiduciary Manager calculate the effects of pension fund policy changes on the sponsoring company's balance sheet. Because of IFRS rules, they say, these independent, third-party calculations can be useful to the plan sponsor. Building some distance between the plan sponsor and the pension plan can be useful for many reasons, including the extreme case, when the plan sponsor contemplates an outright sale of the pension fund.

The size of the Fiduciary Management organization is definitely an issue. The largest firms have enough resources to provide for every aspect of the Fiduciary's role, while smaller players have to specialize. This is especially noticeable in the area of manager selection. The largest suppliers have teams of analysts who can carry out extensive research on portfolio construction and investment returns as well as another large department in which manager selection is carried out by a team large enough to cover the whole world. The smaller players need to have a narrower focus, and they have to find a way to make effective use of their limited capacity in selecting managers. Often this is done through strategic relationships with specialists in this area. But sometimes Fiduciaries choose the opposite approach and create a strategic alliance with a specialist who can translate a neutrally defined risk budget into a strategic asset mix with the desired active components. Implementing and monitoring the investment policy is then carried out in house. Experience shows that this limited capacity can sometimes be a reason why institutional investors choose a combination of two suppliers as a Fiduciary, with one of the parties restricting its activities to selecting and monitoring external asset managers.

One of the more striking features of the service providers listed here is that all of them stress the search for alpha. Only a few years ago, excess returns over a benchmark did not have the importance they now seem to have. But several years of limited returns on beta exposure in "old" markets combined with low correlation between alpha and beta portfolios has induced Fiduciaries to convince their clients that a combination of the two products is a necessity for an investment portfolio. This is yet another indication that Fiduciary Management is a key mechanism for ensuring that a pension fund is able to have timely responses to changing market conditions while continuing to be focused on enduring investment principles.

Notes

Chapter 1   The Pendulum Swings Back in Asset Management

1. Harvey D. Shapiro, "At General Mills: Now there's whole wheat with pension élan," *Institutional Investor* (April 1969), p. 40.
2. See Gary Brinson, Randolph Hood, and Gilbert Beebower, "Determinants of Portfolio Performance," *Financial Analyst Journal*, Volume 42, No. 4 (July/August 1986). See also Gary Brinson, Brian Singer, and Gilbert Beebower, "Determinants of Portfolio Performance II: an update," *Financial Analysts Journal* (May/June 1991).
3. This argument was put forward by Harry Markowitz in his doctoral dissertation in 1952 and again in his 1959 book *Portfolio Selection: Efficient Diversification of Investments*. In this book and other writings, Markowitz provided the bedrock for modern financial management. In 1990 he was awarded the Nobel Prize in economics for his work.
4. See "Managing Educational Endowments: Report to the Ford Foundation" (The Educational Endowment Series) Advisory Committee on Endowment Management New York, 1969.
5. See William L. Cary, Craig B. Bright, Esq. "The Law and Lore of Endowment Funds," The Ford Foundation, New York, 1969.
6. Harvey D. Shapiro, "General Mills: Now There's Whole Wheat with Pension Élan," *Institutional Investor*, April, 1969.
7. "Learning to live with 75 money managers," *Institutional Investor* (February 1974), p. 79.
8. Steven A. Schoenfeld, "Active Index Investing, Maximizing Portfolio Performance and Minimizing Risk through Global Index Strategy," New Jersey, 2004.

Chapter 2   Pension Plans: The Principle Setting for Fiduciary Management

1. Peter Flora & Arnold J. Heidenheimers Eds., The Development of Welfare States in Europe and America (New Brunswick: 1982).
2. R.H., *Maatman,* see for instance, *Het pensioenfonds als vermogensbeheerder* (Deventer: Kluwer 2004), where it is stated that Dutch pension funds are legally entitled to the assets of the fund. The fund is the fiduciary owner: "The pension capital belongs to the pension fund; the economic risk lies with the stakeholders" (p. 266).

3. C. E. Kortleve, "De meerwaarde van beleidsopties," *Economische Statistische Berichten*, No. 4421 (December 12, 2003): "In principle, a pension fund has no surplus or deficit. As far as the balance sheet shows a surplus or deficit, this refers to nondistributed values, for which certain stakeholders bear responsibility. These values can incorporate guarantees by the sponsor."

4. OECD, *Pension Markets in Focus*, No. 3, (October 2006), p. 12.

5. In describing some relevant features of the countries of this paragraph, I have, among other, made use of material provided by the study of Dambise F. Moyo, "The Impact of Pension Fund Reform on the Capital Markets," Goldman Sachs Global Economics Paper, No. 128, September 2005.

6. See B.Wiesner, "Investivlohn in global investierende Pensionsfonds," *Deutsche Pensions & Investmentnachrichten* (März/April, 2007).

7. In a fine article Waring and Siegel take the same stance. In their "Don't kill the golden goose: Why DB retirement plans CAN AND SHOULD BE SAVED, and HOW TO DO SO," they state: "In contrast (to DB plans, AvN), almost all DC plan investors—employees managing their own money—cannot get to the efficient frontier. . . . They don't have the knowledge, and even if they had it, they typically lack the tools to build a portfolio on the efficient frontier." See M. Barton Waring and Laurence B. Siegel, "Investment Insights," *Barclays Global Investors*, Volume 10, No. 1 (February 2007); a reprint of their article appears in *Financial Analysts Journal*, Vol. 63, No. 1 (January/February 2007).

8. See C. Keating, "The True Cost of the FTK: Part One, Research from SEI in conjunction with Con Keating, Principal of the Finance Development Centre" (London: 2006).

9. See also Sebastian Schich, "Two simple measures of potential 'scarcity' of pension fund investments," *OECD, Pension Markets in Focus*, No. 3 (October 2006). There it is stated that the demand for long-term government bonds may exceed the supply by a large margin. Daniel Brooksbank of Investment Pensions Europe, in his electronic message of October 10, 2006, quotes the OECD as saying that new accounting standards may have set up a "vicious circle" of bond demand from pension funds. "In the UK, the FRS 17 require immediate recognition of actuarial gains and losses. Under FRS 17 volatile assets such as equities introduce more volatility onto corporate balance sheets creating a preference for bonds. This arguably can create a vicious circle as the greater the demand for bonds, the lower the yield, and the lower the yield, the greater the pension liabilities, given that liabilities are discounted using bond yields."

10. See also Juliette Rieff-den Boer, " FTK: Consequences for Pension Funds," *The European Pension Fund Investment Forum Tenth Anniversary handbook 2005–6* (London: 2005).

11. See R. Verall, T. Sithole and S. Haberman, Mortality Assumptions used in the Calculation of Company Pension Liabilities in the EU" (London: Cass Business School, November 2005).

Chapter 3 The Role of the Fiduciary Manager as Chief Advisor

1. This argument gains ground in the UK in lawsuits filed against certain pension funds that locked in returns, by buying long-term bonds with relatively low yields, in order to immunize the balance sheet. The suits argue that the interests of future retirees have not been taken into account appropriately in buying bonds offering such low returns.

Chapter 4 Shaping the Fundamental Investment Policies

1. In fact, even this statement does not necessarily hold in all circumstances; it depends on the level of interest rates that are earned by a portfolio as well as the inflation rate (if pensions are indexed), and longevity risk. In a Dutch daily, Wuijster put the issue very clearly: if interest rates are equal to the inflation rate, it takes 40 active years of saving one third of one's income in order to be sure to be able to live 20 inactive years on an average income. See R. Wuijster, *Het Financieele Dagblad*, March 7, 2007.
2. For a discussion of these issues, see Jeremy Siegel, *Stocks for the Long Run: The Definitive Guide to Financial Market Returns and Long-Term Investment Strategies.* (New York: McGraw-Hill, 2002).
3. G. Boender and L. Van Lieshout, "Fiduciary management: backgrounds and challenges by an ALM-consultant," contribution to J.P. Morgan's Annual Dutch Pension Fund Seminar, *"Fiduciary Management—The Ultimate Answer?"*, Polo Club Vreeland, September 8, 2006.
4. See Harvey D. Shapiro, "'At General Mills' Now There's Whole Wheat with Pension Élan," *Institutional Investor* (April 1969), p. 40.
5. A few years later it appears that the company has moved back again to partly investing in equity. One of the main reasons is that it is impossible to offer attractive pensions with acceptable contribution levels in the long run by investing the complete portfolio in bonds with their low yields. So, in the end, the whole move at Boots may not have been structural or strategic, after all, but unintended timing paid a handsome dividend.
6. See George Oberhofer, "Active or passive management? A Logical Decision Model." *Russell Research Commentary*, April 2001.
7. Richard C. Grinold, and Ronald N. Kahn, *Active Portfolio Management*, 2nd ed. (New York: McGraw-Hill, 2000).
8. See Robert B. Litterman, *Modern Investment Management: An Equilibrium Approach* (Hoboken, New Jersey: John Wiley & Sons, Inc., 2003).
9. Ibid, page 481.

Chapter 5   Asset-Liability Modelling and the Fiduciary Manager

1. This refers to a disadvantage present in most measures of risk. They are calculated using historic data and depart from the idea that returns are distributed normally. Probabilities calculated under these conditions do not hold when data cannot be summarized in the well-known bell-shaped distribution curves. In those cases more advanced ways of calculating future outcomes are possible with the disadvantage of being rather complicated and hard to interpret.
2. That, at least, is the case in theory. Actually in the UK most schemes were started with significant deficits as employees were granted past-service benefits. Full funding can take a long time then.
3. For a much more extensive description of the methodology, see, for instance, C.G.E. Boender, Asset Liability Management, in C. Petersen, ed. *Bestuur en Management van Pensioenen,* Sdu Uitgevers, The Hague, the Netherlands. (Den Haag, 2002).
4. Ortec (Operations Research Technology) is a leading, independent consulting firm based in Rotterdam. It provides advice and planning systems. It has a strong market position in the asset-liability management business, along with other consultants such as Hewitt, Watson Wyatt and Mercer. Ortec is cited as a source here because it carried out the asset liability study for the pension fund that is being used as an example.

Chapter 8   Performance Measurement and Benchmarking

1. One of the most explicit examples of recognizing the need for cost accountability is Cost Effectiveness Measurement Incorporated, founded in 1992 by Keith Ambachtsheer and John McLaughlin. This company provides data on cost, return, risk, and liability performance of defined benefit and defined contribution plans all over the world.
2. The Z-score is a yearly measurement of the investment results of all compulsory industry pension funds. Calculating a Z-score is preceded by determining a norm portfolio, before the beginning of each year, in which account is taken of the risks the board of the fund can and wants to take. At the end of each investment year the actual return is compared to the return of the norm portfolio. Employers can leave the compulsory fund if the investment results over the last five years are insufficient. The investment results are benchmarked by the sum of the successive yearly Z-scores, divided by the square root of the number of years.
3. R. Kleynen, *Asset Liability Management binnen Pensioenfondsen* (Maastricht: Datawyse, 1996).
4. The fiduciary manager, in his advisory function, will have already indicated the possibilities afforded by tactical investment policies and their risk characteristics.
5. Mn Services, *Beleggingsplan Yarden Uitvaartverzekeringen,* Rijswijk, July 2005.

6. One problem with direct real estate is the unlimited downside risk. There can be no rent income and continuous costs in the case of a totally wrong investment decision. This is not dealt with here.
7. Gary P. Brinson, L. Randolph Hood and Gilbert L. Beebower, 1986, pp. 39–48.
8. Mn Services, *Beleggingsplan Yarden*, Rijswijk, July 2005.
9. R.C. Grinold and R.N. Kahn, *Active Portfolio Management* (New York: McGraw-Hill, 2000), p.96.
10. A.J.C. De Ruiter and J. Van As, "Beleggingspraktijk," in C. Petersen *Bestuur en management van pensioenen*, Sdu Uitgevers, The Hague, the Netherlands. (Den Haag, 2002), p. 226.
11. Louis Finney, "New Developments in Rebalancing: Techniques and Applications," Mercer Investment Consulting, August 2002.

Chapter 9   The Fiduciary Manager Experience in the Netherlands and Beyond

1. See F.Bosch, "Pensioenfondsen verliezen de regie," *Het Financieele Dagblad*, March 29, 2007. For a reaction, see A. Van Nunen, "Fiduciair versterkt juist de regie," *Het Financieele Dagblad*, April 10, 2007.
2. Erik Van Ockenburg, "Fiduciary Management: Staying in Control," contribution to the J.P. Morgan's Annual Dutch Pension Fund Seminar, "Fiduciary Management—The Ultimate Answer?", Polo Club Vreeland, September 8, 2006.
3. H.P. Van der Horst and E. Snieder, "De pensioenwereld in 2007," KPMG Financial Services, Amstelveen, January 2007.

Chapter 10   Summing Up Fiduciary Management: What It Is and Is Not

1. William O'Barr and, John M. Conley, *Fortune and Folly: The Wealth and Power of Institutional Investing* (Homewood, IL.: Irwin Professional Publishing, 1992).
2. Keith Ambachtsheer, Boice, Don Ezra, and John McLaughlin, *In Search of Pension Fund Excellence—Creating Value for Stakeholders* (New York: John Wiley & Sons, Inc., 1996).
3. Keith Ambachtsheer, R. Capelle and T. Scheibelhut, "Improving Pension Fund Performance," *Financial Analysts Journal* (vol. 54, no. 6, pp. 15–21, November/December, 1998).
4. Don Ezra, "Fiduciary management: An update," speech at Russell Investment Conference, "Celebrating 10 Years of Building a More Certain Future," Huis ter Duin, Noordwijk aan Zee, May 12, 2006.
5. Ibid.
6. K. Ambachtsheer, R. Capelle, H. Lum, "Pension Funds, Governance, and Organization Design," International Centre for Pension Management, in collaboration with the Joseph L. Rotman School of Management of the University of Toronto, October 2005.

7. P. Risseeuw and J. ter Wengel (with the cooperation of J. Rutte), Fund governance
    in Nederland, "Bestuurlijke structuur en beleggingsstrategie bij de Nederlandse
    pensioenfondsen," ESI-VU, co-production of Free University of Amsterdam and
    Russell Investment Group, Amsterdam, 2001.

Chapter 11   A Guide to Fiduciary Managers

1. Given the assumptions made and data used in this study.

Bibliography

Ambachtsheer, Boice, Ezra, and McLaughlin. *Pension Fund Excellence—Creating Value for Stakeholders*. New York, 1996.

Ambachtsheer, Capelle, and Scheibelhut. "Improving Pension Fund Performance," *Financial Analysts Journal* (November/December 1998).

Ambachtsheer, K., Capelle, R., Lum, H. "Pension Funds, Governance, and Organization Design," International Centre for Pension Management, in collaboration with the Joseph L. Rotman School of Management of the University of Toronto, October 2005.

Boender, C.G.E. Asset Liability Management, in C. Petersen, ed. *Bestuur en Management van Pensioenen*, Den Haag, 2002.

Boender, G., and Van Lieshout, L. "Fiduciary Management: Backgrounds and Challenges by an ALM-Consultant," contribution to the J.P. Morgan's Annual Dutch Pension Fund Seminar, "Fiduciary Management—The Ultimate Answer?", Polo Club Vreeland, September 8, 2006.

Bosch, F. "Pensioenfondsen verliezen de regie," *Het Financieele Dagblad*, March 29, 2007.

Brinson, B., Hood, R. and Beebower, G. "Determinants of Portfolio Performance," *Financial Analyst Journal*, Vol. 42, No. 4, (July/August 1986).

Brinson, G., Singer, B., and Beebower, G. "Determinants of Portfolio Performance II: An update," *Financial Analysis Journal* (May/June 1991).

Brooksbank, D. "OECD Sees 'Vicious Circle' of Pension Fund Demand," *Investment Pensions Europe*, October 10, 2006.

Cary, W.L., Bright, C.B. *The Law and Lore of Endowment Funds*, The Ford Foundation, 1969.

Cass Business School, *Mortality Assumptions used in the Calculation of Company Pension Liabilities in the EU*, November 2005.

De Ruiter A.J.C., and Van As, J. "Beleggingspraktijk," in Petersen C., *Bestuur en management van pensioenen*. Den Haag, 2002, p. 226.

Ezra, D. "Fiduciary management: An update," speech at Russell Investment Conference, "Celebrating 10 Years of Building a More Certain Future," Huis ter Duin, Noordwijk aan Zee, May 12th 2006.

Finney, L. "New Developments in Rebalancing: Techniques and Applications," Mercer Investment Consulting, August 2002.

Flora, P., & Heidenheimer, A.J., Eds. *The Development of Welfare States in Europe and America*, New Brunswick, 1982.

Grinold, R.C., and Kahn, R.N. *Active Portfolio Management*, 2nd ed., New York, 2000.

Keating, C. "The True Cost of the FTK: Part One, Research from SEI," in conjunction with Con Keating, Principal of the Finance Development Centre, Wassenaar, 2006.

Kleynen, R., *Asset Liability Management binnen Pensioenfondsen.* Datawyse: Maastricht, 1996.

Kortleve, C. E., "De meerwaarde van beleidsopties," in *Economische Statistische Berichten,* No. 4421, December 12, 2003.

Litterman, R. B. *Modern Investment Management: An Equilibrium Approach,* New Jersey, John Wiley & Sons, Inc., 2003.

Maatman, R.H. *Het pensioenfonds als vermogensbeheerder.* Deventer, 2004.

Managing Educational Endowments. New York: The Ford Foundation, 1969.

Markowitz, H. *Portfolio Selection: Efficient Diversification of Investments,* 1959.

Mn Services. *Beleggingsplan Yarden Uitvaartverzekeringen.* Rijswijk, July 2005.

Moyo, D. F. "The Impact of Pension Fund Reform on the Capital Markets," Goldman Sachs Global Economics Paper, No. 128, September 2005.

Nunen, van A. "Fiduciair versterkt juist de regie," *Het Financieele Dagblad,* April 10, 2007.

O'Barr, W. and Conley, J.M. *Fortune and Folly: The Wealth and Power of Institutional Investing.* Homewood, 1992.

Oberhofer, G. "Active or Passive management? A Logical Decision Model." *Russell Research Commentary* (April 2001).

OECD. "Global Pension Statistics," *Pension Markets in Focus* No. 1 (June 2005).

OECD. "Global Pension Statistics," *Pension Markets in Focus* No. 3 (October 2006).

Rieff-den Boer, J. "FTK: Consequences for Pension Funds," in The European Pension Fund Investment Forum, *Tenth Anniversary Handbook 2005–2006,* London, 2005.

Risseeuw, P., and ter Wengel, J. (with the co-operation of Rutte, J.). "Fund governance in Nederland, Bestuurlijke structuur en beleggingsstrategie bij de Nederlandse pensioenfondsen," ESI-VU, co-production of Free University of Amsterdam and Russell Investment Group, Amsterdam, 2001.

Schich, S. "Two simple measures of potential 'scarcity' of pension fund investments," *Pension Markets in Focus* No. 3 (October 2006).

Schoenfeld, S.A. *Active Index Investing, Maximizing Portfolio Performance and Minimizing Risk through Global Index Strategy,* New Jersey, 2004.

Shapiro, H. "At General Mills: Now there's whole wheat with pension élan," *Institutional Investor* (April 1969), p. 40.

Shapiro, H. "Learning to Live with 75 Money Managers," *Institutional Investor* (February 1974), p. 79.

Siegel, J. *Stocks for the Long Run: The Definitive Guide to Financial Market Returns and Long-Term Investment Strategies.* New York, 2002.

Van der Horst, H.P. and Snieder, E. "De pensioenwereld in 2007," KPMG Financial Services, Amstelveen, January 2007.

Van Ockenburg, E. "Fiduciary Management: Staying in Control," contribution to the JP Morgan's Annual Dutch Pension Fund Seminar, "Fiduciary

Management—The Ultimate Answer?", Polo Club Vreeland, September 8, 2006.

Waring, M.B., and Siegel, L.B. "Don't kill the golden goose: Why DB retirement plans CAN AND SHOULD BE SAVED, and HOW TO DO SO," *Investment Insights,* Barclays Global Investors, Volume 10, No. 1 (February 2007), a reprint of their article appears in *Financial Analysts Journal,* Vol. 63, No. 1 (January/February 2007).

Wuijster, R., *Het Financieele Dagblad,* March 7, 2007.

Index

Absolute returns, 133
Active investment policy: *See also* Investing
  strategies
  active overlay management as part of, 143
  choosing to employ, 52–55
  completion account as necessary adjunct
    to, 58–59, 61–62
  detailed benchmarks in context of,
    140–142
  fiduciary platform to integrate into
    portfolio, 59, 62–67
  "fundamental law of active management,"
    56
  integrating into overall portfolio, 55–57
  measurement of, 145–149
  mixing passive and, 56
  portable alpha strategy replacing the, 59
Alpha:
  definition of, 54
  strategy transporting, 59
Ambachtsheer, K., 172
Asset classes:
  described, 55
  rebalancing, 144–145
  securities within individual segments of, 55
Asset-liability model (ALM):
  basic calculations/decision-making used in,
    82–102
  basic ingredients and framework of,
    75–77
  calculating effects of uncertainty, 80–81
  described, 73–74
  Fiduciary Manager role in using, 74–75,
    102–103
  importance as pension fund tool,
    81–82
  policy changes and, 102
  policy instruments used in, 78–80
Asset-liability modeling practices:
  balance sheet of Pension Fund X, 83
  economic data provided by ALM, 83–84

  future financial situation with changes in
    investment policy, 100–102
  future financial situation with flexible
    premium levels under compound rates
    equal to market interest rates, 88–100
  future financial situation with flexible
    premium levels under fixed compound
    rate, 85–88
  prognosis of future reserves without policy
    changes, 84–85
Asset-liability study:
  benefits of using, 76–77
  described, 39–41
  optimal asset mix determined by, 55
Asset managers (The Netherlands),
  153–154
Asset mix policy level, 55
Association for Investment Management and
  Research, 128
AT&T pension plan, 8
ATP (Arbejdmarkedets Tillaegs Pension)
  [Denmark], 23
Australian pension system,
  33–34

Balanced fund approach, 2–3
Balanced manager, 1
Balance sheets:
  pension fund example of, 28–29
  Pension Fund X example of, 83
Banz, R., 5
Beebower, G., 4
Benchmarks: *See also* Investment
  performance
  active investment policy context of,
    140–142
  active policy, 145–149
  detailed, 132
  equities markets, 137–139
  example of detailed portfolio and relevant,
    147–148

Benchmarks: *See also* Investment
      performance *(Continued)*
   Fiduciary Managers role in establishing,
      43–44, 112–114, 127–128
   liability-driven, 131, 133–134
   reasons behind growing importance of,
      128–131
   risks of industries compared to, 71
   strategic, 131–132, 134–135
Benefits policy, 78
Beta returns, 54
Bismarck, O. von, 16
Black box investment strategies, 118–119
Bond market:
   balanced fund approach to stocks and,
      2–3
   efficient market hypothesis on
      performance of, 9–10
   stocks as outperforming, 4–6
Bonds:
   immunizing portfolios by buying, 48–51
   junk, 112
Boots the Chemist (UK), 49–50
Bottom-up investing approach, 8–9
Brinson, G. P., 4
BSP (basic state pension) [UK], 31

Campina (The Netherlands), 151
Capelle, R., 172
Center for Research in Securities Prices
   (University of Chicago), 5
Closet indexing, 9–10
Collaterized Debt Obligations (CDOs), 112
Communication:
   implementing policies and processes of,
      172
   The Netherlands Fiduciary Management
      experience with, 154
Completion account, 58–59, 61–62
Conley, J. M., 167, 169
Contribution policy:
   as ALM ingredient, 76, 78
   changing level of, 78
Costs/fees issue, 155–156, 178
Custodians, 156–157

Defined benefit (DB) plan, 17
Defined contribution (CD) plans, 17–18
Denmark pension system, 23–25
Detailed benchmarks, 132

Diversification strategy, 139
Dow-Jones Industrial Average, 10
Drexel Burnham Lambert, 112
Duration gap, 67–68

Efficient market hypothesis, 9–10
Employees' Retirement Income Security Act
   (ERISA) [U.S.], 4
Equitable Life, 35
Equities markets: *See also* Stocks
   benchmarking performance of, 137–139
   different criteria/scores for factor ranking
      of, 139
Ezra, D., 171

Fiduciary Management: *See also* Pension
      plans
   claims regarding benefits of, 176–179
   commonalities of pension fund asset,
      36–37
   compared to other investment
      management models, 175–176, 177
   comparing best management practices to,
      169–173
   complexity and depth of, 174
   Financial Management synthesis context
      of, 1
   increased costs/fees related to, 155–156,
      178
   KPMG survey on (2007) on, 159–164
   Netherlands experience with, 151–166
   productivity enhanced by, 173–174
Fiduciary Manager reports: *See also*
      Portfolios
   on daily movements in active return, 70
   on current/proposed active alpha
      portfolio, 69
   on manager performance summary, 71
   on manager risk/return summary, 72
   on risks of industries compared to
      benchmark, 71
   on weights, means, and targets, 70
Fiduciary Managers:
   ALM role by, 74–75, 102–103
   asset-liability study role by, 39–41
   bridging the duration gap, 67–68
   educating plan sponsor role by, 44–45
   increased costs/fees related to, 155–156,
      178
   measuring and benchmarking role by,
      43–44, 113–114, 127–128

need for, 12–13
portfolio construction by, 42–43
selecting investment managers, 43, 62,
    116–117, 121–122
supervision of investment managers by,
    43, 123–125
thinking through risk and return by,
    41–42
trusted counselor role by, 46
Fiduciary platform:
active management and value of, 64–65
avoiding active management pitfalls
    through, 66–67
Financial Analysts Journal, 4
Financial Management:
comparing Fiduciary Management to
    other models of, 175–176, 177
definition of, 1
history driving development of, 1–3
thesis, antithesis, and synthesis context of,
    1
Fixed income portfolios:
apportioning, 112
decisions to be made about, 136–137
Flora, P., 18
Ford Foundation reports (1969), 5–6
401(k) plans (U.S.), 323
France:
early pension plans in, 16
National Retirement Fund of, 16
pension system in, 25
"Fundamental law of active management,"
    56

GARP (Growth At a Reasonable Price), 111
GDP (gross domestic product):
equities market performance and,
    137–139
pension funds' investments relative to,
    20–21
General Mills Employee Retirement System
    Pension Fund, 3, 8, 49
Germany:
early pension plans in, 16
pension system in, 26–27
GIPS/AIMR (Global Investment Performance
    Standards), 128
Governance matrix:
Ambachtsheer, Capelle and Lum surveys
    on, 172–173
general, 170

institutional investor's, 170
pension fund's investment, 170
Grinold, R. C., 56
Growth stock investing, 111
GTE, 11–12

Hedge funds, 106–109, 120
Heidenheimer, A. J., 18
Hood, R., 4

IFRS-rules, 129
Indexing (closet), 9–10
Institutional investors:
governance matrix of, 170
investment performance and, 117
planning cycle of, 132
Insurance:
as ALM ingredient, 78
pension funds/life-insurance assets in
    OECD countries, 24
Interest rates:
future financial situation with flexible
    premium levels under compound rates
    equal to market, 88–100
pension fund balance sheet and, 28–29
Investing: *See also* Portfolios
balanced fund approach to, 2–3
bottom-up approach to, 8–9
discontent with MPT-driven paradigm,
    10–12
efficient market hypothesis on, 9–10
growth stock, 111
international, 110
new paradigm for, 6–8
process and philosophy of, 117–118
Investing strategies: *See also* Active
    investment policy
black box, 118–119
liability-driven investments (LDI), 51–52
portable alpha, 59
Investment managers:
benefits of using multiple, 63
changing aggregate factor risk exposures
    of, 64
Fiduciary Manager supervision of, 43,
    123–125
formulating mandates for, 114
investment process and philosophy of,
    117–118
managing transition to new, 122–123

Investment managers: (*Continued*)
  process of choosing, 62, 116–117,
    121–122
  reasons for terminating, 115–116
  sample size/style chart for, 65
  tactical asset allocation (TAA), 143
Investment performance: *See also*
  Benchmarks
  assessing reasons for, 117
  equities, 137–139
  fixed income portfolio, 112, 136–137
  principal drivers of pension fund's,
    168–173
  real estate investments, 139–140
  rebalancing asset classes to improve,
    144–145
Investment policy:
  ALM predictions on changes in, 100–102
  ALM and range of, 75, 78
  assets-liabilities relationship managed by,
    79
  determining the basic, 171
  determining ways of implementing, 171
  The Netherlands Fiduciary Management
    experience and, 152

Jones, A. W., 107
Junk bonds, 112

Kahn, R. N., 56
KPMG survey of pension funds (2007),
  159–164

The Law and the Lore of Endowment Funds
  (Ford Foundation report), 8

Legislative statutes:
  Employees' Retirement Income Security
    Act (ERISA), 4
  Uniform Management of Institutional
    Funds Act, 8
Liabilities:
  as ALM ingredient, 75
  asset-liability study of, 39–41
  buying bonds to immunizing pension,
    48–51
  longevity issue of, 40
  making changes in, 78
  smoothing techniques for accounting, 50
Liability-driven benchmarks, 131, 133–134

Liability-driven investments (LDI), 51–52
Litterman, R. B., 58
Longevity issue, 40
Long Term Capital Management, 106–107
Lum, H., 172

McKensey & Company, 159
Markowitz, H., 3
Maxwell, R., 35
MBA (Master of Business Administration)
  degree, 3
Milken, M., 112
Mirror Group, 35
Modern Portfolio Theory (MPT):
  computer technology allowing
    applications of, 4–6
  discontent with, 10–12
  Financial Management antithesis context
    of, 1
  origins and rise of, 3–4
  on risk, 4
Morgan Stanley Capital Markets
  International Index, 111
MSCI EAFE, 111
Multi-manager investing:
  benefits of using, 63
  changing aggregate factor risk exposures
    of, 64

National Conference of Commissioners on
  Uniform State Laws, 8
National Retirement Fund (France), 16
The Netherlands:
  compounding rate adopted by, 129–130
  Fiduciary Management adopted in,
    151–166
  pension system in, 27–28
  sufficiency test required in, 28, 29–30
The Netherlands Fiduciary Management
  experience:
  benefits of, 165–166
  changes in communication process, 154
  changes in discussions with asset
    managers, 153–154
  changes in importance of custodian,
    156–157
  changes in investment policy, 152
  changes in level and structure of costs,
    155–156
  changes in role of fund's investment
    committee, 153

future developments of market for
    fiduciary services, 159–164
overseeing the fiduciary, 157–158
New York Stock Exchange, 48

O'Barr, W., 167, 169
OECD countries:
    general picture of pension provision
        structure in, 36
    importance of pension funds in, 22
    pension funds investment in, 20–21
    pension funds/life-insurance assets in, 24
    pension funds similarities/differences in,
        34–36
    pension system organization/regulation in
        specific, 23–34
    private pension plans assets by type of
        financing vehicles (2004), 23
Operational risk, 119–121

Passive investment management, 56
Pension Benefit Guaranty Corporation, 47
Pension fund industry:
    Ambachtsheer, Capelle, and Lum surveys
        on, 172–173
    general picture of European, 36
    international organization/regulations of,
        23–34
    international similarities/differences,
        34–36
    KPMG survey on (2007) Fiduciary
        Management of, 159–164
Pension fund investment committee (The
    Netherlands), 153
Pension funds:
    balanced fund approach to, 2–3
    commonalities regarding management of
        assets, 36–37
    custodian of, 156–157
    discontent with MPT paradigm on, 10–12
    importance in OECD countries, 22
    interest rates and balance sheet for, 28–29
    investment governance matrix of, 170,
        172–173
    new paradigm adopted for, 7–8
    OECD investment relative to GDP, 20–21
    origins of, 2
    principal performance drivers of, 168–173
    research on management of, 167–168
    sufficiency test of, 28, 29–30

Pension Fund X balance sheet, 83
Pension Markets in Focus, 22
Pension plans: *See also* Fiduciary
    Management
    historical development of, 15–18, 20
    international development of provisions
        of, 18–23
Plan sponsors:
    asset-liability study benefits to, 76–77
    concerns and objectives of, 47
    decision-making and education of,
        44–45
    definition of, 20
    establishing benchmarks for, 43–44,
        112–114
    Fiduciary Management communication
        approach to, 154
Portable alpha strategy, 59
Portfolio construction:
    defining appropriate asset classes task of,
        106
    defining sub-allocations, 109–111
    establishing benchmark measures,
        112–114
    Fiduciary Manager role in, 42–43
    growth and value issues of, 111
    hedge funds used in, 106–109, 120
    investing internationally for, 110
    tasks listed, 105
Portfolios: *See also* Fiduciary Manager
        reports; Investing
    diversification of, 139
    example of relevant benchmarks for
        detailed, 147–148
    fixed income, 112, 136–137
    immunizing by buying bonds, 48–51
    integrating active investing policy into
        overall, 55–57
Premium policy:
    ALM predictions on compound rates
        equal to market interest rates and
        flexible, 88–100
    ALM predictions on fixed compound rate
        with flexible, 85–88
Productivity issue, 173–174
"Prudent man rule," 4

Ralfe, J., 49–50
Range rebalancing, 145

Real estate investment performance,
139–140
Rebalancing strategy, 144–145
Returns:
absolute, 133
alpha, 54, 59
assessment of risk and, 41–42
beta, 54
measurement/benchmarking, 43–44
mixing active and passive management in
case of volatile, 56
stocks as out performing bonds, 4–6
Risk:
assessment of return and, 41–42
measurement/benchmarking,
43–44
MPT on, 4
operational, 119–121
"prudent man rule" for, 4
strategies for underfunding,
48–51
tracking errors, fitting different attitudes
toward, 142

S2P (State Second Pension) [UK],
31–32
Social Security (U.S.), 17
Soros, G., 107
Standard & Poor, beginnings of, 10

Stocks: *See also* Equities markets
balanced fund approach to bonds and,
2–3
efficient market hypothesis on
performance of, 9–10
as outperforming bonds, 4–6
Strategic benchmarks, 131–132, 134–135
Style drift, 12
Sub-allocation definition, 109–111
Sufficiency test, 28, 29–30
Sweden pension system, 30
Switzerland pension system, 31

Tactical asset allocation (TAA) managers,
143
Time rebalancing, 145
T. Rowe Price, 8

Uncertainty, 80–81
Uniform Management of Institutional Funds
Act (U.S.), 8
United Kingdom pension system, 31–32
United States:
early pension plans in, 17–18
legislative statutes affecting pension plans
in the, 4, 8
pension system in, 32–33

VGZ-IZA (The Netherlands), 151